SCUBA
DIVING
IN
SAFETY
AND
HEALTH

SCUBA DIVING IN SAFETY AND HEALTH

by
Christopher W. Dueker,
M.D.

Diving Safety Digest
P.O. Box
Menlo Park, CA 94026

With appreciation to my parents

"Praise the Lord from the earth
you sea monsters and all deeps,
fire and hail, snow and frost,
stormy wind fulfilling his command!"
Psalms 148. 7–8

Library of Congress Cataloging in Publication Data

Dueker, Christopher Wayne, 1939–
    Scuba diving in safety and health.

    Rev. ed. of: Medical aspects of sport diving. 1970.
    Includes bibliographies and index.
    1. Scuba diving—Physiological aspects.   2. Scuba
diving—Safety measures.   3. Skin diving—Safety
measures.   I. Dueker, Christopher Wayne, 1939–
Medical aspects of sport diving.   II. Title.
[DNLM: 1. Diving. WD 650 D852s]
RC1220.D5D8   1985   616.9'8022   85-12926
ISBN 0-9614638-0-5

Produced by Madison Publishing Associates

Diving Safety Digest
P.O. Box 2735
Menlo Park, CA 94026

Contents

Foreword

This book was conceived more than nineteen years ago in the belief that recreational divers would enjoy their sport more if they understood the physiological considerations of swimming underwater. In 1970 *Medical Aspects of Sport Diving* was published to provide an introduction to the physiology and medicine of diving.

Scuba Diving in Safety and Health is both a revision and an extension of *Medical Aspects of Sport Diving*. Each subject has been reinvestigated and the text changed to reflect new knowledge. Some older concepts, such as Dr. Albert Behnke's prediction of "silent bubbles" in decompression sickness and Dr. Edgar End's concepts of impaired blood flow in decompression injury, have been proved significant. The book has two new chapters. One emphasizes the special importance of the ear in diving. The other reflects the modern fascination with drugs and discusses how this affects safe diving. The former chapter on mixed gas and deep diving has been deleted since this subject now warrants its own text and because deep diving is not for SCUBA divers. Since the 1960s enormous progress has been made in extending the depth limits for military and commercial diving. For the recreational diver, however, the dangers of deep diving have scarcely changed.

In 1967 the Undersea Medical Society was founded and has been instrumental in expanding research and practice in diving medicine. With the encouragement of the Undersea Medical Society, the Diving Alert Network (DAN) was founded at Duke University. DAN provides an invaluable service to the diving community through education and coordination of accident treatment. In Chapter 20, Health Requirements, the role of DAN is discussed further.

This book is designed for the diver who wants to know more than the techniques of diving. Since the underwater world is a foreign environment, no diver is unaffected by the issues of immersion and compression.

This book is designed to be understandable to the nonmedical reader while providing sufficient references to make it useful as an introduction to diving medicine.

Understanding the principles of diving physiology will make the sport both safer and more enjoyable for you.

ACKNOWLEDGMENTS

Several diving friends have contributed to this book. Garry Gerick provided the diving rescue photograph. My diving buddy, Jack Witt, has been unceasing in his interest in promoting diving safety and in encouraging me. Jack's students know that safety is part of the fun of diving.

The following persons and organizations graciously permitted me to include previously published material: Dr. Karl E. Schaefer (deceased), Dr. E. H. Lamphier, Dr. W. B. Wood, Dr. J. H. Comroe (deceased), National Academy of Sciences, American Physiological Society, Year Book Medical Publishers, University of Hawaii Press, W. H. Freemen Co. (for Scientific American, Inc.), and the U.S. Navy.

As before, my wife, Joyce, with her support and editing skill, made this book possible.

Gloria R. Mosesson, our valued literary agent, assumed the monumental task of steering this book through the shoals between writing and publication.

1 | Marine Life Hazards

Despite popular tales of sea monsters, the danger from marine animals is much less than that from careless diving. Of course there are dangerous animals—some can cause mortal wounds—but avoiding them is generally possible. Divers will find that a basic knowledge of unfriendly inhabitants of the sea will make diving more tranquil and interesting. The danger from marine life stems from encountering carnivorous animals, or venomous animals, or from eating poisonous animals. In this chapter these three dangers will be discussed, with emphasis on their more common life forms.

CARNIVORES

Sharks

Undoubtedly, the marine animal people fear most is the shark. Sharks are elasmobranchs, differing from fish in several ways. Primarily, they have a cartilaginous skeleton rather than a bony one. Ranging in size from 18 inches to over 50 feet, sharks may be found throughout the world, even in fresh water. As might be expected from their size differentiation, shark danger varies greatly. Of the 250 species of sharks, only about twenty-seven have been definitely identified in human attacks.[1]

Sharks cause injury both with their rough skins and their sharp teeth; these teeth are arranged in rows from front to back, with four to five rows in use at any one time. Reserve rows of teeth, covered by a membrane, move forward to replace lost teeth. These, mounted in large, strong jaws, can cause tearing wounds with massive loss of flesh, and since they are relatively loose, they may pull out and be left in wounds. The wound appears to depend on the nature of the attack; attacks from anger leave slashing wounds.

Sharks, reportedly, have poor vision.[2] But apparently they can detect some color. Even if blinded, a shark shows remarkable ability to find food. The sense of smell is so well developed that pungent food may be sensed up to a quarter of a mile away.[3] The most unique sensory mechanism is the lateral line system. Along each side of the shark's body runs a longitudinal canal (lateral line), which contains a watery fluid and sensory cells with hairlike processes that extend into the fluid. Vibrations in the water seem to be detected through this system, by which means the shark probably finds his victims.

Assessing the risk of shark attack is difficult. The worldwide yearly attack rate probably ranges between fifty and one hundred victims.[4] In a thirty-year period in California, twenty-five skin divers (including five using SCUBA) were attacked by sharks.[5] Fifteen of these attacks occurred within a 100-mile section of the north central coast.

Some divers openly deride the danger of sharks; a few even consider sharks cowards. Because only a few types of shark are *known* to be attackers, the others are considered safe. Unfortunately, sharks are highly unpredictable beasts; an individual may be unaware that he belongs to a "harmless" group. Furthermore, it is not easy to distinguish a "safe" shark from a "dangerous" one. Perhaps the risk of attack is not high, but the severity of a given attack cannot be doubted. The risk cannot be justified by a desire to prove bravery. As a general rule, if sharks are sighted, diving in that area should be stopped. Approximately 35 percent of shark attacks are fatal.[6] And even with nonfatal attacks, prevention is infinitely more pleasant and satisfactory than treatment.

Methods of preventing attack vary and do not always meet with success. In proved high-risk areas, antishark nets and bubble barriers are sometimes erected; but nets work only until torn or carried away by the tide, and bubble barriers stop only some sharks while others pass through unbothered. Shark repellent dyes deter some sharks under some conditions, but dyes are ineffective in frenzy feeding.*

If sharks are sighted, an *unhurried* retreat to boat or shore is indicated; thrashing will only attract the sharks. SCUBA divers should leave the area swimming submerged; although submerged swimmers have been attacked, this seems to be somewhat safer than surface swimming. An attacking shark, *may* be sometimes repelled by blowing bubbles, shouting, or striking the shark with a spear gun or billy.

The risk of attack can be diminished by following these rules—a compilation of the most authoritative advice.

1. Avoid known dangerous waters.
2. If sharks are sighted, leave the water *quietly*.
3. Avoid murky water.
4. Do not play with any type of shark.
5. Do not swim alone.
6. If you have a bleeding wound, leave the water.
7. Do not tow speared fish as you swim.
8. Do not dangle hands or feet from boats or floats.
9. Avoid carrying shiny objects (these attract the curiosity of a dim-visioned shark).

To survive a shark attack, the victim must have prompt and vigorous attention; the lone swimmer, unable to help himself, often dies in the water from blood loss or drowning. Get the victim to shore. The rescuer's next step should be to stop the loss of blood. Shark wounds are deep and extensive, and major arteries may be severed. No time can be lost. Ideally, blood flow is stopped by applying direct pressure to the wound. If this is inadequate (as it may be in arterial bleeding), a tourniquet may be necessary. Tourniquets are dangerous, since they may cause ischemia, which will later result in loss of the limb; however, in severe wounds, where death will result from uncontrolled bleeding, a tourniquet may save a life. Eventually, blood replacement will be needed, but in the meantime plasma or plasma substitutes

---

*Sharks have two feeding patterns. The first, individual feeding, though destructive, is fairly orderly. The other is mob feeding, or feeding frenzy, in which masses of sharks wildly attack a bleeding victim.

should be used to maintain blood pressure. Says a British writer on shark attacks: "The greatest factor involved in the saving of shark victims is timely emergency treatment."[7]

In South Africa and Australia physicians initiate treatment on the beach, using intravenous sets which are stored along the coast.[8,9] Unhurried transportation to a hospital follows. Hospital medical care requires adequate blood volume replacement and wound debridement (removal of unhealthy tissue). X rays are used to detect fractures or teeth left behind by the shark. Because of the danger of infection, wounds may be left open initially and then later closed. Prevention of wound infections may involve use of antibiotics plus prophylaxis for tetanus and gas gangrene.

Barracuda

Barracuda, in an array of twenty species, range from under 2 to over 9 feet in length; they are vicious carnivores found in all warm-water areas. Their ability to inflict harm is beyond question. They have strong, long jaws with three rows of teeth—two above, one below. The actual risk from barracuda eludes pinpointing even more than that for sharks. Gudger and Breder report that barracuda are, indeed, more dangerous and more feared than sharks.[10] Certain varieties in some areas are aggressive, but cases of actual attack cannot be easily documented. Unlike the shark, the barracuda is considered more dangerous when alone than when in company of others.[11] The pattern of attack is similar to that of the shark; the wounds look alike except that the barracuda leaves a straighter incision. If barracuda are nearby and appear at all curious, the diver should be ready to leave the water. Treatment is the same as for shark wounds.

Moray Eels

Divers frequently find moray eels in rock areas. Morays have sharp teeth in powerful jaws, which can cause severe lacerations. Once the eel has bitten, he may not release his hold while he's alive and must be pried off after death. Eels will not attack swimmers unless provoked by a too curious hand or a careless foot. When speared, they have a disquieting tendency to writhe their way up the shaft in an all-out effort to bite their attacker. A skin diver, bitten by an eel, may be held underwater until he drowns. If he escapes, the wounds, which are prone to secondary infection, are treated basically like shark wounds. A current diving fad is the taming of morays by petting and hand feeding them. Time will tell if the moray has an undeserved notoriety. Until then, the cautious diver will continue to leave eels alone.

Sea Lions and Whales

Normally, sea lions do not threaten divers, although they may swim playfully at them. But occasional attacks have been reported, particularly during mating season. At those times, their company probably should be avoided. Killer whales could be dangerous if encountered by a diver,[12] but these animals rarely enter shallow, diving waters. Recent work has indicated that killer whales may not be as vicious as previously believed.[13]

Tridacna Clams

These notorious "killer clams" of the tropical Pacific may weigh as much as 400 pounds. In fiction they have been represented as "snapping" shut on an unsuspecting diver, holding him until drowned. In fact, this "snapping" usually requires 10 to 20 seconds, sufficient time for the diver to extricate his limbs. The closure, even then, is not tight, and a knife can be inserted to sever the adductor muscles and permit escape. Experiments in Australia with fins, gloves, and sticks did not induce tridacnas to close quickly or tightly. However, when the closeup framer of an underwater camera was placed in a clam shell and the strobe fired, the clam closed immediately, completely, and persistently. It seems that tridacna's usual sluggishness may not represent his true potential.

VENOMOUS ANIMALS

The ability to administer poisons by biting or stinging assists in self-defense and/or the obtaining of food. The number of venomous sea animals is vast, and marine poisons are very complex. Russell estimates that there are 40,000 venomous marine animal injuries each year.[14] Fortunately, the number of fatalities is quite low, probably fewer than seventy-five yearly, excluding sea snakes.[15] The following discussion concentrates on those animals likely to be a problem to sport divers.

Venomous Invertebrates

These animals, lacking backbones, include representatives from the phyla Coelenterata, Echinodermata, Mollusca, and Annelida. Their stings vary widely in potency from minor skin irritation to death.

Coelenterates

Three classes are involved—the Hydrozoa, the Scyphozoa, and the Anthozoa. The Hydrozoa include "fire coral" (not a true coral) and the Portuguese man-of-war *(Physalia physalis)*, which is commonly mistaken for a jellyfish. Scyphozoa are the true jellyfish. Anthozoa include sea anemones and the true corals.

All of the coelenterates sting with nematocysts, which are tiny capsules on the tentacles containing a coiled thread tube with a sharp point. When the tentacle is stimulated, the nematocyst opens, and the tube strikes the victim, transmitting venom into him. Each tentacle contains numerous nematocysts, so the effect is greatly magnified.

Fire coral (from the Milleporina order of Hydrozoa) is frequently encountered by the tropical diver. A burning pain and then a rash result from contact with Millepora. Prevention involves wearing a protective suit with gloves and avoiding intimate reef encounters.

Unlike true jellyfish, the Portuguese man-of-war *(Physalia physalis)* has no independent method of locomotion. Each Physalia is actually a colony of specialized animals and depends on wind and sea currents to move. A beached Physalia maintains its stinging capability. Stinging causes severe pain and a rash in the area of tentacle contact. The toxin is experimentally lethal, but no human deaths from Portuguese men-of-war (with one possible exception) have been documented.[16, 17]

The jellyfish (Scyphozoa) include a myriad of species. Injuries range from minor stinging to rapid death. The toxins often leave a rash and some cause actual skin destruction in the area of contact.

As with the Portuguese man-of-war, beached specimens are still quite capable of stinging.

The only known human fatalities from coelenterates have been caused by the box jellyfish *(Chironex fleckeri)*, sometimes misleadingly called the sea wasp. This animal, found in the tropical Indo-Pacific of northern Australia and the Philippines, is one of the world's most poisonous animals. In mice experiments, it was found that box jellyfish toxin is 300 times as potent as that from the Portuguese man-of-war.[18] Death from cardiac and respiratory failure may ensue only a few minutes after a stinging. These jellyfish become very large, and they are strong swimmers. Their complex protein toxin has direct effects on the heart and also causes central respiratory inhibition.[19] Modern cardiopulmonary resuscitation has saved some swimmers, but the pain of first contact with the box jellyfish is so severe that swimmers may become incapacitated and drown before help can reach them. An antivenin is now available.[20] Because of its production in horse serum, it has a serious allergic liability, but in Australia life savers have been trained in antivenin use, since the course of serious Chironex poisoning is so swift.

Complete protective clothing is the best defense against all jellyfish. Eye injuries have occurred in swimmers who were not using goggles or masks. All jellyfish should be given a wide berth, especially box jellyfish. Divers on trips to Indo-Pacific areas should heed the seasonal warnings of sightings of this creature.

If an injury occurs, the tentacles should be removed. For many years it was believed that liberal amounts of alcohol poured over jellyfish tentacles would inactivate the nematocysts. Recent investigations with Chironex showed that alcohols actually cause nematocysts to fire.[21] Acetic acid or vinegar (which contains acetic acid) inactivates Chironex nematocysts. This appears to be true for Physalia also.[22,23] A wide variety of folk remedies has been used in treatment of jellyfish injuries. The most prudent course might be drenching with vinegar and then removing tentacles with a gloved hand. Gentle scraping may be necessary to remove adhering tentacle fragments. Two of the leading authorities on marine poisoning have taken opposite positions on the use of papaya-containing meat tenderizers for jellyfish sting treatment.[24,25] Meat tenderizers may injure human skin.[26]

In the class Anthozoa sea anemones and true corals cause trouble for divers. Sea anemones normally use their nematocysts to obtain food. Their toxin may affect man. Anemones, especially the large, tropical ones, should be enjoyed at a distance. Coral can sting skin. (Isolated toxin affects rabbit heart function.) Most coral injuries, however, result from secondary infection of coral cuts. Again, prevention requires a protective suit and careful swimming. Even small coral cuts should be vigorously cleansed with antibacterial soaps.

Echinodermata

Starfish and sea urchins belong in this group. Urchin spines, from a few inches in length to a foot, often break off after piercing a swimmer's hand or foot, and because of their brittleness, they are difficult to remove. Some types also have small barbed organs, called pedicellariae, interspersed among the spines. The spines can penetrate gloves, flippers, or shoes. The most common symptom is an intense burning sensation, followed by swelling and aching. Some tropical species are venomous and can cause paralysis or occasionally death from respiratory failure.[27] When possible, the spine should be removed. If left in the wound, it will eventually be absorbed anyway. However, on occasion foreign-body reactions may develop to retained spines. Crown of thorns starfish can cause painful wounds directly and from toxin action both.

Mollusca

The venomous Mollusca include squid and octopus (cephalopods) and cone shells (gastropods). Large squid do exist but not within diving depths. Octopus are probably the most misunderstood of all sea animals. We have all read of the fearful monsters who crush ships or attack divers. In truth most octopuses are small and nonaggressive. The risk from octopus comes more from their bite than from their grip. Venom, produced in salivary glands, is injected through the biting beak. A burning pain results which may spread out from the wound. Bleeding, more severe than could be expected from the size of the bite, implies some interference with the mechanism of blood coagulation.[28] In Australia the small and attractive blue-ringed octopus has a toxin that has caused human deaths.[29] The toxin interferes with nerve conduction and with the neuromuscular junction. The scarcely noticeable bite causes muscle paralysis, thus making breathing impossible. There is no antidote, but artificial ventilation can be lifesaving.

There are over 400 species of cone shells, all with venom apparatus. In 1958 Kohn identified ten species that had caused human injury: *C. geographus, C. textile, C. striatum, C. tulipa, C. aulicus, C. leppardus, C. anoria, C. obscurus, C. nanus,* and *C. pulicurium.*[30] *C. mormoreus* is also considered dangerous. The cone shell's venom is produced in the venom duct and then is transported to the pharynx. Radula (needlelike) teeth are formed in the radula sheath and moved through the pharynx to the proboscis, which holds a tooth. In attack, the tooth is jabbed into the victim, and venom is injected through it by means of a venom bulb, which acts like a pump.

Human injury usually results from stepping on a cone shell or from picking one up. Initially, the wound site is ischemic (pale); later, it becomes cyanotic (bluish), with swelling and numbness or sharp stinging and burning. Numbness and tingling may spread from the wound to involve the whole body up to the lips and the mouth. Muscle coordination may be lost, followed by paralysis of the voluntary muscles. Speech and swallowing become difficult; there may be visual blurring and double vision. Generalized itching is not uncommon. Severe cases end in coma and death from respiratory failure and cardiac arrest.[31] There is no specific method of therapy. Severe injuries may require prolonged mechanical support of ventilation. The exact composition of the cone toxin is unknown.[32,33] Since it is very difficult to make a quick identification of dangerous cones, great care should be taken in handling them.

Some cones can extend their proboscis to the broad end of their shells, so there is no completely safe place to grab a cone. With improved ventilatory care the 25 percent fatality rate should be reduced.[34]

Annelida

The segmented roundworms include blood worms with biting jaws and bristle worms with stinging bristles. Contact with either results in an inflamed wound with swelling and numbness.

VENOMOUS VERTEBRATES

Venomous vertebrates include elasmobranchs, fish, and reptiles. Again the severity of the attack varies widely as does treatment.

Elasmobranchs

Elasmobranchs include the venomous rays, the largest of which—the manta—may weigh 3,500 pounds and have a "wing" span of 20 feet. The graceful mantas have no venom apparatus and are completely nonaggressive; but because of their size and extremely rough skin, an accidental encounter would be painful at best. Venomous rays are found in seven families with wide distribution.

The ray has a modified caudal spine (stinger) near the base of the tail, which can be raised up and thrust into the victim. The spines vary in size. Because of its serrated surface and forward curvature, the spine can cause a wound six to ten times its own diameter. The venom is found in and excreted from two glandular grooves in the ventral lateral surface of the spine. Normally the spine is covered by a sheath, which detaches itself and remains in the wound.

Stings most often result from stepping on an unseen stingray. When walking in the water, it is best to shuffle the feet along—"the stingray shuffle"—rather than lift the feet normally. This shuffling disturbs the rays, and they swim away.

Stingray injuries are common. Fortunately, most of them cause only pain. Almost immediately, severe pain develops in the area of the wound. This pain persists for several hours and may last for more than two days. Initially the wound is cyanotic, but then it becomes red and swollen. Secondary infection, with sloughing of the tissues around the wound, is common. Systemic symptoms may include faintness, sweating, weakness, nausea, and muscle cramping. In severe cases, cardiac dysrhythmias, hypotension, and respiratory failure may develop. Large rays may cause penetrating wounds of the abdomen or chest.[35]

Stingray toxin affects both the heart and the central respiratory centers. It does not affect neuromuscular transmission.[36]

The wound should be well cleansed and the sheath removed. Soaking the wounded area in hot water for 30 to 90 minutes partially inactivates the toxin and relieves the pain.

If symptoms progress beyond localized pain, medical consultation is advisable.

Fish

Several diverse fish varieties inject venom through their body spines. Venomous fish are found throughout the world, over 220 species; space limits our discussion to the most common types.[37] Divers traveling to new areas should make it a general practice to inquire locally as to what poisonous fish may exist there. Some fish use protective camouflage while others are vividly colored. These fish are not large, but their lack of fear toward man is a tipoff to their insidious natures. Some of them, like the European weever fish, may be aggressive. Venomous fish include scorpion fish, weever fish, catfish, rabbitfish, stargazers, and toadfish.

Scorpion fish (Scorpaenidae)

The most frequently encountered venomous fish are members of the scorpion fish group: scorpion fish proper, lion-fish, and stonefish. Scorpion fish live along both United States coasts, while all three types may be found in the subtropics and tropical Pacific and Indian Oceans.

The fish radically differ in appearance and behavior. The showy lion-fish (zebra, turkey fish) swim freely, while the camouflaged scorpion and stonefish sit and wait. Their venom apparatus basically consists of dorsal, pelvic, and anal spines with attendant venom glands. When contacted, the spine penetrates the victim's skin, injecting the poison. The lion-fish has long slender spines among its lacy fins. Both the scorpion fish and the stonefish have shorter, heavier spines. The venoms appear to be heat-labile proteins.[38]

Intense, intolerable pain immediately follows an encounter with these fish. The pain, lasting 8 to 12 hours, may be so severe at the outset as to make swimming to shore impossible. The wound itself progresses from paleness to cyanosis. Numbness develops around the wound as pain radiates up the affected limb; the limb swells quickly and may stay swollen for weeks or months. In severe cases, the victim suffers from paralysis with respiratory and cardiac depression, delirium, convulsions, and coma.[39] Respiratory failure causes death. If the patient survives 24 hours his prognosis is good, although complete recovery may require weeks to months. The area of the wound often sloughs.

Stonefish cause the most severe injuries while scorpionfish stings generally result only in pain. Treatment of the injuries involves pain relief, wound care, and advanced therapy. Injectable analgesics seem to be less helpful than the infiltration of the wound with local anesthetics. Soaking in hot water helps relieve pain, inactivates the toxin, and initiates wound cleansing. Tetanus prophylaxis and systemic antibiotics are valuable because of the high incidence of infection.

Despite extensive research, the pharmacology of these fish venoms has not been satisfactorily elucidated. There are important primary and secondary effects on the respiratory and cardiovascular systems.[40] An antivenin for stonefish is available from the Commonwealth Serum Laboratories in Australia.[41] This antivenin has been very valuable in minimizing the effects of stonefish poisoning. It must be used with care because of its allergic potential due to its production in horses.

Reptiles

Marine snakes encompass over fifty species, several of which threaten man. These snakes live mainly in tropical waters. Like all other reptiles, they are air breathers; however, they can swim submerged for long periods. Their sizes range from 4 to 9 feet. The tail characteristically flattens into a paddlelike shape, helping in propulsion. Fangs in the upper jaw inject the venom. A sea snake carries about five times as much venom as that required to kill an adult man.[42] Fortunately, the snake's small jaws make his bite usually ineffective. Severe poisoning results in about 22 percent of the cases.[43]

Unlike what happens with most other venomous animals, snake bite symptoms do not result immediately. The wound area remains inconspicuous; generalized symptoms develop only after a latent period, 30 minutes to several hours. The victim notes a feeling of heaviness in his limbs, along with muscle stiffness and pain on motion. Serious cases develop ascending muscle paralysis. Paralysis of the respiratory muscles may result in death. The venom can cause red blood cell lysis (disintegration) and muscle fiber necrosis.

The patient should be kept absolutely inactive. Tourniquets are advised if the injury is promptly diagnosed. Fluids should be given, since this increases venom excretion and partially protects the kidneys from deposition of hemolyzed blood products. Tetanus prophylaxis should be given. If respiratory paralysis develops, ventilatory support will be necessary. Commonwealth Serum Labs has developed an antivenin that is effective even after symptoms have developed, but it must be used with care because of allergic potentials. Other snake antivenins, particularly tiger snake, are effective in sea snake poisonings. With the introduction of antivenin, the fatality rate in Malaya in cases of serious poisoning was reduced from over 50 percent down to 20 percent.[44]

Most epidemiological research on sea snakes has been done in Southeast Asia. There the majority of bites occur in waters of limited visibility, especially in river mouths. Reid discovered no cases occurring in persons actually swimming, although several bathers were bitten when they stepped on snakes.[45] In Australia, there have been only two fatalities from sea snake bites.[46] Australian waters are usually clear, so accidental encounters are less likely. Most sea snake injuries occur to fishermen, who catch the snakes in their nets.

Free swimming snakes are generally not aggressive and actually appear eager to investigate divers. They are particularly attracted to swim fins. Snakes may be more aggressive during their mating season. It is tempting to pet and hold these graceful animals, but their great potential should never be forgotten.

GENERAL COMMENTS

Many marine animals can cause injury, but, in fact, the risk of injury is slight for the average diver. A coral cut or minor jellyfish sting is the worst that most will suffer. The most toxic specimens are not found in continental United States waters. If a diver avoids coral, keeps his eyes open for rays and urchins, and refrains from baiting sharks, he is unlikely to be injured.

These animals—with the exception of sharks and barracuda—do not attack; if left alone, they will be no problem. Size does not determine danger. Sea animals usually are shy; if they are *not* wary, the careful diver will consider them poisonous until he has identified them. Shells should be picked up only by a gloved hand. Snakes and eels should be left alone.

First aid is vital in the treatment of attacks from all these animals. First, stop the bleeding; then, clean the wound. Have someone call a physician. Try to identify the guilty animal. Contact with most varieties is obvious to the diver. A stinging, painful wound while swimming is almost always due to a jellyfish. Generalized distress following some time after a mild wound is most likely due to a sea snake.

ANIMALS POISONOUS TO EAT

Poisonous marine animals include some very popular food fish as well as those not normally considered edible. Toxicity of a given animal may differ from area to area, depending on the season. Symptoms range from mild discomfort to death. Since many divers enjoy catching and eating animals, they need to know the risks of poisoning.

Mollusks

At certain times of the year, many forms of shellfish are poisonous; this may follow a "red tide," in which the mollusks are exposed to large numbers of microscopic dinoflagellates (*Gonyaulax catenella* or *Gonyaulax tamarensis*). These tiny animals are harmless to shellfish, but they cause man to become sick—cooking makes no difference.[47] Poisonous mollusks cannot be differentiated from nonpoisonous ones, but most regions do publicize dangerous periods.

The mollusks which may be involved are the bivalves: mussels, clams, oysters, and scallops. These animals should never be consumed during shellfish quarantine periods.

After eating a poisonous mollusk, symptoms of numbness and tingling of the lip occur within 30 minutes; this tingling may spread to the limbs. Nausea, vomiting, and diarrhea are common. In extreme cases, paralysis gradually develops; fatalities are produced in 2 to 12 hours from respiratory failure.[48] The potent toxin, saxitoxin, interferes with transmission through the nerves. Its action is like that of maculotoxin (from the blue-ringed octopus) and tetraodontoxin (puffer fish).[49]

There is no specific antidote to saxitoxin. Survival is likely if ventilatory support can be provided when necessary. The Center for Disease Control reported no fatalities in fifty-five cases between 1970 and 1974;[50] unfortunately, there have been fatalities in California subsequent to the CDC report.

Sharks

Eating shark meat happens to be less dangerous than the threat of being eaten by them; however, shark poisoning does exist and can be serious. The liver seems to be the most toxic organ, although poison in muscle tissue has been recorded also. Symptoms appear within about 30 minutes and include nausea, vomiting, tingling about the mouth, and burning of the tongue.[51] Severe cases suffer muscular incoordination and paralysis. Fatalities may occur from respiratory failure. The toxin has not been identified, and there is no specific mode of treatment. Flesh from American sharks has not been considered a problem.

Fish

Fish poisoning includes ciguatera, tetrodont, and scombroid.

Ciguatera

Over 400 species of fish reportedly cause ciguatera, the most common form of fish poisoning. The list includes common fish such as snappers, bass, jacks, pompano, parrotfish, and barracuda. It appears that the fish become poisonous from eating toxic dinoflagellates *(Gamberdiscus toxicus)*.[52] Toxin accumulates in the fish, causing him no harm, but when man catches and eats him, this stored toxin causes the poisoning. Distribution of toxic fish is not consistent even within a small area.

Because of toxin accumulation, older and larger fish of a given species are more likely to be dangerous than small ones. The liver and gonads contain most of the poison, but some may also be found in the fish's flesh. Cooking does not inactivate toxicity.

Symptoms from ciguatera poisoning vary from individual to individual.[53] Within 3 to 12 hours of ingestion, there is usually numbness and/or tingling around the mouth. Most victims will have disturbances in sensation. Cold objects may appear hot—one person blew on ice cream to cool it off. Joint and muscle aching is very common as are vomiting and diarrhea. Other complications include weakness, dizziness, ataxia, chills, and headache. Most cases resolve themselves within a few days, but weakness, itching, and pain may persist for months. Bradycardia (abnormally slow heart rate) and hypotension may develop. In severe poisoning, respiratory paralysis may be fatal.

Ciguatoxin has been identified, but its exact mode of action in man remains undefined. At one time it was thought to be an anticholinesterase but this has been discounted.[54]

There is no specific treatment. Gastric lavage may be useful if the onset of symptoms is prompt. Atropine helps abdominal complaints, but not the other disturbances. Severe cases require ventilatory support. Halstead cites a 12 percent fatality rate[55] but this is very high compared with figures from Hawaii (no fatalities),[56] Center for Disease Control (no fatalities),[57] and the South Pacific (three deaths in 3,009 cases).[58]

Ciguatera is a very large problem throughout the warm water regions of the world. It afflicts many common food fish as well as moray eels and some turtles. No simple method has been devised to determine whether or not a given fish is poisonous. Natives find it useful to try parts of a suspect fish on stray cats or dogs. It is not necessary to travel far away to experience ciguatera; it is common in Hawaii, Florida, the Bahamas, and the Caribbean. Withers states that ciguatera is the "most frequently foodborne disease of chemical nature in the U.S."[59]

Tetraodont Poisoning

Many species of puffer fish, box fish, and trigger fish contain tetraodontoxin. In Japan where fugu (puffer fish) is considered a delicacy, the most problems have developed. Between 1967 and 1976 Japan had 1,015 patients with puffer poisoning. Thirty-seven percent died.[60] This establishes tetraodont as the most dangerous form of fish poisoning. The toxin is concentrated in the gonads and liver, but traces are also found in the skin and flesh. Cooking does not inactivate the poison.[61] Because the toxin is water soluble, progressive soaks in fresh water will reduce the fish's danger, as will not eating the liver, skin, or gonads.

Tetraodontoxin acts by depressing nerve conduction. This is one of the most potent toxins known.[62] Its action resembles that of saxitoxin and maculotoxin. Symptoms begin minutes after eating. As with ciguatera, the initial symptom is tingling about the mouth. This gradually becomes numbness, which spreads through the limbs. Gastrointestinal symptoms may be present. Heavy salivation may be followed by difficulty in speaking and swallowing. Paralysis may develop along with respiratory failure, which causes death. Large doses affect nerve conduction within the heart. There is no antidote. Treatment is for respiratory failure and hypotension. The course is shorter than in ciguatera, and death may result within 30 minutes.

Puffer fish should not be eaten. Despite supervision, in Japan over half the food poisoning deaths resulted from eating fugu.

Scombroid Poisoning

Scombroid poisoning can be eliminated by proper storage techniques. Fish with dark flesh—tuna, mackerel, dolphin, bonita, etc.—carry this type of poisoning. It originates from histamine and a histaminelike substance formed in the fish.[63]

A bacteria (proteus) metabolizes histidine, which is stored in the dark flesh. This transformation forms histamine and saurine. If the fish are promptly cooked, canned, or refrigerated, the bacteria are killed before they can produce these toxic products.

Even if you are made ill by eating a scombroid fish, this poses the least danger of all forms of fish poisoning. The period of illness lasts only 8 to 12 hours. The most characteristic symptom is a sharp, peppery taste in the mouth, after ingestion. Hives and a red rash may possibly develop. Abdominal pain may be felt. Fast heart rate and respiratory distress plague severe cases. Gastric lavage should be performed, and antihistamines should be given by mouth or injection to relieve symptoms. Divers who spear scombroid fish should be careful to store them properly.

GENERAL PREVENTION

Because of the potential seriousness of marine animal poisoning and the absence of specific therapy, preventive measures should be heeded. Of first importance is the knowledge of which animals prove dangerous. Since this varies from area to area, a thorough investigation should be made before eating the fish of that area. If ciguatera is known, fish commonly infected—especially barracuda—should be avoided. Large fish of a given type are more dangerous than small ones.

Fish should be cooked, and internal organs ought not to be eaten. Fish should be cleaned promptly and kept cold if not prepared immediately. Puffer fish and moray eels should never be eaten.

NOTES: MARINE LIFE HAZARDS

1. Bruce Halstead, *Dangerous Marine Animals* (Centreville, MD: Cornell Maritime Press, 1980).
2. P. M. Gilbert, "The Behavior of Sharks," *Scientific American,* 207: 60–68, 1962.
3. *Ibid.*
4. Bruce Halstead, *op. cit.*
5. D. Miller, "Shark Attacks," *CenCal Diver,* 20: 1, 6–8, 1979.
6. Bruce Halstead, *op. cit.*
7. D. Davies, G. Campbell, "The Aetiology, Clinical Pathology, and Treatment of Shark Attack," *Journal of the Royal Navy Medical Service,* 48: 110–136, 1962.
8. N. Goodwin, J. White, "First Aid for Shark Attack Victims," *South African Medical Journal,* 52: 981–82, 1977.
9. C. Edmonds, "Dangerous Marine Animals," *Australian Family Physician,* 5: 381–407.
10. E. Gudger, C. Breder, "The Barracuda (Sphyraena): Dangerous to Man," *Journal of the American Medical Association,* 90: 1938–43, 1928.
11. W. Miner, "The Noxious and Obnoxious Marine Life of the Tropical Pacific," unpublished thesis, 1967.
12. S. Dalton, "Understanding Killer Whales," *Pacific Diver,* August 1977, pp. 18ff.
13. Miller, *op cit.*
14. F. Russell, Poisonous and Venomous Marine Animals and Their Toxins," *Annals of the New York Academy of Science,* 245: 57–64, 1975.
15. *Ibid.*
16. R. Southcott, "The Neurologic Effects of Noxious Marine Creatures," *Topics on Tropical Neurology,* Contemporary Neurology Series, R. Hornabrook, ed. (Philadelphia: F. A. Davis, 1975), 165–258.
17. R. Goldhahn, "Scuba Diving Deaths: A Review and Approach for the Pathologist," *Legal Medical Annual,* 1976: 109–32, 1977.
18. Southcott, *op cit.*
19. J. Williamson et al., "Serious Envenomation by the Northern Australia Box Jellyfish (Chironex fleckeri)," *Medical Journal of Australia,* 1: 13–15, 1980.
20. *Ibid.*
21. R. Hartwick, "Disarming the Box-Jellyfish, Nematocyst Inhibition in Chironex Fleckeri," *Medical Journal of Australia,* 1: 15–20, 1980.

22. B. Turner, "Disarming the Bluebottle Treatment of Physalia Envenomation," *Medical Journal of Australia*, 2: 394–95, 1980.
23. J. W. Burnett et al., "First Aid for Jellyfish Envenomation," *Southern Medical Journal*, 7: 870–72, 1983.
24. Bruce Halstead, *op. cit.*
25. Russell, *op. cit.*
26. Burnett, *op. cit.*
27. Bruce Halstead, *op. cit.*
28. Bruce Halstead, *op. cit.*
29. S. Sutherland, W. Lane, "Toxins and Mode of Envenomation of the Common Ringed or Blue-Banded Octopus," *Medical Journal of Australia*, 1: 893–98, 1969.
30. A. Kohn, "Cone Shell Stings, Recent Cases of Human Injury Due to Venomous Marine Snails of the Genus Conus," *Hawaii Medical Journal*, 17: 528–32, 1958.
31. Southcott, *op. cit.*
32. A. Kohn et al., Preliminary Studies on the Venom of the Marine Snail, Conus," *Annals of the New York Academy of Science*, 90: 206–25, 1960.
33. B. W. Halstead, "Current Status of Marine Biotoxicology—an Overview," *Clinical Toxicology*, 18: 1–24, 1981.
34. Kohn, "Cone Shell Stings."
35. T. Cross, "An Unusual Stingray Injury—the Skindiver at Risk," *Medical Journal of Australia*, 2: 947–48, 1976.
36. B. W. Halstead, *op. cit.*
37. F. Russell, "Comparative Pharmacology of Some Animal Toxins," *Federal Proceedings*, 26: 1206–24, 1967.
38. Edmonds, *op cit.*
39. Southcott, *op. cit.*
40. R. Carlson, "Some Pharmacological Properties of the Venom of the Scorpionfish Scorpaena guttata-II," *Toxicon*, 11: 167–80, 1973.
41. Edmonds, *op. cit.*
42. H. Reid, "Sea Snake Antivenene: Successful Trial," *British Medical Journal*, 2: 576–77, 1962.
43. *Ibid.*
44. H. Reid, "Epidemiology of Sea-Snake Bites," *Journal of Tropical Medical Hygiene*, 78: 106–13. 1975.
45. *Ibid.*
46. H. Heatwole, "Sea Snake Attack: Myth or Menace?" *Skin Diving in Australia and New Zealand*, April 1978, pp. 40–45.
47. Southcott, *op. cit.*
48. J. Hughes, M. Merson, "Fish and Shellfish Poisoning," *New England Journal of Medicine*, 295: 1117–20, 1976.
49. Southcott, *op. cit.*
50. Hughes and Merson, *op. cit.*
51. Bruce Halstead, *op. cit.*
52. Bagnis et al., "Clinical Observations on 3,009 cases of Ciguatera (Fish Poisoning) in the South Pacific," *American Journal of Tropical Medical and Hygiene*, 28: 1067–73, 1979.
53. *Ibid.*

54. F. Russell, "Ciguatera Poisoning: A Report of 35 Cases," *Toxicon*, 13: 383–85, 1975.
55. Bruce Halstead, *op. cit.*
56. P. Helfrich, "Fish Poisoning in Hawaii," *Hawaii Medical Journal*, 22: 361–72, 1963.
57. Hughes and Merson, *op. cit.*
58. Bagnis, *op. cit.*
59. N. W. Withers, "Ciguatera Fish Poisoning," *Annual Review of Medicine*, 33: 97–111, 1982.
60. S. Tsunerari et al., "Puffer Poisoning in Japan—A Case Report," *Journal of Forensic Science*, 25: 240–45, 1980.
61. Southcott, *op. cit.*
62. *Ibid.*
63. Hughes and Merson, *op. cit.*

2 | Physical Environment

The water surrounding the diver makes up his physical environment. The effects of this medium will manifest themselves in many ways: direct and indirect effects of pressure plus the differences in temperature, vision, etc. Physical changes result in the diverse physiological modifications observed during diving.

PRESSURE

Certainly, high pressure is the most noticeable property of the fluid environment. Living under water is often referred to as living in a hyperbaric (high pressure) environment. Almost every swimmer has had ear pains while under the water and been vaguely aware that "pressure" caused the pain. Pressure, defined as force per unit of area, is commonly expressed as pounds per square inch (psi) or grams per square centimeter (gm/cm²). These measurements reflect the power which a gas or liquid exerts in all directions. Pressure in a vertical column can be spoken of as weight, since the force exerted by it depends upon the weight of the column.

The column of air that reaches from the earth's surface to the upper limits of the atmosphere exerts pressure due to its weight. The total weight of this column of air is equivalent to 14.7 psi; it has sufficient force to raise a column of mercury (Hg) 29.92

inches or 760 mm. Pressure gauges other than mercury manometers (as in barometers) do not measure this pressure and hence read zero at the earth's surface. We speak, then, of "gauge" versus absolute pressure. To obtain the absolute pressure, one must add 14.7 psi to the gauge reading, thus allowing for atmospheric air pressure. Atmospheric pressure (14.7 psi) is called *1 atmosphere* or *1 atmosphere pressure.*

Water is much heavier per unit of volume than is air; therefore water exerts more pressure for each foot of depth. Thirty-three feet of salt water weighs as much as the entire atmospheric height of 18,000 miles. Each 33 feet of descent into water will add 14.7 psi to total pressure.* For example, at 66 feet, the water alone has a pressure 2x atmospheric or 29.4 psi. Total pressure acting on an object at this depth includes the air pressure exerted on the water's surface and will be 14.7 plus 29.4 or 44.1 psi. Since each 33 feet of salt H_2O equals 1 atmospheric pressure, dividing depth by 33 will give the number of atmospheres in a given depth. To find the total number of atmospheres, simply add 1 to account for the pressure of air pushing down on the water. Thus 66 feet can be called 3 atmospheres. In this book, depth will frequently be given in atmospheres, and unless otherwise noted will mean absolute pressure.

Because of the constant relationship of 14.7 psi per 33 feet of salt water, each foot of descent equals .445 psig (gauge). The pressure resulting from a known depth can be found by multiplying depth in feet by .445; absolute pressure adds 14.7 psi to the product.

The proportionate increase in pressure becomes less per unit of depth change as depth increases, despite the fact that each foot still adds .445 pounds of pressure. As total pressure increases, each added increment represents a smaller percentage of the total. For example, at 33 feet pressure has increased 14.7 pounds and is twice surface pressure; this increase is 50 percent of the total pressure. At 66 feet pressure has increased another 14.7 pounds, but this is only one third of the total. (See table.)

---

*All of these figures hold true at sea level. In the mountains, the altitude reduces ambient pressure. For example, atmospheric pressure in Denver is 640 mmHg. Pressure in mountain lakes is diminished because of the lower air pressure.

DEPTH AND PRESSURE

Depth	Atmospheres Absolute	Pressure	Percent total Pressure added by each 33 feet descent
Surface	1	14.7 psi	—
33 feet	2	29.4	50 percent
66 feet	3	44.1	33
99 feet	4	58.8	25
132 feet	5	73.5	20
165 feet	6	88.2	17

The average man's body has a surface area of 19.4 square feet. With 14.7 psi at sea level, the total force on the body is then 41,000 pounds. At 33 feet it would be 82,000 pounds, and at 165 feet 246,000 pounds. The body can withstand this enormous pressure with ease since it transmits the pressure, thus exerting an equal force outward. (See diagram, page 36.) Fluids are not compressed, and the body has a fluid content of approximately 65 percent. Pressure changes are of significance only when a differential pressure exists, as in a gas cavity. For example, though the chest is quite compressible, an excessive amount of pressure will compress lung volume to intolerable limits. Creation of unequal pressure causes the ear pain of diving. In theory, the body can tolerate infinite pressures as long as these pressures are equalized in the air spaces. In fact, extreme pressures will slightly compress fluids. Uneven compression can cause forces that may be both painful and destructive. In some dives, approaching 600 feet, divers have experienced joint pain during the descent; slowing the descent eased the pain, which implies that pressure equalization occurred slowly. Experimental animals have been subjected to 4,000 feet pressure with no ill effects directly attributable to pressure.[1]

Weight per unit volume, density, represents the number of molecules of a substance contained in a given volume; this may be expressed as pounds per cubic foot (pound/foot^3) or grams per cubic centimeter (gm/cm^3).

Rising temperature activates molecules, thus increasing intermolecular distance. Fewer particles will be contained in the same volume, so the weight per unit volume decreases. Warm water

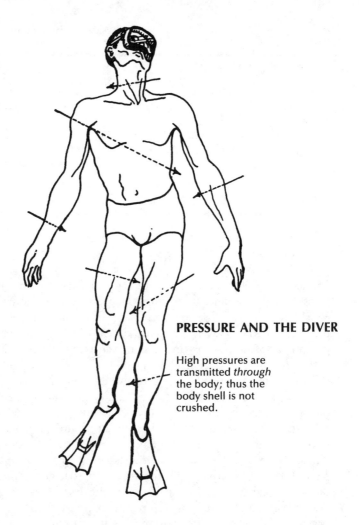

PRESSURE AND THE DIVER

High pressures are transmitted *through* the body; thus the body shell is not crushed.

thus floats on cold water. Because of water's complex structure, density does not follow temperature in the lower ranges. Ice at 0° Centigrade floats on melted water (0–4°C).

High pressure reduces the intermolecular distance, thus increasing the number of molecules in a certain volume. Fluids are virtually noncompressible, but can form gas if pressure on them is sufficiently reduced. Water turns to steam at a lower temperature in the mountains because of reduced atmospheric pressure.

Salt water weighs 64 pounds/foot^3, and fresh water weighs 62 pounds/foot^3; the difference is due to dissolved salts.

BUOYANCY

Water density determines an object's buoyancy. According to Archimedes' principle, *an object immersed partially or wholly in a liquid is buoyed up by a force equal to the weight of the liquid displaced.* Object volume determines the amount of water displaced, and water density determines the buoyant force. Displacement of one cubic foot of salt H_2O creates an upward force of 64 pounds. Comparison of the density of the object with the water determines the state of buoyancy. Neutral buoyancy at a given depth means that the object floats with no tendency to rise or to sink. The weight of the object is the same as the amount of H_2O displaced—that is, the densities are the same. Positive buoyancy means that the object tends to rise in the fluid. In negative buoyancy, the object sinks. At the surface, neutral and positive buoyancy are equivalent, although more of a positively buoyant mass will be out of the water because less displacement is required to maintain buoyancy.

The human body has a density close to that of water; this is not surprising, since the body is largely made of water. Density varies among individuals in relationship to fat content. Fat has a low liquid content and is thus less heavy than an equivalent quantity of muscle. Obese persons float better than lean ones. Women have a proportionately higher fat content at a given weight and are generally good floaters. A Navy study found a range of 1.021 gm/cm^3 to 1.097 gm/cm^3 in men. The average for lean men was 1.081 and 1.056 for obese men.[2] Salt water density is 1.027 gm/cm^3 (64 pounds/foot^3) and fresh H_2O is 1 gm/cm^3. All but the very fattest men hence would be slightly negatively buoyant in salt water, and all would sink in fresh water; however, by taking a deep breath the swimmer increases his volume (by chest expansion) while adding little weight. His displacement rises, and in all persons, this will be sufficient to permit floating. This can be demonstrated by lying in the water and breathing through a snorkel tube. During inhalation you will rise slightly and then will sink a bit during exhalation. A deep inspiration decreases body density by increasing volume. During a breath-hold dive, increasing sea pressure compresses the chest, thus reducing lung volume; this decrease raises body density, and buoyancy becomes negative. A "bottom drop" is made by taking a deep breath and pushing off from the surface. The initial velocity will carry the person to the point where lung compression causes negative buoyancy, and a deep "fall" can be made with no effort. Negatively buoyant persons do not require an initial push off.

Wearing a wet suit creates a positive buoyancy from the air in the cells of the suit. It is difficult to dive in a wet suit unless added weights are worn. At very great depths, pressure compression eliminates this buoyant force.

SCUBA bottles, when charged, are slightly negatively buoyant; however, when their air has been used, they have a density less than that of salt water. Empty tanks have a positive buoyancy of 3 to 10 pounds, depending upon their composition and size.

TEMPERATURE

Upon entering the water, one is almost always aware of a chilling sensation. Body heat passes directly through the water, just as it passes through the handle of a tin cup. Because water conducts heat much better than air, water feels colder than air of the same temperature.

The ocean is divided into three winter and four spring and summer temperature bands (thermoclines). In winter, at midlatitudes, temperature stays at a fairly constant 59 degrees F to a depth of 1,500 feet. From 1,500 feet down to 4,000 feet, the temperature drops steadily to about 39 degrees. Below this depth there is little temperature change. In spring and summer, the sun warms the surface water and forms another thermocline. Temperature in the upper 50 to 70 feet may reach 77 degrees and there may be nearly a 20 degree F temperature change from the surface to 200 to 300 feet.[3] In diving, the greatest change is noted in the shallow depths, since the majority of solar heat absorption occurs within 15 feet in summer and 30 feet in winter.

In almost all cases, diving will be done in water where chilling, rather than overheating, is the problem. Heavy work in some tropical waters with temperatures over 86 degrees F might cause overheating and heat exhaustion. With the exception of this warm water diving, temperature maintenance is one of the biggest problems in diving.

Upon immersion, heat begins to be lost to the water. Skin

temperature quickly decreases but the central body (core) temperature falls slowly. Several mechanisms permit core temperature maintenance. Blood flow to the skin is reduced; this means that the skin and subcutaneous fat form an insulating shell. Heat production increases. As warm blood leaves the core, it heats blood that is returning to the core (counter current heat exchange). These heat conserving mechanisms are not sufficient to prevent heat loss permanently. Blood flow to the scalp is not markedly reduced, and the head thus accounts for 50 percent of heat loss.[4] The SCUBA diver has to warm his cold inhaled air, and this may account for 25 percent of total heat expenditure.

In addition to being uncomfortable, cold water can be quite dangerous. Chilling of the hands quickly reduces manual dexterity. The diver may be unable to use his equipment. With sufficient chilling it may be difficult even to hold a SCUBA mouthpiece between the teeth.

Cold has a "distraction effect," which takes the diver's mind from the dive and focuses it on the sensation of cold. This distrac-

THERMOCLINES

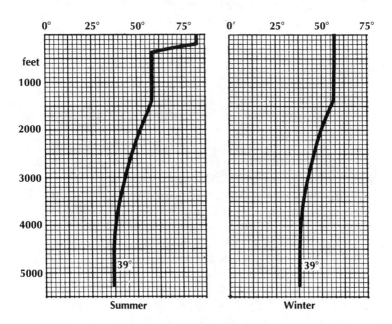

Summer   Winter

tion is obviously dangerous in itself and may also interact with fatigue, nitrogen narcosis, or anxiety.

Core temperature will not significantly fall during the usual recreational dive. Working dives or involuntary immersions can cause severe heat loss (hypothermia). When core temperature falls about 2 degrees F, shivering begins.[5] This increases heat production but also increases heat loss since skin blood flow increases. The net effect is a loss of body heat. With further decreases, mental changes are more serious and at about 90 degrees F, serious disturbances in the rhythm of the heart develop.[6] Immersion in very cold water (below 40 degrees F) can be fatal even before central body temperature falls. The victim of a cold water immersion is overwhelmed by the cold, has muscle rigidity, and breathes very rapidly. He will be unable to swim even a few yards.[7] Keatinge suggests that sudden exposure to cold water may cause heart rhythm disturbances.[8]

It is impossible to predict tolerance times precisely for immersion in water normally encountered by divers. This is affected by activity, since exercise in waters warmer than 75 degrees F reduces heat loss through increased heat production. In colder water, activity may increase heat loss because exercise causes more blood flow to the previously vasoconstricted skin. Very heavy exn 75 degrees F reduces heat loss through increased heat production. In colder water, activity may increase heat loss because exercise causes more blood flow to the previously vasoconstricted skin. Very heavy exercise in cold water may offset the heat loss.[9] Any clothing worn will reduce heat loss by adding insulation. A person's body composition is also important, since thicker fat layers improve insulation. People vary in their voluntary tolerance to cold. Finally, there appears to be some physical adaptation to cold conferred by frequent cold water diving.[10, 11] Cessation of cold stress causes loss of this adaptation.[12]

Divers reduce cold's insult by using exposure suits. Basically, these suits reduce heat loss by providing more insulation. The types of suits are discussed in Chapter 3, Equipment.

It is very important that divers understand the dangers of cold. When a dive becomes uncomfortable, it is time to stop. After leaving cold water, body temperature typically falls further ("after drop") as cold blood from the periphery once again enters the central circulation. Divers should wrap up after diving to reduce further chilling. After a dive it takes at least an hour to restore the lost heat. Even if body temperature is normal, there may be heat loss. During a multidive day, this heat loss may accumulate dangerously, unless care is taken to rewarm after each dive.

VISION AND LIGHT

In air, light rays are refracted by the cornea and focused on the retina. Proper focusing depends upon a difference in the refractive properties of the cornea and the air. Water has almost the same refraction index as the cornea, so light passes through it and the cornea with almost no bending. Because this light does not focus on the retina, images are blurred. Visual acuity underwater without a mask is one tenth of the surface acuity.[13] Use of a mask places an air layer between the water and the cornea, thus reestablishing a refractive difference.

Water bends light rays in such a fashion that the perceptions of size, distance, and relative distance of objects (stereoacuity) are disrupted. The eye interprets objects as 25 percent larger than their true size.[14] This magnifying property of masks may lead to the spearing of small fish or to the exaggeration of a "sea monster's" size. Light refraction makes objects appear 25 percent closer. Other considerations, however, result in distant objects actually appearing farther away than the true distance.[15] Stereoacuity may be reduced to 20 percent of normal. Interestingly, experienced divers are partially able to adapt to many of the underwater visual disturbances.[16]

Peripheral vision is markedly impaired in diving, chiefly because of reflection from the flat face plate. Goggles almost completely eliminate peripheral vision.

When light enters the water, its intensity is reduced by scattering, by water absorption, and by the absorption by suspended particles. Depth of light penetration varies, but in clearest water, light cannot maintain photosynthesis below 656 feet.[17]

Light attenuation first affects both ends of the wave-length spectrum of visible light; with increasing depth, the range is further constricted, leaving only a midrange light. Below about 40 feet red and orange fade; yellow and green are eliminated at about 120 feet. Blue persists the longest. Objects appear to lose their colors, but artificial light, used for work or photography, will restore normal colors.

SOUND

Water transmits sound four times as fast as air, because of the high rate of sound energy loss in H_2O; thus normal speech is impossible. At depth, the deepest basso has a preadolescent voice. The reason for this remains unclear. The most likely explanation would seem to relate to the changes in density.

GASES

The force of water pressure is transmitted throughout the body and affects the body's gas spaces. In diving, changes in sea pressure and temperature will be reflected within the body's gas spaces. As water pressure increases, lung compression will occur, unless the air supply pressure is increased correspondingly. Increases in gas pressure augment gas uptake by the blood. These changes—all due to the rising ambient pressure—cause the major maladies of diving: decreased respiratory efficiency, carbon dioxide intoxication, decompression sickness, nitrogen narcosis, oxygen poisoning, lung rupture, and the various forms of "squeeze."

The relationships among temperature, pressure, and volume are expressed by the general gas law and its derivatives. These laws apply to "ideal" gases and are not strictly true for actual gases. They make three untrue assumptions: 1. The gas molecules, themselves, occupy no space; volume is accorded only to the space between molecules. (Because gases have such large intermolecular spaces, the volume of the molecules is insignificant in comparison with the intermolecular volume.) 2. The molecules do not interact. (If molecules combined, their energy would be reduced and intermolecular volume would decrease. Some interaction does exist but it is generally not significant.) 3. The collisions are perfectly elastic; no energy is lost through collision. (Perfectly elastic collisions do not occur, but the slight energy loss need not be considered.)

The general gas law states that the product of absolute pressure and volume equals the number of moles (1 mole = 22.4 l) times absolute temperature* times the universal gas constant:

$$PV = n \text{ (moles) } R \text{ (gas constant) } T$$

---

*Temperature is changed to absolute by adding 273 to Centigrade readings to give degrees Kelvin, or by adding 460 to Fahrenheit readings.

The universal gas constant (R) is expressed in liter atmospheres/gm molecules Kelvin and has a value of .082. It is derived from solving the gas formula at standard conditions:

$$1 \text{ mole, } 1 \text{ atm, } 273 \text{ K, } 1 \text{ liter}$$

Since for a given situation, NR is constant, the equation can be rewritten:

$$\frac{PV}{T} = NR \quad \text{or} \quad \frac{PV}{T} = K$$

A second set of P, V, and T will also yield the constant K:

$$\frac{P_1V_1}{T_1} = K \quad \frac{P_2V_2}{T_2} = K \quad ; \quad \frac{P_1V_1}{T_1} = \frac{P_2V_2}{T_2}$$

Simple algebra permits the solving for any of the three factors when two are known.

GAS PRESSURE

Boyle's law can be derived from the general equation that states *at constant temperature, volume of gas is inversely proportional to the pressure placed on it*. High pressure pushes the gas molecules together. The equation becomes

$$\frac{P_1V_1}{T_1} = \frac{P_2V_2}{T_1}$$

Since T is constant it can be dropped to give

$$P_1V_1 = P_2V_2$$

If pressure is known, $V_2 = \frac{P_1V_1}{P_2}$. Obviously, a fall in pressure from P_1 to P_2 will increase V_2 while a rise will lower it. In a simple example, a diver's chest holds 6 liters of air at 1 atmospheric pressure. What is its volume under 2 atmospheric pressure (33 feet)?

$$V_1 = 6 \quad P_1 = 1 \qquad \qquad (6)\ (1) = (V_2)\ (2)$$
$$\text{so}$$
$$V_2 = ? \quad P_2 = 2 \qquad \qquad V_2 = 3L$$

In diving the pressures involved are those of the water acting on the body. Since pressure is directly proportional to depth, volume is also dependent on depth. The importance of Boyle's law in understanding diving physiology can hardly be overstated; it permits explanation of "squeeze," lung overexpansion during ascent, formation of gas bubbles, and duration of air supply.

A balloon provides a ready model to examine the effects of water pressure on volume. Take this compressible sphere with a hypothetical volume of 10 down to 33 feet in salt water. Here its volume will be reduced by 50 percent. $(1) (10) = (2) V_2$; $V_2 = 5$. At 66 feet one more atmosphere of pressure has been added, and volume will be 3.33. At 99 feet, or 4 atmospheres absolute, the balloon's volume is reduced to 2.5.

On ascent to the surface, the balloon will expand to its original volume of 10. If it were inflated to 10 at 99 feet, it would expand four times during ascent to a volume of 40, which might well result in its explosion. This, as will be discussed later, is the basis of lung rupture in noncontrolled ascents made after breathing high pressure air.

Although volume is directly proportional to pressure, the rate of volume change decreases with depth. Each foot comprises a larger portion of the total pressure in the shallow range and hence causes a greater proportionate change in volume. Thirty-three feet from the surface doubles pressure, but going from 33 feet to 66 feet raises total pressure by only 33 percent. Graphic representation of volume to depth gives a hyperbolic curve. (See graph.) This explains why the effects of pressure differential are more noticeable during the early stages of descent.

A sphere demonstrates one further point. For a sphere

$$V = 4/3\pi r^3 \qquad \text{or } R = \sqrt[3]{\dfrac{V}{4/3\pi}}$$

Since $4/3\pi$ is constant, sphere radius is a function of the cube root of volume. As volume is directly affected by pressure, radius is affected by the cube root of pressure. By substituting $4/3\pi r^3$ for V in the equation for Boyle's law, it can be seen that

$$r_2 = r_1\sqrt[3]{P_1/P_2}$$

In the balloon with V of 10, the radius would be 1.34. When V is 2.5 (at 99 feet) radius is .843. Thus while volume is reduced to ¼, radius remains over half of the initial value. In decompression and air embolism, bubble radius is more significant than volume.

SPHERE VOLUME & RADIUS RELATED TO DEPTH (PRESSURE)

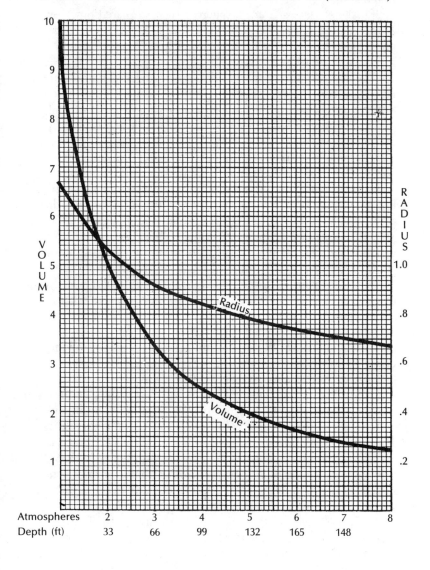

It can be seen that after a point, increases in P cause little reduction in radius. Radii for different pressures are included on the graph.

Finally, surface area for a sphere is radius squared times 4π. Since volume is related to radius cubed, changes in r have a greater effect on volume than on surface area. Pressure causing a given bubble radius change will cause a greater reduction in volume than in surface area. This has practical significance in recompression therapy of decompression sickness. Recompression can reduce radius to the point of permitting blood flow while still maintaining a surface area effective in gas diffusion from the bubble.

The reduction in gas volume by increasing pressure explains why surface supplied diving requires more air at increasing depths and why SCUBA tanks have a shorter supply duration. Discounting the effect of increasing respiratory needs in diving, the amount of air in each breath (tidal volume) does not change with depth. The average amount at rest is 500 ml, with a respiratory rate of about 12 per minute, so that volume per minute is 6 l, regardless of depth. Air, supplied from the surface, must be released to the diver at pressure equivalent to dive pressure in order to prevent lung compression. Because pressure reduces volume, the intake volume of the air compressor must be increased so that after pressurization, the supplied volume will be equal to body needs. For a diver at 99 feet (4 atmospheres) requiring 6 l/min under 4 atmosphere pressure, the surface requirement is 24 l.

SCUBA bottles are rated in cubic feet at maximum pressure. A so-called 72 cubic foot tank will hold slightly less than half a cubic foot of air at atmospheric pressure. Compression fills the tank with ½ cubic foot of air at 2150 psig, 147 times atmospheric. This small volume of high pressure air will expand to 72 cubic feet if discharged on the surface. At 33 feet, the discharged volume is halved by the higher outside pressure. Since air use remains constant with depth change, the decrease in effective bottle capacity proportionately reduces supply duration.

With moderate exertion, as in SCUBA diving, the body requires abourt 28 l (1 cubic foot) of air per minute. Thus, at the surface, a 72 cubic foot bottle will last approximately 72 minutes, and this will decrease with depth; at 33 feet the 36 cubic foot effective value only lasts 36 minutes. The following graph shows

SUPPLY VOLUME RELATED TO DEPTH

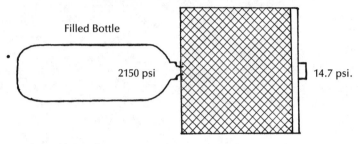

Filled Bottle

2150 psi

14.7 psi.

1 Opened at surface

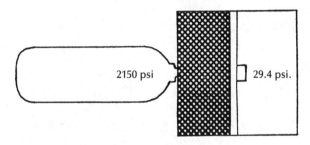

2150 psi

29.4 psi.

2 At 33 ft. the doubled ambient pressure limits
volume expansion to ½ surface value

the relationship of duration and depth. Obviously an incompletely filled tank lasts a shorter time at any depth.

A second part of Boyle's law relates gas density to pressure: *Under constant temperature, density is directly proportional to absolute pressure.* (Reduction of intermolecular distances by pressure allows a greater weight of molecules to be contained in a given space.) High density of air at depth increases airway resistance, thus making breathing harder.

TEMPERATURE

Charles's law states that *with constant pressure volume is directly proportional to absolute temperature:*

$$V_2 = \frac{V_1 T_2}{T_1}$$

Higher temperatures increase the intermolecular distance by causing greater activity. An inflatable surf mat, therefore, becomes fuller when left in the hot sun. If the volume is held constant, raising the temperature will similarly elevate pressure. In charging SCUBA bottles, high pressure air forced into a rigid tank results in high temperatures within the bottle. Placing a warm SCUBA bottle in cold water will lower its internal pressure.

PARTIAL PRESSURE

Dry air contains 79.03 percent nitrogen (N_2), 20.92 percent oxygen (O_2), .04 percent dioxide (CO_2), and traces of rare gases and carbon monoxide. As total gas pressure is changed, the constituents' percentages will remain constant, but the pressure of each will change. The pressure of each gas—partial pressure—is found by multiplying the total gas pressure by the percentage of component gas. Dalton's law states: *In a gas mixture the pressure of each gas is that which it would exert if it were the only gas in the mixture.* Also: *the total gas pressure is the sum of the pressures of each component.* In surface air, O_2 has a partial pressure (pO_2) of 760 mm (atmospheric pressure) times 20.9 percent = 159 mm. After raising pressure to 2 atmospheres (33 feet of salt H_2O), O_2 percentages remain at 20.9 percent but the total pressure becomes 1520 mm, and pO_2 is 318 mm. Pressure, not percentage, determines the extent of gas uptake and its elimination from the body. For example, under high pressure a small percentage of O_2 will provide the body with normal amounts of oxygen, while high percentages of it at low pressures may be insufficient. At 18,000 feet in the air, the pO_2 provided by 20.9 percent O_2 falls to 80 mm. Similarly, at 33 feet underwater, an O_2 percentage of 10.45 would maintain normal pO_2. Each breath of this 10 percent O_2 air contains the same volume of O_2 as does 21 percent O_2 air at the surface, since the number of molecules in a given volume—density—is doubled at 33 feet. At 4.78 atmospheric absolute (125 feet) the partial pressure of 20.9 percent air would be 760 mm—equivalent to breathing pure O_2 at the surface. Oxygen, under high pressure, can be poisonous. In deep diving the percentage of O_2 must be reduced so that toxic pO_2s are not reached. Although a person can do quite well on only 5 percent O_2 at 400 feet, a match will not burn in this atmosphere. Combustion requires a minimal percent of O_2 regardless of total atmospheric pressure.[18]

GAS SOLUBILITY

Gases in the lungs equilibrate with gases dissolved in the blood (gas tension). Oxygen is removed from the blood as it passes through the body, so that when it returns to the lungs, its tension is lower than pO_2 in the lungs. Nitrogen, though the major component of air, is not used in the body. At atmospheric pressure, N_2 passes from the tissue to blood at the same rate that it enters the tissues from the blood. Hence, venous and arterial tensions are the same; with each breath the same amount of N_2 enters the body from the lungs as passes out through the lungs.

When the partial pressure of inspired N_2 rises, a gradual rise in blood N_2 follows, and tissue N_2 levels increase. A gradient from lungs to blood continues until equilibration among lung, blood, and tissue results. If gas pressure is then reduced, N_2 leaves the tissues and blood, flowing into the lungs until equilibrated at the new pressure. Increased uptake of N_2 under high pressure accounts for nitrogen narcosis and is important in the development of decompression sickness.

Solubility of a given gas depends upon partial pressure and upon the solubility of that gas in a given liquid. Henry's law relates pressure to solubility: *The weight of a slightly soluble gas which can be dissolved in a given volume of liquid at constant temperature is almost directly proportional to the partial pressure of that gas.* This is not true in cases of chemical combinations between gas and liquid, as in O_2 transport by hemoglobin. The solubility of a gas varies, depending on the liquid involved. For instance, fat and water solubility are quite different. Furthermore, temperature must be constant, since solubility decreases as temperature increases. The question of relative solubilities is important in nitrogen narcosis and in decompression sickness. Heightening pressure will raise the amount of all gases in solution, but the extent of increase reflects the properties of each gas involved.

Highly soluble gases are carried in large quantity under relatively low pressure. Similarly, a slightly soluble gas will require high pressure for the solution of small volumes. Knowing the tension of a dissolved gas does not indicate the quantity of gas since quantity depends on solubility. Let us assume that two gases, X and Y, are present in the lungs at 100 mm and that the solubility of X is twice that of Y; then at equilibrium the blood tensions of each gas will be the same—100 mm. However, at this pressure, twice as much X can be carried as Y. Because of X's greater solubility, equilibrium takes longer than for Y. X will diffuse faster within the blood and tissues since it has a higher pressure gradient. The Bunsen coefficient of a gas relates its solubility to pressure.

Living underwater involves far more than mere acclimatization to wetness. The many physical differences discussed in this chapter have extensive significance for both skin and SCUBA divers.

NOTES: PHYSICAL ENVIRONMENT

1. J. MacInnis, "Living Under the Sea," *Scientific American,* 214: 24–34, 1966.
2. A. Behnke, "The Absorption and Elimination of Gases of the Body in Relation to Its Fat and Water Contents," *Medicine,* 24: 359–79, 1945.
3. J. Williams, *Oceanography, An Introduction to the Marine Sciences* (Boston: Little Brown & Co., 1962).
4. E. Beckman, "Thermal Protection During Immersion in Cold Water" in *Proceedings of the Second Symposium on Underwater Physiology,* (Washington, D.C.: National Academy of Science, 1963) pp. 247–66.
5. P. Webb, "Thermal Stress in Undersea Activity," *Underwater Physiology,* vol. 5, C. J. Lambertsen, ed. (Bethesda, Md., FASEB, 1976), pp. 705–24.
6. F. Preston, "Water Hazards or How to Avoid a Watery Grave," *Practitioner,* 211: 209–19, 1973.
7. W. Keatinge et al., "Sudden Failure of Swimming in Cold Water," *British Medical Journal,* 1: 480–83, 1969.
8. W. R. Keatinge, M. Hayward, "Sudden Death in Cold Water and Ventricular Arrhythmia," *Journal of Forensic Science,* 26: 459–61, 1981.
9. A. Craig, M. Dvorak, "Thermal Regulation of Man Exercising During Water Immersion," *Journal of Applied Physiology,* 25: 28–35, 1968.
10. J. Hanna, S. Hong, "Critical Water Temperature and Effective Insulation in Scuba Divers in Hawaii," *Journal of Applied Physiology,* 33: 770–73, 1972.
11. S. Hong, "Pattern of Cold Adaptation in Women Divers of Korea (Ama)," *Federal Proceedings,* 32: 1614–22, 1973.
12. Y. Park et al., "Time Course of Deacclimatization to Cold Water Immersion in Korean Women Divers," *Journal of Applied Physiology,* 54: 1708–16, 1983.

13. S. Luria, J. Kinney, "Vision in the Water Without a Facemask," *Aviation Space Environmental Medicine,* 46: 1128–31, 1975.

14. D. Williamson, "Correction of Ametropia in Skin and Scuba Divers," *Journal of the Florida Medical Association,* 56: 98–103, 1969.

15. S. Luria, J. Kinney, "Underwater Vision," *Science,* 167: 1454–61, 1970.

16. *Ibid.,*

17. D. Williamson, "Underwater Vision," *Skin Diver,* September 1967, pp. 24.

18. T. Schmidt et al., "Chamber Fire Safety," Technical Memorandum UCRI 721 Oceans Systems Inc., Tarrytown, New York, 1973.

3 | Equipment

The skin diver uses a minimum of equipment: mask, fins, and usually a snorkel. His diving depth and duration will be limited since he has no continuous supply of fresh air. Because of its simplicity, skin diving is ideal for the beginner and the occasional diver. For sheer excitement nothing equals the sport of spear fishing—pursuing fish with minimal equipment.

SCUBA (Self-Contained Underwater Breathing Apparatus) adds an air supply to the skin diver's equipment, thus opening new vistas of depth and duration. With these advantages go the problems of more complicated equipment and the risk of more diving maladies. The following table shows which diseases apply to skin diving and which to SCUBA.

DIVING DISEASES

Problem	Skin	SCUBA
drowning	yes	yes
squeeze	yes	yes
lung squeeze	yes	no
decompression sickness	unlikely	yes
air embolism	no	yes
nitrogen narcosis	unlikely	yes
oxygen poisoning	no	unlikely
carbon monoxide	no	yes

Some diving equipment is essential—for example, a mask. Other equipment makes diving more enjoyable—for example, a camera. Equipment that improves diver comfort such as a wet suit may also increase diver safety. This chapter is not designed to be an exhaustive discussion of all diving equipment. The focus is on those aspects of equipment that specifically affect health.

VISION EQUIPMENT

The visual problems of diving are discussed in Chapter 2, Physical Environment. No person can see well underwater without placing an air space between the eyes and the water. Swimmer's goggles don't work because they cannot be "equalized" and will cause eye squeeze. Furthermore, goggles severely restrict peripheral vision. Diving masks also restrict peripheral vision, but this has been reduced in some models. Masks are available in a myriad of styles. Some persons are allergic to the antioxidants in rubber and should use hypoallergenic masks made of silicone rubber.[1]

At one time there was interest in contact lenses for divers, which could be worn without a mask and would eliminate loss of peripheral vision. Unfortunately, these lenses were never perfected.

The diver with naturally poor vision will find that the magnifying properties of water diminish his handicap. But corrective lenses help even more. Corrective lenses can be bound directly to the faceplate and these are very satisfactory. Attempts to fasten glasses inside a mask usually fail. Mask faceplates can be made with ground-in corrections.

The finest vision is obtained with contact lenses worn under a mask. Hard contact lenses are easily displaced and have been associated with corneal swelling resulting from bubble formation during decompression.[2] Soft contacts do not cause decompression corneal problems and are much less likely to become displaced during a dive. An ophthalmologist, testing out soft contacts, deliberately flooded his mask during 100 dives and never lost a soft lens.[3] This is not a recommended practice, however, as soft lenses can be lost. Mask fogging is common and there are many home remedies for preventing it. Commercial defogging agents must be used properly since improper use has caused temporary visual impairment.[4]

TEMPERATURE CONTROL

In almost all diving, chilling becomes a problem. Chilling makes diving both uncomfortable and dangerous. The physiology of cold is discussed in Chapter 2, Physical Environment.

Most divers use a wet suit. These tight-fitting cellular rubber suits trap a thin layer of water next to the skin. This is warmed and then combines with the wet suit itself to provide insulation from the cold water outside the suit. Wet suits work well for most divers in moderately cold water. Thicker suits provide more insulation, but their bulk restricts mobility. Vigorous motion usually lets in a rush of cold air. Nylon lining makes a wet suit easier to doff and don but reduces its insulative property. The same is true for zippers. Hoods are valuable since up to 50 percent of heat loss is through the head. Mittens are warmer than gloves (less surface area for heat loss), but mittens may impair dexterity.

Better thermal protection is possible with a dry suit. The diver is surrounded by air, which requires less heat to keep warm. Most dry suits are made of rubber, which insulates as with a wet suit; dry suits made of fabric have no intrinsic insulative property and must be used with underwear or a rubber suit, to reduce heat loss further. Generally there is some water leakage with dry suits. They are more expensive than wet suits and much more complicated to use. But on the whole, dry suits are more effective than wet suits. Commercial diving often requires warmed suits.

The insulative use of cellular rubber decreases with depth as pressure compresses the rubber. At 33 feet, insulation is 58 percent of surface with a decrease to 37 percent at 99 feet.

The diving suit provides two other benefits. It helps protect against abrasions and stinging animals, and it provides an emergency source of buoyancy; if the weights are dropped, the diver will find it almost impossible to sink.

BUOYANCY EQUIPMENT

In the early days of sport diving, divers were advised to use a safety vest. These vests, often aviators' life vests, were small and were intended only for emergency flotation. They could be inflated by the user's own breath through a narrow hose or automatically by means of a small carbon dioxide cylinder. Unfortunately, the carbon dioxide inflating system quickly corrodes in salt water and is rarely functional. The small size of the vest and the small inflating cylinder provide insufficient lifting power to bring a diver up from a very deep dive. A distressed diver would find it difficult to inflate the vest himself, even on the surface. If properly maintained, these small vests are of value to skin divers who do not use wet suits or weights, but more reliable buoyancy is provided by a wet suit and weights: In distress, the diver ditches the weights and lets the wet suit hold him up.

Gradually the safety vest has given way to a buoyancy compensator. This large, inflatable device can be used to adjust buoyancy during a dive as well as to provide surface flotation. It can be inflated in a variety of ways: by mouth, by carbon dioxide cylinder, by low pressure connection to the air tank, or by its own air cylinder. Buoyancy compensators are large, complicated, and expensive, but they are handy, and many people enjoy diving with them. Maintenance is necessary to ensure that the device functions properly. Careful use is necessary to prevent too rapid an ascent when it is used to trim underwater buoyancy. The compensator is not a substitute for proper weight checking. These flotation devices provide quite a lot of surface support for a distressed diver. Unfortunately, some of them will float an unconscious diver face down in the water.

Flotation equipment is sometimes considered suitable for emergency ascents. The small size of safety vests and their small inflation cylinders mean that they would not provide much lift except in very shallow diving. The large compensators can provide abundant lift if air is available for inflation. Buoyant ascents, however, are very difficult to control and are dangerous.

WEIGHT SYSTEMS

As discussed, almost all divers must wear extra weights if they use a rubber diving suit. On the surface, buoyancy is most positive, and neophytes tend to wear too much weight in an effort to make the dive easy. But deep under water, suit and chest compression decrease buoyancy, and less weight is necessary. It is thus safer to dive with less weight, in order to prevent being dangerously heavy at depth.

In emergencies, the weights must be easy to release. This requires an easily unbuckled belt, worn on top of other equipment.

AIR SUPPLY

The modern SCUBA diver, with reliable equipment readily available, often takes his regulator and air tank for granted. But air supply is too vital a part of diving to neglect. As discussed in Chapter 7, Respiration, breathing becomes more difficult as dives deepen; increasing exercise requires more ventilation. Equipment that works in shallow diving may be inadequate for a vigorous, deeper excursion. Moreover, regulators vary widely in quality and especially in ease of use as depth or work increases.

Until recently it has been difficult to obtain accurate information on regulator function. High quality regulators are more reliable under conditions of increased demand than less sophisticated equipment. But in general, regulator failure is more apt to be caused by improper maintenance than by initial poor quality. Well-maintained regulators rarely fail when used properly.

Quite often, testing of a regulator that has "failed" during a dive reveals that the regulator functions normally. The failure was actually caused by improper breathing technique. If, for example, a diver tries to breathe rapidly—in a state of fright, say—it is quite possible that the air delivery will seem inadequate. Slower, deeper breathing would solve the problem.

Even the finest regulator is useless without a source of clean air—a well-maintained tank properly filled. Only clean air should be used for sport diving. Oxygen or other gas mixes are not suitable. Air should be free of oil, carbon monoxide, and other contaminants, and tanks should be filled with proper compressor technique, to avoid carbon monoxide contamination. Have your tank filled at a certified air station.

The SCUBA tank is among the most neglected pieces of equipment. Tanks must be kept clean. Visual inspection should be carried out at least once a year and hydrostatic testing every five years. Corrosion in a tank may weaken it and increase the possibility of a tank explosion. Corrosion consumes the oxygen in stored air and has been known to cause hypoxic death.[5] Both steel and aluminum tanks corrode, although the risk is less with aluminum. With proper tank maintenance, corrosion should not be a problem.

The tank should be completely filled before it is used. Amazingly, many divers don't check to see that this very basic rule has been followed. For example, on a boat dive, used tanks are frequently placed near the air-filling station and left to a mate's attention. If the tank has been filled "hot," the air will later cool down and contract, thus shortening the dive of the man who uses it. Occasionally there is insufficient pressure in the compressor to fill the tank or some other problem. Before a tank is used, the air pressure in it must be checked by the diver who will be using it.

The development of the submersible pressure gauge, which tells a diver how much air pressure he has left, has made diving easier than it used to be and much safer. Because the rate of air consumption changes during a dive, it is hard to predict how long a tank will last. The J valve reserve system works well for divers who are careful to check the valve position during filling (down) and during the dive (up, until needed), but, the submersible gauge is best. How many pilots would fly without a fuel gauge? Naturally, if a gauge fails to function, that could be dangerous to an unsuspecting diver. But that is rare. More often, a gauge works, but the diver never looks at it.

SUPPLEMENTARY BREATHING EQUIPMENT

Many divers now use "octopus" regulators. This second regulator on a tank provides an emergency air source for a buddy. Proper octopus technique requires training and practice. It has advantages over "buddy breathing" but is still far from perfect. If one diver has run out of air, the second is likely to be quite low.

For some specialty diving (such as cave diving) an entire extra tank and regulator system may be useful.

OTHER TYPES OF BREATHING EQUIPMENT

The open circuit SCUBA used in sport diving exhausts three quarters of each breath since there is no rebreathing; because not all of the oxygen in each breath is used, open circuit is wasteful. However, its simplicity and safety more than offset the loss of gas.

For specialized use, semiclosed and closed circuit SCUBA prove of value. In semiclosed SCUBA, part of each expiration passes into the water, while the majority of it goes through a carbon dioxide absorber and is rebreathed. A continuous supply of fresh gas adds oxygen. Semiclosed SCUBA permits the use of synthetic gas mixes rather than air. These mixes—usually helium and oxygen—have a lower inert gas level than does air; this helps prevent decompression sickness and inert gas narcosis. Rebreathing extends the supply duration of a given tank volume.

In closed circuit SCUBA all of the expiration, less the CO_2 removed by the carbon dioxide absorber, is rebreathed. The gas used is pure oxygen. Because closed circuit rigs leave no bubble trail, they are of military value. Oxygen does not cause decompression sickness or gas narcosis; however, the possibility of oxygen poisoning severely limits the depth at which closed circuit SCUBA can be used. (The normal U.S. Navy limit is 25 feet for 75 minutes, with exceptional exposure permitted to 40 feet with 10 minutes maximum duration.) Semiclosed SCUBA reduces the risk of O_2 poisoning by the use of only part O_2.

Mixed gas and oxygen SCUBA has no place in sport diving. In semiclosed SCUBA, the regulation of gas mix and flow requires extensive training. Decompression sickness continues to be a problem, and proper methods of decompression are not widely enough promulgated. With depth changes, flow and oxygen percentage may require adjustment, so that a diver cannot simply use a predetermined mix in open circuit tanks. Furthermore, mixed gas diving is expensive.

In closed circuit SCUBA, oxygen poisoning represents the greatest danger; it does not require deep diving. Besides the danger of O_2 poisoning, any oil in the tank could form an explosive mixture with oxygen. Oxygen must *not* be used to fill open circuit SCUBA tanks. Both closed and semiclosed systems depend upon perfectly functioning carbon dioxide absorbers; any defect can be fatal. Many deaths among recreational divers have stemmed from home-devised rebreathing systems.

SURFACE SUPPLIED DIVING

Hookah diving extends diving duration by supplying air from a surface compressor to the diver through a hose. A regulator, worn by the diver, adjusts supply pressure as in SCUBA. The low pressure capacity of the compressor limits depth to under 50 feet.

Another form of equipment, known in the Navy as the lightweight diving outfit (Jack Brown apparatus) utilizes surface air supplied to a full face mask. The diver can adjust air flow with a control knob. This equipment has great value for light work at shallow depths. Usually, lightweight equipment is restricted to 60 feet, but it can be used to 130 feet.

OTHER EQUIPMENT

Divers use fins, whatever type the individual prefers. SCUBA divers need a means of determining dive depth and duration. Knives may be helpful in escaping entanglements; however, avoiding entanglements is to be preferred.

SUMMARY

Diving, especially SCUBA, does involve quite a wealth of equipment. In the early days of SCUBA diving accidents resulting from homemade apparatus were frequent. Today, most divers are using equipment that is satisfactory as long as it is properly maintained. Accidents caused by equipment malfunction are rare.

Unfortunately, in many accidents, the proper equipment was present but was not correctly used. Often, a distressed diver is found with air in his tank, the expensive compensator unused, and his weight belt still in place. This could have resulted from accidents occurring without warning, failure to recognize the problem, psychomotor failure, which renders rational activity impossible, or unfamiliarity with the equipment.

NOTES: EQUIPMENT

1. A. Fisher, "Water-Related Dermatoses," *Curtis,* 25: 132ff, 1981.
2. D. Simon, M. Bradley, "Adverse Effects of Contact Lens Wear During Decompression," *Journal of the American Medical Association,* 244: 1213–14, 1980.
3. D. Williamson, "Soft Contact Lenses and Scuba Diving," *Eye, Ear, Nose, Throat Monthly,* 50: 24–27, 1971.
4. W. L. Wright, "Scuba Diver's Delayed Toxic Epithelial Keratopathy from Commercial Mask Defogging Agents," *American Journal of Ophthalmology,* 93: 470–72, 1982.
5. J. Temple, Jr. et al., "Scuba Tank Corrosion as a Cause of Death," *Journal of Forensic Science,* 20: 571–575, 1975.

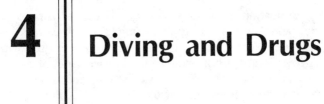

4 Diving and Drugs

Good divers must be able to be comfortable in an alien and challenging world. Challenges come from the water itself, cold, motion, exertion, sensory deprivation, direct pressure effects, and indirect pressure effects. As discussed in the preceding chapters, every dive causes change within the body. Adding the effects of drugs complicates the matter.

A drug is any chemical substance that affects mental and/or physical function. This includes chemicals used in therapy (medicines), recreation (tobacco, alcohol), or abuse. For a diver the most important effects concern capacity for vigorous exercise, mental acuity, and coordination. Often a drug taken for one purpose will affect another organ system. For example, antihistamines are used to ameliorate the symptoms of environmental allergy, such as hay fever, but they frequently cause drowsiness. This type of drug would help the diver by reducing nasal congestion, but would be dangerous because of its mental effects.

In determining which drugs are suitable for divers, one must eliminate any that would impair exercise capacity, mental acuity, or coordination. Unfortunately the task is difficult: (1) Divers may not realize that they are using drugs (cigarettes, for example). (2) Side effects of drugs may be subtle. (3) There is enormous individual response to drugs. (4) Drug effects are modified by variables such as fatigue and cold. (5) Emotional stability may modify, as well as be modified by, a drug's action. (6) Pressure can modify drug action. (7) Changes in nitrogen, oxygen, and carbon dioxide affect drug action.

Evaluation of drugs is very complicated. Physicians must be constantly aware of drug interaction, unusual reactions, and individual response. The medical reader is inundated with new discoveries about both new and old drugs. And, of course, controversy is common. All this leads to the conclusion that little is known about drugs and diving.

The importance of the problem is well recognized, and scientific investigation continues to be vigorous. There is no doubt that high pressures and changes in body gas tensions affect drug action. This has been well demonstrated in the laboratory. Unfortunately, lab results cannot be assumed to apply to humans who are diving rather than just undergoing pressure exposures.

A major discovery is that a drug's actions underwater cannot be predicted by its actions on the surface.[1] This means that any drug for use underwater must be individually evaluated, instead of being considered a part of a general drug type. For example, some mental depressants are made more potent by pressure while others seem to be counteracted. It would be virtually impossible to evaluate every drug, so decisions must be made as to which are most relevant to diving. Then one must determine which effects are to be investigated. Is it more important to know if the predicted effects of a medicine have been modified by pressure or to know if that medicine causes unsuspected behavior under pressure? In most experiments, it is possible to look for only a few types of changes. Finally, different depths have different influences. Investigations at very high pressures may not be applicable to shallow SCUBA diving. Relatively few investigations have been made of drug actions at SCUBA depths. Much more has been done at very high pressures and at depths comparable to deep saturation diving.

Divers use drugs for three basic purposes: to make diving more pleasant, because they routinely use them, or to prevent or treat diving maladies.

DRUGS USED TO FACILITATE DIVING

Since ear and sinus squeeze are the most common problems in diving, it is not surprising that decongestants are popular. By constricting blood vessels, they reduce tissue swelling and improve sinus and middle ear gas flows. However, repeated use of many of these medicines leads to a "rebound phenomenon," in which congestion is worse than before treatment started. Many decongestant preparations are combinations of several medicines. Those that contain antihistamines can cause mental dulling and drowsiness. Persons vary widely in their susceptibility to sedation by antihistamines; some people use them as sleeping pills. Pressure testing in rats with standard doses showed no performance decrement with pseudoephedrine (Sudafed), a popular non-antihistamine decongestant.[2] (High doses did affect performance.) In rats, this was also true for the antihistamine diphenhydramine (Benadryl). But humans had impaired performance with Benadryl.[3]

Rough water dives frequently cause motion sickness. There are several classes of drugs used (with limited success) for its prevention. Antihistamines such as dimenhydrinate (Dramamine) impair function in some divers. Central stimulants (amphetamines) may add to nitrogen's effects.[4] Scopolamine has been used to prevent motion sickness. A skin patch scopolamine preparation permits continuous transcutaneous absorption of the drug at a slow rate. This has been popular in boating and fishing, but its safety in diving is questionable since scopolamine is a sedative. Even undetected degrees of sedation can be dangerous, especially where there is concomitant nitrogen intoxication.

DRUGS USED INCIDENTALLY

This is the largest group of drugs used by divers. It includes the recreation drugs as well as medicines used for acute and chronic diseases.

Coffee, tea, and cola drinkers consume caffeine and other active chemicals. For most persons these should not be a problem in diving, since few people drink so much of these beverages that they are nervous and tremulous. Certain cardiac dysrhythmias (e.g. atrial tachycardia) are more common in heavy caffeine users.

Cigarette smoking is a bad habit for anyone. Smoking hinders cardiopulmonary fitness. Prolonged cigarette use causes permanent damage to lung function. Smoking impairs the clearing of lung secretions, which can lead to obstruction of small airways. In emphysema, air movement is restricted (especially exhalation), and the lung tissues are distended and weakened. This makes diving both more difficult and more dangerous and increases the likelihood of overexpansion injuries. Carbon monoxide levels are higher in smokers than in nonsmokers, and this could compound the problem of using impure air. Finally, smoking appears to accelerate the development of coronary artery disease.

Alcohol is a depressant of the central nervous system. As such it has no place in diving. Experiments in man have demonstrated an interaction of alcohol with the effects of hyperbaric air (at 4 or 6 atmospheres).[5] This occurred even 90 minutes after alcohol ingestion, when the subjective effects of the alcohol were fading. (Interestingly, rats at 7 atmospheres showed some reversal of the surface effects of alcohol.)[6] Divers need their full capabilities and should not impair themselves by drinking on a diving day.

Alcohol is frequently associated with drownings. In analyses of large numbers of drownings in both the United States and Australia, about 50 percent of adult victims had elevated blood alcohol levels.[7] Similar blood studies are not available for those persons who drown while diving.

Alcohol causes blood vessel dilation, and this can interfere with the heat-conserving constriction of blood vessels, which occurs with immersion in cold water.

Exercise followed by drinking is particularly dangerous, since this combination may cause profound falls in blood-glucose levels.[8] Low blood glucose leads to weakness and confusion, and interferes with temperature maintenance.

It has often been theorized that alcohol consumption may increase the risk of decompression sickness, but this has not been experimentally established.

Drugs that affect mental function are the most commonly prescribed medicines in the United States. These psychoactive drugs are used for sedation, tranquilization, sleep, and mood elevation. Abuse of them is also very common. Sedatives and tranquilizers should never be used when diving is planned. These drugs are an excellent example of the difficulties in evaluating underwater drug effects.

Individuals vary widely in their susceptibility to these medicines. At the surface, minor performance decrements, which could be very serious under water, might go undetected. Animal experiments reveal that pressure effects are not the same for all sedatives and tranquilizers.[9] Some appear unchanged by pressure; others have their properties enhanced, and still others may be counteracted. Results from different experiments are not always consistent.[10, 11, 12] One type of performance may be affected differently from that of another within the same animal by the same drug. Human experimentation is sparse in this area and will probably remain so. There is little reason to study sedatives and tranquilizers in divers. Persons who are habituated to them are not suitable diving candidates. Divers need to face reality without sedation.

Mood elevators or psychic energizers are an interesting class of drugs for divers. It had been theorized that the mental activation caused by amphetamines might counteract the narcotic properties of nitrogen. Unfortunately, this was proved untrue in rats. Rats trained for high pressure performance had poorer function when they were administered amphetamines and then pressurized.[13]

The tricyclic antidepressants have a tendency to cause cardiac dysrhythmias. Since cardiac rhythm disturbances are not uncommon in divers, this is reason enough to avoid these drugs.

Drugs of abuse such as narcotics and hallucinogens have not been extensively studied under pressure. No one would recommend them for divers. Realistically, however, there is no denying that some divers use these drugs. Their predictable effects would be dangerous under water. They might also have unpredictable effects, since this is true of other mood-changing drugs. Anecdotal reports of marijuana use by divers describe unpleasant psychic effects and interference with heat conservation.[14] Rats, given the active ingredient in marijuana and then pressurized, demonstrated some reversal of the drug's usual effects.[15] But this definitely does *not* mean that marijuana is safe in diving, even for rats.

A further problem with the psychoactive drugs is their complicated systems of absorption, metabolism, and elimination. These drugs still may be active in the human body for quite a while after their last use.

Medicines used for acute and chronic illnesses may also influence fitness for diving. The problems associated with decongestants, which are used in the treatment of infections or allergic upper respiratory disorders, have been discussed. Similarly, use of sedatives, tranquilizers, or antidepressants in any illness would make diving inadvisable.

Most often it is the disease itself, rather than the medicine used to treat it, that affects diving safety. For example, in determining whether a person with epilepsy should or should not dive, the underwater effects of his anticonvulsant drugs are not important. The very presence of a convulsive disorder by itself makes diving unsafe; medicines do not modify this truth. Many similar examples can be mentioned. The patient with heart disease should not dive; digoxin's underwater effects are not the issue. Pulmonary disease makes diving unsafe, and this again is inherent to the disease, not the medicines used in its treatment.

High blood pressure (hypertension) is a common affliction. Mild hypertension, without impairment of cardiac function, may be tolerable in sport divers. However, several of the medicines used in hypertension therapy may be dangerous under water. Sedatives have been discussed. Diuretics can cause excessive fluid loss, and this may compound the partial dehydration seen with decompression sickness. Often divers neglect to drink enough to compensate for fluid loss associated with vigorous exercise while breathing dry compressed air. Electrolyte deficiencies not infrequently accompany diuretic use, and this may increase the risk of cardiac dysrhythmias. Some of the newer antihypertensive drugs limit cardiac response to exercise. This restriction of exercise capacity may be dangerous in diving. Cardiac output sufficient for daily activity may be inadequate in a rough sea. These drugs have not been investigated for possible pressure interactions.

The Undersea Medical Society has found that questions about oral contraceptives and diving are the most frequent ones asked. Some fear has been voiced because of the association of oral contraceptives and vascular thrombosis. This risk is one that deserves careful consideration. Unfortunately, "There is [*sic*] no data in the literature on the effects of oral contraceptives in the hyperbaric environment."[16]

DRUGS USED TO PREVENT OR TREAT DIVING MALADIES

Medicines may be important in the treatment of diving accidents and illnesses. Specific examples are discussed in the appropriate chapters.

There has been a continual search for medicines to prevent those maladies which limit or impair diving.[17] For the sport diver, the most applicable drugs are those that facilitate ear and sinus equalization. As discussed above, these drugs are far from perfect.

Decompression sickness is a serious problem in both recreational and professional diving. The sport diver can almost eliminate the risk by *carefully* adhering to standard decompression practices. Professional diving often requires profiles that are on the very edge of tolerable exposure. The great expense of commercial diving makes it important to maximize diving while minimizing the acute and chronic effects of decompression sickness. A great variety of drugs has been evaluated for efficacy in preventing bubble formation or in reducing the secondary effects of bubble formation. None of these has become clinically useful. Particular interest has centered on aspirin's ability to interfere with blood platelet aggregation. This aggregation, initiated by gas bubbles, may be important in decompression sickness. Laboratory results were encouraging, but in man aspirin has failed to modify platelet changes caused by decompression to any significant degree.[18] Aspirin has not been shown effective in the prevention of decompression sickness.[19]

This is an important discovery since some sport divers feel they are protecting themselves by routinely using aspirin. Aspirin is not without hazards. It is quite irritating to the gastric mucosa, and occult gastric bleeding is a common complication of aspirin use. Aspirin also has a significant allergic potential.

Nitrogen narcosis severely restricts maximum safe diving depth for divers using air. Substitution of less narcotic inert gases solves the problem, until divers reach those depths associated with the high pressure nervous syndrome. Sport divers are very susceptible to the dangers of nitrogen narcosis. The only safe preventive is to avoid deep diving. Mixed gas diving is not suitable for sport diving. No medicine has been found that will eliminate inert gas narcosis in humans.

Oxygen toxicity is not a problem in air SCUBA diving unless it becomes necessary to activate recompression therapy for decompression sickness or air embolism. Modern recompression therapy utilizes amounts of oxygen that can be toxic to the lungs or central nervous system. Extensive research has been done to find drugs to counteract these biochemical effects of hyperbaric oxygen, but no drugs have been shown to be of clinical value. Anticonvulsants delay the onset of oxygen seizures, but they only mask the toxicity of oxygen.[20] Even if seizures are prevented, permanent brain damage can result.

The search continues for medicines that can prevent diving maladies. Today, prevention must depend on conservative diving rather than on drug therapy.

SUMMARY

It is not feasible to discuss every illness and its therapy in relation to diving. Basically any illness that limits alertness or exercise capacity makes diving unsafe. Chapter 20, Health Requirements, is a further guide. Medicines used for any illness must be carefully evaluated by a physician who knows that the patient will be diving.

Basic principles of drug use for divers include the following:

1. Effects tolerable in ordinary activity may be dangerous in diving.
2. Drug action on the surface may be changed unpredictably under water.
3. Individuals vary in their responses to drugs.
4. No drug should be used under water without its first being used on the surface. (But remember principle number 2.)
5. When accepting a prescription medicine, be certain that the physician knows you will use it under water in vigorous, stressful activity.
6. When choosing a nonprescription drug, carefully read the label.
7. Do not exceed the recommended dose.

Drug use in diving is a complex, confusing subject. The unpredictability of drug action under pressure must be recognized by all divers. Experimental data are still sparse and have often been obtained in experiments with animals at depths that are not encountered by sport divers. Sport diving is an optional activity that is intended to be pleasurable. When drugs must be used, the benefits of diving are often less than the risks. Diving requires the utmost in mental and physical capability. Drugs that reduce these capabilities add to the inherent risks of diving. The prudent diver limits drug use to those few that have been established as generally safe when properly used.

NOTES: DIVING AND DRUGS

1. J. M. Walsh, "Behavioral Effects of Drugs in the Hyperbaric Environment," *Interaction of Drugs in the Hyperbaric Environment*, J. M. Walsh, ed., (Bethesda, Md.: Undersea Medical Society, 1980), pp. 17–21.

2. *Ibid.*

3. *Ibid.*

4. J. Thomas, "Amphetamine and Chlordiazepoxide Effects on Behavior Under Increased Pressures of Nitrogen,"*Pharmacologic Biochemical Behavior,* 1: 421–26, 1973.

5. A. Jones, "Combined Effects of Ethanol and Hyperbaric Air on Body Sway and Heart Rate in Man,"*Undersea Biomedical Research,* 6: 15–25, 1979.

6. J. Thomas, J. M. Walsh, "Behavioral Evaluation of Pharmacological Agents in Hyperbaric Air and Helium-Oxygen" in *Underwater Physiology VI,* C. Shilling, and M. Beckett, eds. (Bethesda, Md.: FASEB, 1978), pp. 69–77.

7. I. Mackie, "Alcohol and Aquatic Disasters," *Practitioner,* 222: 622–65, 1979.

8. *Ibid.*

9. Thomas and Walsh, "Behavioral Evaluation."

10. *Ibid.*

11. R. Philip, "Drugs and Diving," *Interaction of Drugs in the Hyperbaric Environment,* pp. 11–16.

12. H. F. Nicodemus et al., "Dose-responses of Guinea Pigs to Diazepam at Recompression Depths," *Undersea Biomedical Research,* 7: 1–9, 1980.

13. Thomas, "Amphetamine."

14. P. Tzimoulis, "Drugs and Diving Don't Mix," *Skin Diver,* September 173, p. 4.

15. J. M. Walsh, L. Burch, "Reduction of the Behavioral Effects of D^9—

Tetrahydrocannabinol by Hyperbaric Pressure," *Pharmacologic Biochemical Behavior,* 7: 111–16, 1977.

16. Anonymous, "Effects of Drugs in the Hyperbaric Environment," *Interaction of Drugs in the Hyperbaric Environment,* p. 51.
17. P. Bennett, "Review of Protective Pharmacological Agents in Diving," *Aerospace Medicine,* 43: 184–92, 1972.
18. Philip, *op. cit.*
19. P. W. Catron, E. T. Flynn, Jr., "Adjutant Drug Therapy for Decompression Sickness: A Review," *Undersea Biomedical Research,* 9: 161–74, 1982.
20. Bennett, *op. cit.*
21. J. Harp, Jr., et al. "Effects of Anesthetics on Central Nervous System Toxicity of Hyperbaric Oxygen," *Anesthesiology,* 27: 608–14, 1966.

5 || Squeeze

The solids and liquids of the body transmit water pressure evenly. Blood vessels are not compressed, since pressure inside them rises at the same rate as does outside pressure. Blood pressure readings reflect the differential between internal and external pressure on the vessel, and since this remains constant, blood pressure does not change from normal. High pressure does not crush the fluid portion of the body.

Pressure differentials across air spaces can result in pain and damage (squeeze or barotrauma). In diving, the tissues surrounding these spaces are under high pressure. Since the spaces are noncollapsible, with the exception of the lungs, pressure cannot be maintained by a reduction in volume. Unless high pressure air can be admitted to the spaces, tissue pressure will exceed pressure in the space, and a relative pressure gradient will be created. Actual pressure in the space is unchanged, but relatively its pressure drops as the surrounding pressure increases. Since there is no air flow, there is no volume change. Fluid will exude from the blood vessels into the space. If the pressure differential continues to increase, rupture of the capillaries may result. Bleeding into a space will reduce the volume of the space, thus raising the pressure to equalize with tissue pressure. In barotrauma the most painful period is generally the time just before vessel rupture; pain may ease following it.

EAR SQUEEZE

Most frequently barotrauma involves the middle ear. Failure of normal eustachian tube function can occur during either descent or ascent. Ear squeeze is discussed in Chapter 6, Diving and the Ear.

SINUS SQUEEZE

The nasal accessory sinuses, rigid air spaces in the skull, connect with the nose through small ducts. They are lined by a mucous membrane containing many capillaries. There are four sets of sinuses: frontal (above the eyes), maxillary (in the upper jaw), ethmoid (on either side of the nose), and sphenoid (at the base of the skull). Normally, air flows freely to and from the sinuses, pressure equalization being effected automatically. Allergy or sinus infection can result in swelling of the mucous membrane, sufficient to block air flow. In diving, if equalization does not follow, rising tissue and capillary pressure will result in a relatively negative sinus pressure, with the result of exudation and possible capillary rupture. Pain may be felt above, behind, between, and below the eyes. The frontal sinuses have the longest ducts and are most often involved in sinus barotrauma.[1] Blood from the sinus cavity may later be driven out the nose. Sinus barotrauma is twice as common on descent as on ascent. Nosebleed occurs in about 60 percent of the cases of sinus squeeze. On ascent, 25 percent of squeeze cases may have nosebleed without pain.[2] Unlike adjustment in the ears, sinus equalization is not voluntary. Usually, a blocked duct cannot be opened by any maneuver, but sometimes blowing the nose will clear a passage. Diving in the presence of a cold will increase the likelihood of sinus barotrauma. Premedication with decongestants may relieve membrane swelling, making equalization possible, but decongestants sometimes cause drowsiness, and frequent decongestant use may cause "rebound" congestion. Less commonly, persons may have poor sinus air flow because of polyps or a deviated nasal septum.

Occasionally, pressure increases may cause pain in the teeth. This is probably most often due to maxillary sinus squeeze. An air pocket in the pulp of a tooth, or in the tooth bordering on gum tissue could fail to equalize, thus causing true tooth squeeze.

OTHER SQUEEZES

A common form of barotrauma is face squeeze. The space between the goggles or mask must have its pressure equalized with the pressure within the tissues surrounding the eyes. Goggles cannot be equalized because there is no way to admit high pressure air to them. They must not be used in diving. When a mask is used, the diver equalizes by blowing a small amount of high pressure air (from the compressed lungs or SCUBA supply) through the nose into the mask.

SUIT (BODY) SQUEEZE

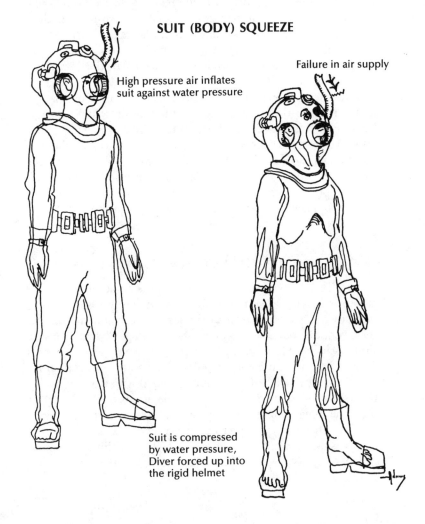

High pressure air inflates suit against water pressure

Failure in air supply

Suit is compressed by water pressure, Diver forced up into the rigid helmet

In cases of face squeeze, cold compresses should be applied promptly to the injured area. These will reduce the extent of swelling; later, warm compresses will speed resolution of any swelling.

Skin squeeze resembles face squeeze in its pattern. Pockets of air may be trapped in folds of the dry suits. These folds may not be evenly compressed during the dive, pinching the skin. Well-tailored wet suits solve this problem by allowing an even layer of water between the skin and the suit.

Anyone with a fondness for diving adventure stories has read about divers being crushed by high pressures. As has been noted, the mere application of high pressure will not crush the body—with the exception of chest compression. So-called body squeeze can occur in surface-supplied diving with hard-hat suits, if air supply pressure suddenly fails or if a sudden fall by the diver is not matched by an increase in air pressure. Outside pressure then exceeds the suit pressure, and it is crushed. The body may be forced up into the rigid helmet by the violent volume change. Because of this danger, hard-hat rigs are used only with a non-return valve in the helmet; air flow can go only into the helmet. If the diver falls off a descending line, or into a hole, the pressure change can cause squeeze, especially in the shallow depths with greatest pressure change per foot. A fall in air pressure with a surface-supplied face-mask rig will cause face squeeze.

THORACIC SQUEEZE

In SCUBA diving the regulator supplies air at a pressure approximately equal to the sea's surrounding pressure. Thus, intrathoracic air pressure matches sea pressure and the flexible chest is not compressed. In breath-hold diving, no high pressure air is available to the lungs. Sea pressure compresses the skin diver's chest and raises his diaphragm. Pressure equalization results from the fall in lung volume, i.e., Boyle's law ($P_1V_1 = P_2V_2$). The chest is a semicompressible air space. In the intact chest the lungs cannot be infinitely compressed without causing damage. That is, they begin to act like a rigid air space such as the ears or sinuses. Further compression will cause fluid exudation and blood vessel rupture. This is known as lung or thoracic squeeze.

LUNG SQUEEZE

SCUBA DIVE

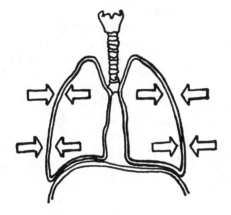

High pressure air
offsets water pressure

SKIN DIVE

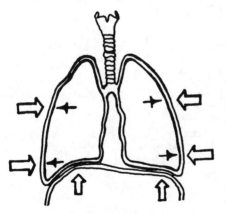

Water pressure pushes
the chest walls inward

No high pressure air to
push outward

Compression of the abdomen
forces the diaphragm up

The depth of a breath-hold dive is absolutely limited by thoracic squeeze, since chest compression is related to depth. Formerly, it was believed that diving to residual lung volume (see Chapter 7, Respiration) would cause barotrauma. After a full inhalation, the lung volume is about five times residual volume. Thus, the average diver would be safe to about 5 atmospheres (132 feet). Since few skin divers ever go that deep, this theory was unchallenged. However, a few adventurers have used special techniques to breath-hold dive deeper than 300 feet.

On immersion, compression shifts blood from the extremities and abdomen into the blood vessels of the chest. Since chest volume is limited, addition to blood volume causes air volume to fall. This raises pressure without causing any lung barotrauma. This mechanism permits lung air volume to fall below residual without damage. Measurements during simulated and actual dives have demonstrated blood shifts from 600 ml to more than a liter.[3,4] This compensation is not unlimited, however. Lung squeeze would still restrict dive depth. Lung squeeze can occur in moderate depth diving if the starting lung volume is low or if air volume is lost during the dive. A person who dives with less than a full inspiration may encounter lung squeeze. A diver who loses consciousness may exhale involuntarily and have lung squeeze. This could occur to a SCUBA diver. Thoracic squeeze may cause only pain, or it may cause fatal lung damage. It is a rare malady, but its rarity does not mean that it should be considered a nonexistent threat.[5,6]

NOTES: SQUEEZE

1. P. Fagan, et al., "Sinus Barotrauma in Divers," *Annual of Otology, Rhinology, and Laryngology,* 85: 61–64, 1976.
2. *Ibid.*
3. K. Schaefer, et al., "Pulmonary and Circulatory Adjustments Determining the Limits of Depths in Breathhold Diving," *Science:* 162: 1020–23, 1968.
4. A. Craig, Jr., "Depth Limits of Breath Hold Diving (an Example of Fennology)," *Respiratory Physiology,* 5: 14–22, 1968.
5. M. Strauss, P. Wright, "Thoracic Squeeze Diving Casualty," *Aerospace Medicine* 42: 673–75, 1971.
6. M. Khan, "Fatal Thoracic Squeeze," *Journal of the Indian Medical Association,* 73: 38–39, 1979.

6 | Diving and the Ear

Ear problems are the most common ailments in diving. They range from minor pain to incapacitation. The ear serves the sense of hearing and is also important in the maintenance of equilibrium.

The ear is comprised of the external ear (ear canal), the middle ear (containing the bones that transmit sound energy), and the inner ear which contains the cochlea, vestibule, and semicircular canals. The hearing and equilibrium organs are in the inner ear.

The tympanic membrane (eardrum) separates the external and middle ears. The round window and the oval window are two membranes separating the middle and inner ears. The bony chain of the middle ear connects to the tympanic membrane and the oval window. The membranous inner ear is comprised of a series of interconnecting ducts, which contain endolymph. The ducts are surrounded by perilymphatic fluid.

EXTERNAL EAR INFECTIONS

Infections of the external ear canal (otitis externa) cause localized pain and swelling. In severe cases the infection may spread beyond the ear canal. Swelling may impair hearing. Normally, the external ear maintains itself. Ear wax (cerumen) has a protective effect on the canal skin because of its acidity. The canal is self-cleaning, and efforts to supplement this are harmful because they remove this protective cerumen.

Swimming and diving disrupt the water-soluble cerumen and cause maceration (softening and wearing away) of the canal skin. The canal normally harbors bacteria, but these do not cause infection. With prolonged wetting, the bacteria population changes, and infection begins. Swimmers are much more likely to have external ear infections than nonswimmers. Continuous moisture, as encountered in saturation diving, causes an infection rate of almost 100 percent.[1]

Most recreational divers do not develop otitis externa, although the incidence may be greater in tropical waters. Drying solutions of acid in alcohol or aluminum and calcium acetate are popular, but their effectiveness is not established, and they do not work in saturation diving.[2] Do not attempt to dry an ear with a swab; this damages the canal lining. The use of dry suits does not eliminate the risk of external ear infections.[3] Ear plugs must not be used in diving, since pressure changes may wedge them in the ear and/or cause injury to the tympanic membrane.

MIDDLE EAR BAROTRAUMA

Pressure is exerted from the water inward on the tympanic membrane and from the surrounding tissues on the middle ear space. (See drawing.) Normally, the eustachian tube permits equalization of pressure. This narrow tube passes from the middle ear to the nasopharynx, permitting air flow to and from the ear. As lung compression raises intrathoracic air pressure, this air passes through the eustachian tube to the ear. In SCUBA or surface-supplied diving, the high pressure air entering the mouth and nose passes directly through the eustachian tube, raising pressure to that of the water. Blockage of this tube eliminates this route of equalization, and a pressure gradient develops. The capillaries of the middle ear become dilated; leakage may occur if the pressure increase continues. The tympanic membrane is flexed inward, and capillaries within it may rupture. The membrane itself may be torn.

As a rule, the only result of ear squeeze is pain. In severe cases—with or without tympanic rupture—there may be a temporary hearing loss. With time, this resolves itself. In polluted waters, a ruptured eardrum may permit the development of a middle ear infection (otitis media). Water rushing into the middle ear may cause stimulation of the vestibular mechanism of the inner ear. Normally this mechanism assists in maintaining postural equilibrium, and stimulation may thus disrupt one's sense of equilibrium. The afflicted diver may be unable to distinguish up from down.

Trauma to the ear can be caused by only a slight increase in pressure. Tympanic membranes may rarely rupture in less than 10 feet of water.[4] If equalization is possible within the first 33 feet, a deeper dive usually can be made without difficulty. The greatest differential per foot develops within the first 33 feet.

Pain results from over two thirds of ear squeeze cases. This becomes so severe that few people will continue to dive in its presence. Blood may drain from the ear through the eustachian tube and be evident after the dive in the mouth and/or the nose.

Any person will have ear squeeze if his middle-ear pressure is not equalized. Some rare persons have such free air flow that they are never consciously aware of pressure changes, for them equalization is automatic. The majority will have pain during pressurization, unless an effort is made to equalize ear pressure with ambient pressure. This process is called clearing the ears.

There are several techniques to equalize the middle ear pressure with water pressure—clearing the ears. These include swallowing, yawning, or moving the lower jaw from side to side. The Toynbee maneuver is swallowing with the nose pinched shut. In the Frenzel maneuver, the tongue is used with a closed nose, mouth, and larynx to raise pressure in the eustachian tube. Perhaps the most popular technique is Valsalva's maneuver, the mouth and nose are shut, and there is exhalation with the larynx closed. The Valsalva raises pressure not only in the eustachian tube but also in the chest. It is inadvisable to perform a prolonged, vigorous, straining Valsalva. Increased chest pressure impairs blood return to the heart and may dangerously interfere with circulation. Furthermore, the high pressure may cause inner ear damage (see p. 83). If clearing requires much effort, the dive technique is faulty or a medical problem is present. If ear pain

EAR SQUEEZE

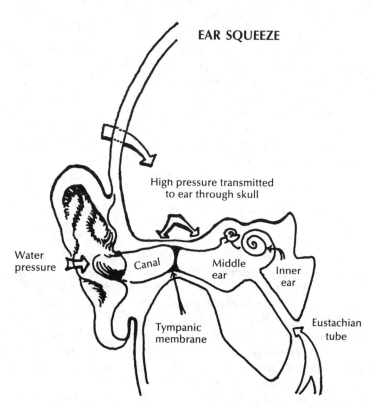

High pressure transmitted to ear through skull

Water pressure

Canal

Middle ear

Inner ear

Tympanic membrane

Eustachian tube

High pressure air passes to middle ear via eustachian tube and counteracts water pressure.

develops during a dive, and the ears cannot be easily cleared, the dive should be terminated.

Pain alone does not mean that barotrauma has occurred. It does, however, serve as a warning that a potentially dangerous situation exists. In a study of submarine school candidates, Alfandre found an incidence of clinical otic barotrauma of 36 percent during pressurization to 4 atmospheres (99 feet).[5] No tympanic rupture was found during the 432 exposures.

For most divers the ability to equalize is a function of experience. It is useful to begin clearing before pain is felt. A closed eustachian tube cannot be opened if a pressure gradient of about 90 mm of mercury develops (equivalent of going from the surface to 4 feet).[6] Posture also affects eustachian tube function. Head-

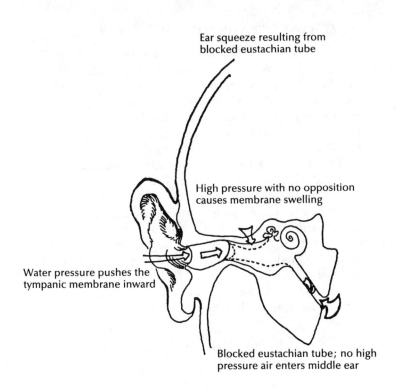

Ear squeeze resulting from blocked eustachian tube

High pressure with no opposition causes membrane swelling

Water pressure pushes the tympanic membrane inward

Blocked eustachian tube; no high pressure air enters middle ear

down descents cause more venous congestion around the tube than feet-first descents, and this makes clearing more difficult. Sometimes equalization can be effected by ascending a few feet, clearing, and then dropping down again.

Some persons have anatomical abnormalities that impede air passage to the ear. Often problems in equalization result from allergies or infections that block the eustachian tube. Submarine candidates with colds had a 61 percent incidence of clinical ear barotrauma.[7]

Use of decongestant tablets, nose drops, or nose sprays before diving may facilitate eustachian tube function. Care must be taken, however, since some of these medicines cause drowsiness, and frequent decongestant use may cause a rebound phenomenon, which worsens the original congestion. The safest path is to avoid diving on those days when clearing is difficult.

After the diver has equalized to an increased pressure during a descent, he must expel the high-pressure air during ascent; otherwise, falling ambient pressure would increase middle ear pressure, flex the tympanic membrane outward, and compress the middle-ear capillaries. This reverse squeeze rarely develops, since flow from the ear to the throat is easier than the reverse; the eustachian tube only occasionally blocks air exit. However, impairment in air release may cause vertigo (see page 84).

Use of decongestant medicines may speed drainage from a damaged middle ear. If an eardrum becomes perforated, it usually heals naturally, but cases of nonhealing are not infrequent. The perforation most often closes in one to two days, but it should not be exposed to pressure for a minimum of a month, and swimming should not be allowed until after the damage has completely healed. Antibiotics may be necessary if the injury took place in polluted water.

The use of ear plugs can cause another type of ear damage: external ear squeeze. The plug forms an air pocket between itself

RESULT OF USING EAR PLUGS

Transmitted pressure causing swelling of canal lining

Water pressure wedges plug into ear

High pressure air

Unopposed air from throat pushes tympanic membrane outward

and the tympanic membrane. As middle ear pressure rises, along with capillary pressure in the external canal, this pocket has a relatively lower pressure, causing capillary exudation and rupture as the eardrum flexes outward. (Note that the eardrum here ruptures outward rather than inward.) Since the plug isolates the air space, no equalization is possible. If middle ear pressurization lags behind water pressure, the plug may be forced deep into the external canal, making removal quite difficult. Under sufficient pressure, the plug could perforate the tympanic membrane. Ear plugs, hence, have no place in diving. Hoods to wet suits may present a similar problem of air pocket formation. Water should be allowed to enter the hood itself so that no air pockets can be formed.

INNER EAR BAROTRAUMA

Damage to the inner ear can cause impairment in hearing and/ or in equilibrium. Obviously any disruption in these functions is very serious.

The inner ear is not an air space, but it is affected by pressure changes within air spaces. Pressure changes are transmitted to the inner ear across the round and oval windows from the middle ear. The perilymph of the inner ear is connected with cerebrospinal fluid and reflects pressure changes within the chest and abdomen.

Excessive pressure gradients can damage the fine cellular structures of the inner ear. Rupture of either the round or oval window causes fluid leakage, which impairs inner ear function.

Within recent years several cases of round window rupture, and a smaller number of oval window tears, have been described.[9] Two mechanisms appear to be involved. A vigorous Valsalva maneuver will increase cerebrospinal fluid pressure, and this is transmitted through the perilymph to the round window. If the diver has not equalized his middle ear, the inner ear pressure will not be matched and the round window may rupture. The second mechanism involves increased pressure on the tympanic membrane being transmitted via the stapes to the oval window. This may directly tear the oval window or cause transmitted pressure to tear the round window.

Proper diagnosis is very important in all ear injuries. It is especially important to distinguish between middle ear and inner ear damage. Both may cause hearing loss, but that from inner ear injury has the pattern of nerve damage. A tuning fork test gives lateralization to the affected ear in middle ear injury and to the unaffected ear in inner ear injury. The treatment of the two maladies is quite different.

Inner ear injury is treated with bed rest and exploratory surgery if there is no spontaneous healing. Ear inflation is used in middle ear barotrauma, but is very dangerous in window rupture.

Prevention is much more effective than therapy. Even with proper therapy there may be permanent deficits in function. The injury can usually be avoided by thorough and gentle ear equalization during the dive. Opinions are varied, but the conservative advice is to avoid further diving if inner ear barotrauma occurs.[10]

INNER EAR DECOMPRESSION SICKNESS

Decompression sickness may involve the inner ear and cause hearing and/or equilibrium defects. This is usually a problem with deep diving on mixed gases.[11] It must be distinguished from inner ear barotrauma, since decompression sickness requires recompression therapy, which would be dangerous in barotrauma. Barotrauma is more commonly associated with descent during shallow diving, while decompression sickness follows ascent from deep dives. Unfortunately, recompression does not always cure inner ear decompression sickness.

VERTIGO

Vertigo is the sensation of rotary movement of self or environment. It is commonly misused as a synonym for dizziness. Vertigo is not uncommon in diving. In some diver surveys the incidence may be as high as 40 percent. The incidence of true vertigo is probably less, since many persons confuse dizziness with vertigo.

Position sense involves integration of impulses from eyes, ears, skin, muscles, and joints. Diving can affect any of the inputs or the integrative ability of the brain. Sensory deprivation from reduced visibility and absence of ground contact is an important factor. The diver's brain may be affected by nitrogen narcosis, impure breathing gas, high inspired oxygen, inadequate oxygen, high carbon dioxide, or low carbon dioxide.

Derangements within the equilibrium system of the inner ear (vestibular system) cause vertigo. This may result from abnormal stimulation or from interference with normal function. Sea sickness (see Chapter 19, First Aid) is a normal reaction to inner ear stimulation. Persons without normal vestibular function do not suffer from motion sickness.

If cold water contacts only one ear, the unequal thermal sensation may lead to vertigo. This can happen if a tightly fitting wet suit hood admits water to only one ear canal. An ear canal obstructed with the swelling of otitis externa or with structural abnormalities may exchange water poorly, thus setting up unequal thermal stimulation to the tympanic membrane. Rupture of a tympanic membrane allows the middle ear to fill with water. This water comes in close contact with the inner ear. The ear is sensed by the brain as being colder than the other ear, and vertigo results.

In the previous discussion of inner ear barotrauma and decompression sickness, disturbances in equilibrium were noted. These result from direct injury to the inner ear.

After eliminating nonear causes of vertigo and the inner ear influences just discussed, quite a few cases of vertigo remain to be explained. Lundgren devised the term "alternobaric vertigo" to describe vertigo resulting from unequal pressure equalization within the middle ears.[13] That is, if one middle ear has a higher pressure than the other, there is unequal inner ear stimulation, which may cause vertigo. Most of this vertigo (up to 60 percent) occurs during ascent, when ear pressure relative to water pressure rises.[14] During ascent the ear air usually vents passively. But vertigo can develop on descent.

Impaired eustachian tube function is frequently found in divers who have experienced alternobaric vertigo. Other divers had normal tube function without evidence of barotrauma, but still developed higher than normal pressures on ascent.[15] It is difficult to ascertain the incidence of alternobaric vertigo. Interestingly, it is more common in experienced divers than in neophytes.[16] Vertigo can be markedly reduced by careful equalization, even on ascent, and by avoiding diving when the eustachian tubes are not functioning properly.

NOTES: DIVING AND THE EAR

1. D. Wright, J. Alexander, "Effects of Water on the Bacterial Flora of Swimmers: Ears," *Archives of Otolaryngology,* 99: 15–18, 1974.
2. S. Alcock, "Active Otitis Externa in Divers Working in the North Sea: A Microbiological Survey of Seven Saturation Divers," *Journal of Hygiene,* 78: 395–409, 1977.
3. I. Brook et al., "Effect of Diving and Diving Hoods on the Bacterial Flora of the External Ear Canal and Skin," *Journal of Clinical Microbiology* 15: 855–59, 1982.
4. A Keller, Jr., "A Study of the Relationship of Air Pressure to Myringorupture," *Laryngoscope,* 68: 2015–27, 1958.
5. H. Alfandre, "Aerotitis Media in Submarine Recruits," U.S. Naval Submarine Medical Center Research Report, March 1966.
6. Keller, *op. cit.*
7. Alfandre, *op. cit.*
8. W. D. McNicoll, "Eustachian Tube Dysfunction in Submariners and Divers," *Archives of Otolargyngology,* 108: 279–83, 1982.
9. J. Farmer, "Diving Injuries to the Inner Ear," *Annals of Otology, Rhinology, Laryngology,* 86 (Supplement 36): 1–20, 1977.
10. P. Taylor, P. Bucknell, "Rupture of the Round Window Membrane," *Annals of Otology, Rhinology, Laryngology,* 85: 105–10, 1976.
11. J. Farmer, et al., "Inner Ear Decompression Sickness," *Laryngoscope,* 86: 1315–27, 1976.
12. L. M. Terry, W. Dennison, "Vertigo Among Divers," U.S. Naval Submarine Medical Center Special Report, No. 62–63, April 1966.
13. C. Lundgren, "Alternobaric Vertigo—A Diving Hazard," *British Medical Journal,* 2: 511–13, 1965.
14 C. Lundgren et al., "Alternobaric Vertigo and Hearing Disturbances in Connection with Diving: An Epidemiological Study," *Undersea Biomedical Research,* 1: 251–58, 1974.
15. Ö. Tjernström, "Function of the Eustachian Tube in Divers with a History of Alternobaric Vertigo," *Undersea Biomedical Research,* 1: 343–51, 1974.
16. J. Vorosmarti, M. Bradley, "Alternobaric Vertigo in Military Diving," *Military Medicine,* 135: 182–85, 1970.

7 | Respiration

Breathing provides the tissues with the required volatile nutrient, oxygen, and removes volatile cellular waste products—chiefly, carbon dioxide.

Alterations in respiratory physiology are significant in diving. Even at shallow depths, the SCUBA diver may notice some difficulty in breathing. As the exertion increases, breathing becomes still harder. Problems related to respiration play an important part in deep-diving research. This chapter will discuss some basic aspects of respiratory physiology and show the effects of underwater breathing. Because it differs in nature, respiration in skin diving will be discussed in the next chapter.

STRUCTURE

The upper respiratory tract reaches from the mouth and the nose to the larynx. Here air is filtered, humidified, and heated or cooled as necessary. From the larynx, air moves through the trachea to its bifurcations into the bronchi. At this point, the conducting tubes enter the lungs. The right lung has three lobes and the left has two; each lobe divides further into pulmonary segments. The bronchi, with cartilaginous ring support as in the trachea, branch into bronchioles, which have no cartilage in their walls. These are strengthened by smooth involuntary muscle, but the next division, the respiratory bronchioles, have no muscular support. Finally, air enters the alveolar sinuses and then the alveoli (air cells).

From the single trachea the respiratory tree branches into a million tiny tubes. The alveoli are the sites of gas transfer with the blood. These microscopic sacs total approximately 300 million. The surface area of the alveolar membrane is 70 square meters (approximately 40 times surface area of the skin). Surface tension forces tend to collapse the alveoli, but they are kept open by pulmonary surfactant. This is a complex chemical substance that acts to reduce the effect of alveolar radius on surface tension. Its action equalizes surface tension on different-sized alveoli so that the small alveoli do not collapse, and the large alveoli do not overdistend.

A serous membrane, the visceral pleura, covers the lungs. Another serous layer on the inner surface of the thoracic wall, the parietal pleura, is linked by a fluid interface to the visceral surface. During inspiration, active muscle contraction pulls the chest wall out, and the lungs are distended by this force acting across the pleural surfaces. Normally, the two pleural surfaces are juxtaposed, but exudates from pneumonia and similar diseases can separate the layers. The pleura may become fibrotic, and thus depth of inspiration may be limited.

The interaction between lung surface and chest wall in inspiration results in an intrapleural pressure, which is subatmospheric. Thus, air flows into the lungs (a negative pressure system). With maximal inspiratory effort, the lung pressure can be reduced from 60 to 100 mm Hg below atmospheric.

Expiration, normally passive, results from the elastic recoil of the lungs when thoracic expansion ceases. The increasing intrathoracic pressure then forces the gases from the lungs into the atmosphere.

From a functional point of view, the lungs can be subdivided into

1. Total lung capacity (TLC), the lung content when lungs are inflated from total collapse to maximum inflation
2. Vital capacity (VC), the amount of air which can be inhaled after maximal expiration
3. Residual volume (RV), amount of air remaining in the lungs after maximal expiration—volume from maximum expiration to collapse

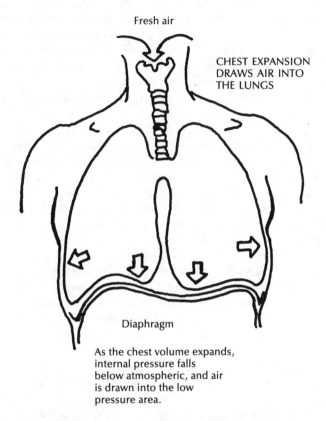

Fresh air

CHEST EXPANSION
DRAWS AIR INTO
THE LUNGS

Diaphragm

As the chest volume expands,
internal pressure falls
below atmospheric, and air
is drawn into the low
pressure area.

4. Inspiratory capacity (IC): amount of air which can be inhaled after normal expiration
5. Functional reserve capacity (FRC), amount of air remaining after a normal expiration
6. Inspiratory reserve volume (IRV), amount of air which can be inhaled beyond normal inhalation
7. Tidal volume (TV), amount of air inhaled and exhaled in a normal breath
8. Expiratory reserve volume (ERV), amount of air which can be exhaled after normal expiration.

The above illustration shows the relative size of these components. In diving, the divisions of chief interest are the tidal volume, residual volume, and total lung capacity.

Residual volume is about 20 percent of total lung capacity in young males and rises with age. Recall that the ratio of residual volume to total lung capacity affects the depth where lung squeeze will develop. (See Chapter 5, Squeeze.) With a high ratio, RV small in comparison to TLC, more compression of lung volume can occur before RV is reached.

The respiratory passage from nose to alveoli does not participate in gas transfer to the blood; it is called dead space. At the end of expiration, this passage is filled with expiratory alveolar gas. Upon inspiration, this old gas enters the alveoli first. It is followed by fresh air, creating a mixture. Upon expiration, the mixed gas flows out and again fills the passages. The volume of dead space is usually figured as 150 ml. Thus, if the tidal volume is 500 ml, only 350 ml of fresh air reaches the alveoli. The final 150 ml remains in the respiratory tree during inspiration and is the first quantity to be exhaled; it never reaches the alveoli.

Ventilation supplies the lungs with air and removes air upon expiration. The gross amount of ventilation per minute is called respiratory minute volume (RMV) and is the product of the respiratory rate and the tidal volume. Alveolar ventilation per minute is less, since it equals rate times tidal volume minus dead space. Obviously, an increase in dead space will reduce alveolar ventilation at a given rate.

Dead space depends upon body position and depth of inspiration. In deep inspiration, the volume of the tubes is increased with the walls distended; dead space is increased.

Diving tends to increase dead space, because the volume of air in the tubes of the breathing equipment comprises one part of the dead space air. Under pressure breathing, the body's air passages expand in volume; if the regulator's pressure is set too high, pulmonary capillaries may collapse, resulting in alveoli without blood supply.

When dead space increases, the tidal volume or rate must increase, or alveolar ventilation will be below normal. Increasing the depth or rate of respiration requires more energy and may cause respiratory fatigue. Typically, the exhausted diver takes rapid, shallow breaths, which further reduce alveolar ventilation.

Uneven ventilation is dangerous in diving, since it may lead to air trapping and air embolism. Ideally, each alveolus should receive the same amount of ventilation. This is never exactly the case because of lung structure—some alveoli are farther from the sup-

STATIC LUNG VOLUMES

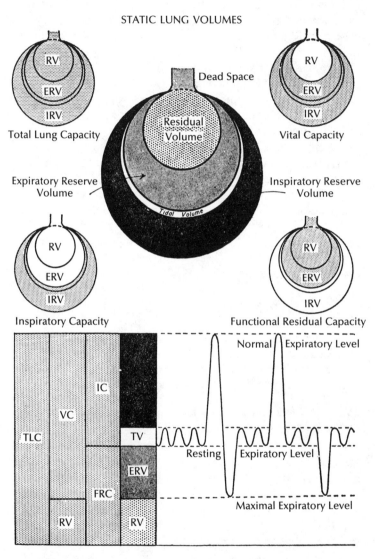

The large central diagram illustrates the four primary lung volumes and their approximate magnitudes. Below are lung volumes as they appear in spirographic tracings; shading in the first vertical bar to the left of the tracing corresponds to that in the central diagram above. From Julius H. Comroe, Jr., et al., *The Lung* (Chicago: Year Book Medical Publishers, Inc., 1962). Used with permission of the publisher.

ply. The distribution may be made more uneven in cases of localized loss of alveolar expansion—fibrosis or breakdown of elasticity. Regional obstruction of the tubular lumen will also reduce ventilation. Walls may be partially collapsed or blocked with mucus plugs, as in asthma. Regional check valves may inhibit free air flow in some regions.

In the upper respiratory tract, the dry, inspired air is humidified by the addition of water-vapor at a pressure of 47 mm Hg. The presence of water vapor reduces the total pressure of N_2, O_2, and CO_2 to 713 mm (760 mm—47 mm), so that pO_2 is less in tracheal air. In the alveoli, as CO_2 is released from the blood and O_2 is absorbed by it, O_2 partial pressure drops to 100 mm Hg and pCO_2 rises to 40 mm. The lungs are perfused by mixed, venous blood whose pO_2 is below alveolar (40 mm) with pCO_2 above alveolar (46 mm). Equilibration of pressure occurs, and the arterial blood, leaving the alveoli, has a composition almost identical to alveolar.

PULMONARY CIRCULATION

Gas exchange takes place in the vast capillary network surrounding the lungs. Oxygen poor blood from the veins enters the right atrium, passes to the right ventricle, and is pumped into the pulmonary artery. This artery is unusual in that it carries venous

RESPIRATORY PARTIAL PRESSURES*

	Dry Air	Tracheal	Alveolar	Venous	Arterial
Oxygen	159.1 mm HG	149.2	104.	40.	100.
Carbon Dioxide	0.3	0.3	40.	46.	40.
Water Vapor	—	47.	47.	47.	47.
Nitrogen	600.6	563.5	569.	573.	573.
Total	760.	760.	760.	706.	760.

Note: Since the tissues cannot produce as much CO_2 as they use of O_2, venous blood has a lower total pressure.

*Julius H. Comroe, Jr., *Physiology of Respiration* (Chicago: Year Book Medical Publishers, Inc., 1965), pg. 18.

CIRCULATION
EXCHANGE OF GASES

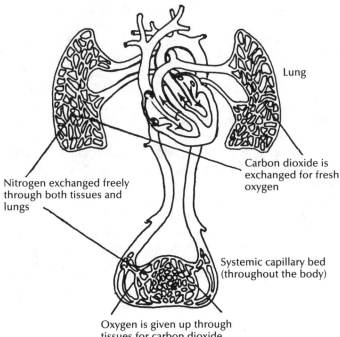

Lung

Carbon dioxide is
exchanged for fresh
oxygen

Nitrogen exchanged freely
through both tissues and
lungs

Systemic capillary bed
(throughout the body)

Oxygen is given up through
tissues for carbon dioxide

blood. The artery branches into smaller arterioles, which further divide to form the pulmonary capillaries. After oxygenation from the alveoli, the blood flows into the pulmonary venules, which form the pulmonary veins leading arterial composition blood to the left atrium. From the left atrium, blood goes to the left ventricle and is pumped, via the aorta, to the systemic arteries, where O_2 is removed in the capillaries and CO_2 is added, thus forming venous blood. Pressure within the pulmonary circulatory system is low in comparison with that in the systemic (approximately 15 mm pulmonary artery pressure vs. 120 mm aortic), but resistance is correspondingly low, so that pulmonary blood flow volume equals systemic. In vigorous exercise, pulmonary blood flow may double, but pressure rises only 25–50 percent, due to low resistance.[1]

IMMERSION EFFECTS

Even shallow immersion markedly affects lung volumes and circulation. Water pressure exerts direct effect on the limbs and abdomen to shift blood into the thorax. Abdominal compression displaces the diaphragm upward and limits lung expansion. Both vital capacity and functional residual capacity are reduced.[2] Large amounts of blood—almost a liter—are shifted from the peripheral circulation into the blood vessels of the thorax.[3] Expansion of this vascular space impinges on alveolar volume and further reduces vital capacity. Residual volume and expiratory reserve volume (the components of FRC) are both decreased. The reduction in residual volume affects maximal breath-hold dive depth. (See Chapter 5, Squeeze.)

When the air volume of an alveolus is reduced sufficiently, it will close. This critical volume is called the closing volume. Normally, even after exhalation, most alveoli are open. With aging, alveoli tend to increase their closing volume and may be shut during some phases of normal ventilation. Not surprisingly, this reduces ventilatory efficiency and impairs gas exchange. With immersion, vascular shifts increase closing volume and may cause uneven lung ventilation.[4] This effect can be partially offset by large inhalations and is less likely in young divers.

The vascular shifting increases blood return to the heart and causes a larger cardiac output and higher pulmonary artery pressure. The augmented cardiac output improves perfusion of the lungs and partially corrects the deleterious effects that immersion has on ventilation.[5]*

GAS EXCHANGE

The alveolar-capillary exchange area is an enormous 70 square meters; the thickness of the border between alveolus and capillary

---

*The above determinations were made in persons immersed to the neck while standing. This situation is not fully comparable to SCUBA diving. In another study, prone immersion had less effect on lung volume: I. Daskalovic et al., "The Effects of Prone Immersion on Lung Function," *Abstracts of the Seventh Symposium on Underwater Physiology,* Athens, 1980.

is microscopic. Gas exchange takes place by diffusion. In this, because of the activity of the gas molecules, regions of different composition equilibrate, as the area of high concentration of gas blends in with the low concentration region. In this same manner, the fragrance of an open bottle of perfume will gradually fill a room. Light gases diffuse faster since their molecules travel faster and collide more frequently. Graham's law states that *the rate of diffusion in air is inversely proportional to the square root of density*. By this law, oxygen diffuses slightly more rapidly than CO_2 within the alveoli; however, when oxygen enters the blood, solubility becomes the determining factor in diffusion rate.

Carbon dioxide is almost 24 times more soluble in blood than O_2. Therefore, the overall rate of diffusion is greater for CO_2, despite its slower diffusion within the alveoli. The combined rate shows CO_2 to diffuse approximately 20 times faster than O_2.

Abnormalities of alveolar walls and faulty capillary circulation impair O_2 diffusion. Inspired gas may freely enter an alveolus with a thickened wall, but diffusion through that wall will be limited. Reduction in effective capillary flow, because of the restriction of blood flow or thickened capillary walls, will similarly reduce diffusion. These changes effectively diminish the surface area for gas exchange. They also increase the dead space volume by adding additional areas without capability for gas exchange.

Gas pressures equilibrate almost completely across the alveolicapillary membrane. Interestingly, at high O_2 pressures, there is a noticeable difference between alveolar and arterial O_2 tensions; the mechanism has not been definitely established.[6]

OXYGEN TRANSPORT

Because of differences in solubility, there are differences in blood content among various gases at a given partial pressure. Highly soluble gases exist in large amounts at relatively low partial pressures, while high pressure may only slightly raise the amount of a poorly soluble gas. The partial pressure represents a driving force for solution, but its effect depends upon the solubility coefficient of the gas.

The blood carries oxygen in two forms: dissolved in plasma and chemically combined with hemoglobin. Plasma solubility is low; at normal temperatures only .3 ml O_2 is carried in each 100 ml of plasma at the normal arterial O_2 tension of 100 mm. A small amount is also carried in the liquid portion of the red blood cells, but it only raises total solubility to .31 ml/100 ml of blood at 100 mm. Since the tissues consume 250 ml of O_2 in a minute, this low solubility would require a blood flow of 83l/min (14 times normal) to provide minimum needs.

By far the majority of O_2 is chemically combined with hemoglobin (about 65 times the amount carried in plasma). The saturation of hemoglobin's capacity to carry O_2 depends upon O_2 partial pressure, but the relationship is not linear. At arterial pO_2 of 100 mm, Hb is 97.5 percent saturated while saturation is 100 percent above 250 mm. As pO_2 falls when the blood reaches the tissues, the hemoglobin saturation does not fall completely. There is thus a reserve of O_2 carried by hemoglobin. At normal venous O_2 tensions of 40 mm, hemoglobin is still 75 percent saturated. The relationship of pO_2 to hemoglobin saturation follows an S-shaped dissociation and association curve. Hemoglobin gives up more O_2 for each millimeter fall in pO_2 at low O_2 tensions. Therefore, O_2 is readily released from hemoglobin in the active tissues since they have a low O_2 tension.

At alveolar concentrations, hemoglobin saturation remains more constant. Moderate decreases in alveolar pO_2 will not radically lower hemoglobin saturation. For example, at 70 mm pO_2, Hb is still 93 percent saturated. The curve is shifted to the right—less saturation per unit pO_2—in regions of high CO_2 (this is called the Bohr effect), high acidity, and elevated temperature.

Normally, there are about 15 gm of Hb/100 ml blood, and each gm can carry 1.34 ml O_2. This is about 20 ml O_2/100 ml and is 19.5 ml at saturation of 97.5 percent. If all of this O_2 were extracted, a cardiac output of about 1.2 l/minute would supply tissue needs. In fact, only about one fifth of the total O_2 content is removed, although the amount rises in highly active tissues.

Breathing air under pressure (SCUBA) raises the blood O_2 tension and will permit more O_2 transport in plasma solution. At 300 feet the amount of O_2 in solution could theoretically meet minimal tissue requirements with a normal cardiac output, even without any O_2 being carried by hemoglobin.

At these high O_2 tensions, hemoglobin would be completely saturated. Tissue requirements would first be met by the dissolved

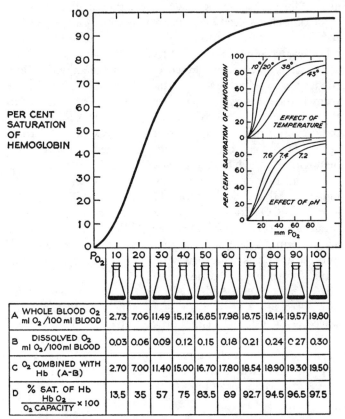

	PO₂	10	20	30	40	50	60	70	80	90	100
A	WHOLE BLOOD O₂ ml O₂/100 ml BLOOD	2.73	7.06	11.49	15.12	16.85	17.98	18.75	19.14	19.57	19.80
B	DISSOLVED O₂ ml O₂/100 ml BLOOD	0.03	0.06	0.09	0.12	0.15	0.18	0.21	0.24	0.27	0.30
C	O₂ COMBINED WITH Hb (A-B)	2.70	7.00	11.40	15.00	16.70	17.80	18.54	18.90	19.30	19.50
D	% SAT. OF Hb $\frac{Hb\ O_2}{O_2\ CAPACITY} \times 100$	13.5	35	57	75	83.5	89	92.7	94.5	96.5	97.5

HbO_2, dissociation curves. The large graph shows a single dissociation curve, applicable when the ph of the blood is 7:40 and temperature 38° C. From Julius H. Comroe, Jr., *Physiology of Respiration* (Chicago: Year Book Medical Publishers, Inc., 1965). Used with the permission of the publisher.

O_2; hemoglobin would not release any of its oxygen until the blood tension fell to 250 mm.

CARBON DIOXIDE TRANSPORT

Venous blood transports CO_2 back to the heart and thence to the lungs. The relationship of pCO_2 to CO_2 content is almost always linear. Carbon dioxide enters the capillary blood, and some of it is dissolved in the plasma. The majority of it enters the red blood cells where it is dissolved, forms compounds with proteins, and combines with H_2O to form carbonic acid (H_2CO_3), which dissociates in the presence of carbonic anhydrase to $H+$ (hydrogen ion) and HCO_3- (bicarbonate). The HCO_3+ then reenters the plasma in exchange for chloride ($Cl-$). Thus most of the CO_2 is eventually carried in the plasma. This form of transfer requires absorption of $H+$ so that acidity is kept within tolerable limits. The major accepter (buffer) of the acid—hydrogen—is hemoglobin, which has released its O_2. Hb thus plays a star role in the elimination of CO_2 and volatile acids from the tissues. In the lungs the Hb takes up alveolar O_2 and cannot accept hydrogen ions. The CO_2 transport reactions are then driven in reverse; bicarbonate (HCO_3-) enters the red blood cells from the plasma and re-forms CO_2, in which form it enters the plasma and diffuses into the alveoli. The decrease in CO_2 transport by the saturated Hb is known as the Haldane effect.

As might be expected, CO_2 transport is impaired in conditions of reduced HbO_2 dissociation. Under high pressure, plasma dissolved O_2 will supply a larger proportion of the tissues O_2 needs, and no O_2 need be supplied from the hemoglobin. This reduction in release of O_2 from hemoglobin lowers the amount of CO_2 that can be transported. Tissue pCO_2 will rise as transport is reduced, thus raising venous pCO_2.

RESPIRATORY STIMULATION

Variations in gas tensions influence ventilation by regulating the rate and depth of inspiration. In the most elementary sense, they act as stimuli to maintain blood gas levels within a normal range.

Oxygen is not very influential at average alveolar levels. Its effects are generally not seen until alveolar (arterial) pO_2 reaches 60 mm. At an inspired percentage of 12 percent, there is only minimal deviation from the normal respiratory pattern with 21 percent O_2.[1] Oxygen acts on respiration through chemoreceptors in the carotid body (a neurovascular structure in the main neck artery) and in the arch of the aorta. Stimuli, then, go to the respiratory center in the medulla (brain stem). Evidently pO_2 is more influential than actual O_2 content. If hemoglobin is reduced but alveolar O_2 remains normal, the O_2 chemoreceptors are not stimulated. The total amount of O_2 in the blood is reduced, but O_2 tension stays normal. At high pO_2 there may be initial respiratory depression, but this is generally transitory.[7]

Carbon dioxide is more effective in modifying ventilation. With minor percentage increases in alveolar CO_2, changes may be seen in tidal volume and frequency. As a rough rule, the average minute volume change is 2.5 l/minute for each mm rise in alveolar pCO_2.[8] High CO_2 acts in the aortic and carotid chemoreceptors. This response appears to be reduced by rising O_2 tensions.[9] At near normal CO_2 pressures, the major effect comes from chemoreceptors in the medulla, which act reflexly on the respiratory center. The medullary receptors are not affected by O_2 tensions. Medullary response to increased pCO_2 is slower than is seen in the carotid and aortic receptors.

THE WORK OF BREATHING

The major work in breathing is done to overcome the elastic recoil forces in the lung; it is this recoil that creates the subatmospheric intrapleural pressure. Inspiration distends the lungs and passageways, allowing the inflow of air. The ratio of change in volume to pressure change is known as compliance. Fibrotic lungs have low compliance; that is, a great deal of pressure is required for small volume changes.

In normal breathing, the work required to overcome elastic recoil is more than twice that needed to overcome frictional resistance in the lung tissues and the air passages; however, as respiratory rate increases, as it does with exercise, the proportion of work done in making up for frictional resistance increases. By far the most frictional work is involved in air movement.

The amount of work is reflected in the pressure required to give adequate ventilatory flow. As airway resistance rises, the pressure required to maintain flow increases. In smooth air flow, pressure required for a given flow rate (v) is directly proportional to the air's viscosity. Where K is a constant to allow for the viscosity of a given gas, $P = KV$. Resistance varies directly with the length and inversely with the fourth power of tube radius. As the airways branch into smaller tubes, resistance is kept from increasing markedly by a corresponding reduction in the length of the tube. As one tube becomes two, each tube has a diameter only slightly smaller than the original. Also, a progressive reduction in flow rate means that less pressure is needed in the small tubes.

In those passageways with irregular surfaces and at points of narrowing, the airflow creates eddy currents and is thus termed turbulent flow. Unlike smooth flow, turbulent flow depends on density, not viscosity. $P = V^2K$ where K applies to density. Note that pressure rises with the square of flow rate. The tendency for turbulent flow depends on flow rate, tube diameter, gas density, and gas viscosity. Mathematically, Reynold's number represents this:

$$N = \frac{\text{density} \times \text{flow rate} \times \text{diameter}}{\text{viscosity}}$$

Thus, high flow rate, density, and large diameter will increase the percentage of flow, which is turbulent, and accentuate the resistance in the turbulent fraction.

Airway resistance increases noticeably during diving, even shallow SCUBA diving. At shallow depths, the breathing equipment accounts for most of the resistance. The narrow tubes and orifices make air exchange more difficult; when breathing is speeded by heavy exertion, the equipment's efficiency falls still further as resistance to flow rises. Slow, deep breathing causes the least resistance.

As the dive becomes deeper, the resistance continues to rise. In chamber experiments, with minimal resistance equipment, pressures of only three atmospheres absolute reduced maximal breathing capacity (the maximum volume of air which can be breathed in and out over a given period of time) by over 36 percent above surface values; at 5 atmospheres MBC was more than halved.[10] Experimental subjects showed impairment in both force and speed of expiration; the timed vital capacity (percentage of vital capacity which can be expired in a given period, done serially for 1 to 3 seconds) and maximal expiratory flow rates showed the effects of pressure. One study showed a 50 percent cut in maximal expiratory flow rate at only 99 feet.[11] Overall resistance at 99 feet was twice the surface value. Furthermore, these marked changes came on while the subjects were at rest and using equipment much more efficient than SCUBA rigs.

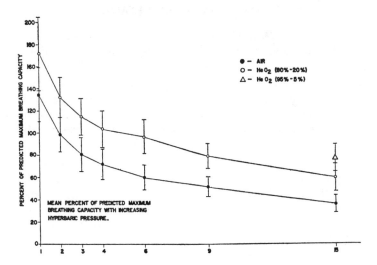

From W. B. Wood "Ventilatory Dynamics Under Hyperbaric States" in *Proceedings of the Second Symposium on Underwater Physiology,* Washington, D. C. 1963. Used with permission.

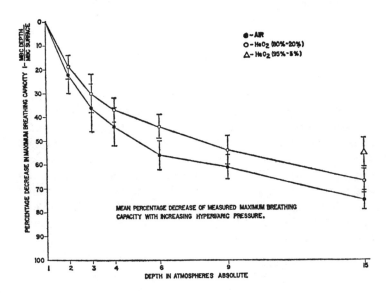

From Wood "Ventilatory Dynamics." Used with permission.

The main reason for increased airflow resistance at deep depths is probably related to density changes in the inspired gas; density rises proportionately with absolute pressure. High density elevates the tendency for turbulent flow (Reynold's number) and then increases resistance in the turbulent flow fraction. As an example, raising the density from 1 to 2 will double the percentage of flow that is turbulent and will then double resistance in this flow.

Conversely, high viscosity gases reduce the tendency toward turbulent flow. Helium has a density about one seventh that of air and a greater viscosity. Even at atmospheric pressure, the use of helium-oxygen will lower resistance below that seen when breathing air. At depth, resistance will rise, but the degree is much less than with air. Experiments with dense gases showed that ventilatory impairment is less at great depths than would be predicted from extrapolation of data obtained at moderate depths.[12]

In the shallow depths of sport diving, the effect of density is much less than that of inefficiency in the equipment. Breathing resistance represents an important problem in diving.

EFFECTS OF IMPAIRED VENTILATION

The larger dead space and the increased airway resistance combine to hinder ventilation in divers; the dead space requires either faster or deeper breathing to provide adequate alveolar ventilation, but the higher resistance makes this breathing more difficult. Alveolar ventilation suffers. As the work of breathing becomes harder, more of the body's energy production must be spent on it. This reduces the amount of energy that can be used for physical exertion. A vicious circle soon develops: Inefficient breathing reduces the production of energy, while the work of breathing requires a larger amount of energy. Any SCUBA diver who has attempted hard work under water can attest to the fact that generalized fatigue soon follows difficult breathing.

RESPIRATORY NEEDS

While the efficiency of breathing falls in diving, the need for efficient ventilation increases. At rest, a tidal volume of 500 ml and a rate of 12 breaths per minute provides a respiratory minute

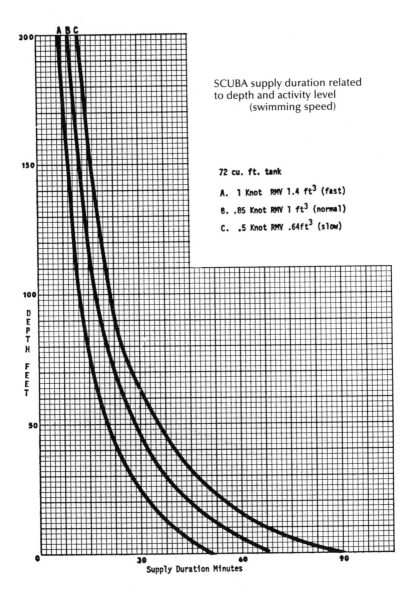

SCUBA supply duration related
to depth and activity level
(swimming speed)

72 cu. ft. tank

A. 1 Knot RMV 1.4 ft^3 (fast)

B. .85 Knot RMV 1 ft^3 (normal)

C. .5 Knot RMV .64ft^3 (slow)

volume (RMV) of 6 liters. Slow walking requires a RMV of 15 l/min. To swim at a comfortable speed of .8 to 1 knot* demands 28 l/min. Oxygen consumption rises similarly; on the average, it goes from .25 l/min. at rest to nearly 2 l/min. when swimming at 1 knot.[13] That swimming is an inefficient means of propulsion is demonstrated by the fact that 1 l of O_2 will suffice for a 116 yard run (8 miles per hour), but only for 14 yards of 1 knot swimming.

Obviously, the rate of air consumption determines the duration of SCUBA air supply at a given depth as shown on the accompanying graph.

EFFECTS OF DECREASED VENTILATION

In the simplest sense, impaired ventilation reduces the amount of oxygen supplied to the tissues and limits carbon dioxide elimination.

Symptoms of inadequate O_2 (hypoxia) develop insidiously. Respiratory stimulation usually does not occur until the inspired O_2 is half the normal amount. At this concentration, unconsciousness may supervene before breathing is increased. Attentiveness, judgment, and muscle function are impaired between .12 and .16 atmospheres. (Recall that normal O_2 is .20 atmospheres.) Thus, the most dangerous aspect of hypoxia is its potential for destruction without warning.

In open circuit SCUBA, hypoxia rarely develops; ventilatory restriction is offset by the rise in partial pressure of O_2. At 33 feet, the O_2 driving force doubles and can compensate for reduced alveolar ventilation. In deep diving, the oxygen percentage in helium oxygen mixes may be cut below 10 percent but will still provide a more than adequate partial pressure.

Unconsciousness from hypoxia presents a major risk in the use of closed-circuit and semiclosed circuit SCUBA. The closed circuit equipment must be thoroughly purged of air and filled completely with oxygen, otherwise the oxygen will quickly be exhausted; but total volume in the supply bag will remain nearly constant since the high concentration of nitrogen remains. The

---

*A knot equals 2,000 yards per hour, slightly faster than 1 mile per hour.

diver breathes the N_2 in and out, unaware that he is receiving no oxygen until it is too late.

When semiclosed SCUBA is used, the oxygen percentage must be carefully regulated. During ascent, failure to increase O_2 may result in hypoxia.

Deficiency in carbon dioxide elimination results far more commonly than inadequate oxygenation. At 132 feet, air that contained the normal .04 atmospheres CO_2 on the surface, will have a CO_2 partial pressure of .2 atmospheres. This high inspired CO_2 adds to the impaired expiration of alveolar CO_2 from inadequate alveolar ventilation. Furthermore, the exertion of diving results in a greater tissue production of CO_2.

OXYGEN CONSUMPTION AND RESPIRATORY MINUTE VOLUME

Activity	O_2 consumption L/min	Respiratory minute volume L.	Cu. Ft.
bed rest	.25	6	.21
sitting quietly	.30	7	.25
walking (2 mph)	.70	16	.57
running (8 mph)	2.0	50	1.8
slow SCUBA swim. (0.5 knot)	.8	18	.64
average SCUBA (0.85)	1.4	28	1.0
fast SCUBA (1 knot)	1.8	40	1.4
peak swimming (1.2–1.4)	2.5–3.4	60–75	2.1–2.7

Note: At a speed of .5 knots it is difficult to maintain headway. Peak speed can be maintained by well trained swimmers for 10 to 15 minutes. These figures are averages.

From:
1. U. S. Navy Diving Manual, Part I, 1963.
2. E. H. Lamphier, and J. V. Dwyer, "Diving with Self Contained Underwater Breathing Apparatus," U. S. Navy Experimental Diving Unit Special Report, Series 1, April 1954.

When air is supplied under pressure, the high oxygen saturates the hemoglobin and reduces its capability to transport CO_2 away from the tissues. When hemoglobin is completely saturated, pCO_2 may rise 5 mm., an equivalent of breathing 6 percent CO_2 (150 times normal).[14]

Elevated CO_2 can stimulate respiration or be mentally depressive. The typical hyperventilation that accompanies high CO_2 serves as a warning, but unfortunately this is not consistent. The depressive effects of CO_2 may predominate over respiratory stimulation when inspired O_2 is high or in exercise; both conditions exist in diving.[15]

In deeper diving, CO_2 retention increases the risk of nitrogen narcosis and oxygen poisoning.

Elevated carbon dioxide may contribute to the development of abnormal heart rhythms. These may strike without warning to cause unconsciousness and drowning.

At shallow depths, the elimination of carbon dioxide generally remains adequate with open-circuit SCUBA. Some divers tend to retain carbon dioxide even with proper equipment.[16] The practice of "skip breathing," i.e., holding the breath to conserve air supply, may raise carbon dioxide to dangerous levels.

Hard-hat diving is frequently accompanied by CO_2 intoxication, unless the helmet is vigorously ventilated with fresh air. Closed and semiclosed SCUBA depend on carbon dioxide absorbers; malfunction in them will result in rapid elevation of inspired CO_2.

Many factors affect ventilatory requirements in diving. Moderate exercise in shallow, warm water causes physiological changes very similar to those seen with exercise on land. However, with falls in water temperature, oxygen demands increase. As depth increases, ventilation becomes more difficult. A neophyte, paralyzed by fear, not infrequently concludes his regulator has failed when the problem really is inefficient breathing. Experienced divers have problems, too, especially if they retain carbon dioxide. Over a wide range of pressures, moderate exercise should be well tolerated. This does not mean that hard work can be demanded for a long period. Increased oxygen demands from cold, exercise, and from the work of breathing itself may limit underwater exercise capacity.

The impairment of breathing increases the fatigue of SCUBA diving and limits the diver's exertions. Respiratory problems have proved to be major obstacles in the extension of diving depth and duration of dives.

NOTES: RESPIRATION

1. J. Comroe, Jr., *Physiology of Respiration,* 2nd ed. (Chicago: Year Book Medical Publishers, Inc., 1974).

2. C. Prefaut, "Human Gas Exchange During Water Immersion," *Respiration Physiology,* 34: 307–18, 1978.

3. M. Arborelius et al., "Hemodynamic Changes in Man During Immersion with the Head Above Water," *Aerospace Medicine,* 43: 592–98, 1972.

4. G. Dahlback, C. Lundgren, "Pulmonary Air Trapping Induced by Water Immersion," *Aerospace Medicine,* 43: 768–74, 1972.

5. C. Perfaut et al., "Influence of Immersion to the Neck in Water on Airway Closure and Distribution of Perfusion in Man," *Respiratory Physiology,* 37: 313–23, 1979.

6. C. J. Lambertsen, "Physiological Effects of Oxygen Inhalation at High Partial Pressures," *Fundamentals of Hyperbaric Medicine,* (Washington, D.C.: National Academy of Science, 1966), pp. 12–20.

7. *Ibid.*

8. Comroe, *op. cit.*

9. C. J. Lambertsen, "Physiological Effects of Oxygen" in *Proceedings of the Second Symposium on Underwater Physiology* (Washington, D.C.: National Academy of Science, 1963) pp. 171–87.

10. W. Wood, "Ventilatory Dynamics Under Hyperbaric States," *Proceedings of the Second Symposium on Underwater Physiology* (Washington, D.C.: National Academy of Science, 1963) pp. 108–23.

11. R. Marshall et al., "Resistance to Breathing in Normal Subjects During Simulated Diving," *Journal of Applied Physiology,* 9: 5–10, 1956.

12. R. Peterson, W. Wright, "Pulmonary Mechanical Functions in Man Breathing Dense Gas Mixtures at High Ambient Pressures—Predictive Studies III," in *Underwater Physiology V,* C. Lambertsen, ed. (Bethesda, Md.: FASEB, 1976), pp. 67–77.

13. E. Lanphier, "Oxygen Consumption in Underwater Swimming," U.S. Navy Experimental Diving Unit Report No. 14–54, 1954.

14. Lambertsen, "Oxygen Inhalation."

15. E. Lanphier, J. Dwyer, "Diving with Self Contained Underwater Breathing Apparatus," U.S. Navy Experimental Diving Unit Special Report Series, 1954.

16. J. Macdonald, A. Pilmanis, "Carbon Dioxide Retention with Underwater Work in the Open Ocean," *Underwater Physiology VII,* C. Lambertsen, M. Matzen, eds., (Bethesda, Md.: Undersea Medical Society, 1981), pp. 197–207.

8 Respiration in Skin Diving

Most skin diving is done with a snorkel tube, which may slightly restrict ventilation because of its small bore. The maximum diving depth possible with a snorkel is about 4.5 feet. In drawing air from the surface (atmospheric pressure) into the lungs, underwater force must be exerted to expand the chest against the hydrostatic pressure of the water. The limit of pressure difference from surface to depth of breathing is about 100 mm/Hg, which equals 4.5 feet. Beyond this, it is not possible to develop subatmospheric intrathoracic pressure, and air cannot be drawn into the chest.

The duration of a breath-hold (apneic) dive is limited by the break point of breath holding. Lung volume, pO_2, pCO_2, physical training, and motivation combine to establish the duration to the break point. Of these, motivation is the least amenable to scientific testing. That it is a factor can be confirmed by any diver who has stayed down longer than he thought possible while in pursuit of a valued fish.

The stimulus to breathe can be either low blood O_2 or high CO_2. The average value for stimulus by CO_2 is 60 mm (normal arterial and alveolar is about 40 mm). Oxygen ends breath holding at 30 mm (normal arterial level is 100 mm). When low O_2 and high CO_2 are combined, a smaller deviation in both values (50 mm for both) will stimulate breathing.[1] Conversely, with elevated O_2, a higher CO_2 can be tolerated during breath holding.

Lung volume decreases during apnea (cessation of breathing), since the volume of O_2 used exceeds the amount of CO_2 given off. The terminal lung volume consists mainly of N_2. As lung volume decreases, a lower blood CO_2 will terminate breath holding. Conversely, an enlarged volume will permit greater CO_2 tolerance.

Exercise decreases the time that the breath can be held.[2] The rate of O_2 use increases so that the break point is reached sooner. Interestingly, a higher tolerance to CO_2 has been reported by some researchers,[3] although the mechanism has not been defined. The combined effect of lowered O_2, falling lung volume due to increased O_2 absorption rate, and rising pCO_2 secondary to exertion, hastens the break point.

Breathing pure oxygen at atmospheric pressure will increase breath-hold time 55 to 80 percent over air breathing. Hyperventilation with pure O_2 extends time to three times that in hyperventilated air.[4] The stimulus for rebreathing is pCO_2, since pO_2 will remain above stimulating levels.

Hyperventilation before diving is a common practice; it is also a dangerous one. Unquestionably, rapid deep breathing before a dive will increase the breath-hold time. Hyperventilation can lower alveolar pCO_2 to 15 (from 40) and raise O_2 to 140 mm (from 100). Blood content of O_2 will not rise markedly with this increase. During the apneic period, blood O_2 levels will fall while CO_2 rises. The low pCO_2 may complicate the situation by constricting cerebral blood vessels, thus reducing O_2 supply to the brain.

After hyperventilation, carbon dioxide may not rise quickly enough to end apnea before loss of consciousness from low O_2. In a study by Craig, after 10 minutes of hyperventilation followed by breath holding, pO_2 dropped to 40 mm, less than half the normal amount, before pCO_2 again reached stimulatory levels.[5] Lung volume will fall faster after hyperventilation since the O_2 removed represents a larger fraction of the total volume. Unconsciousness may occur without warning. Many underwater swimming deaths have been reported after hyperventilation. It is a great danger in underwater distance-swimming contests.

In breath-hold diving, the patterns of gas exchange are more complex than in simple breath holding under water. Water pressure variation during descent and ascent affects lung volumes, and consequently the partial pressures of lung gas are changed.

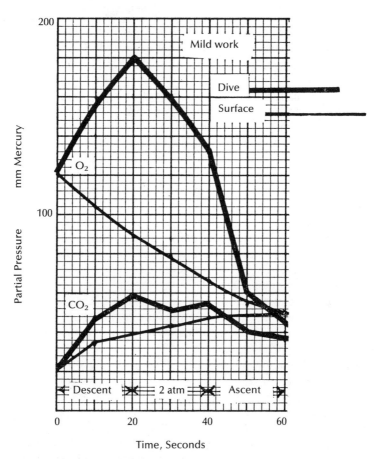

Alveolar pO_2 and pCO_2 in breath holding with air at normal pressure and during simulated dives. Note the difference between breath holding on the surface and under pressure. From Lanphier and Rahn, "Alveolar Gas Exchange." Used with permission.

At depth, lung compression raises the total lung pressure and with it the partial pressure of oxygen. Because of the high pO_2, breath-hold time increases. Davis reports 180 seconds normal at 100 feet—far above the normal duration.[6]

During descent, pCO_2, pO_2, and pN_2 rise. The increase in pO_2 lags behind absolute pressure increases since oxygen is constantly removed by the blood. The rise in alveolar partial pressure of CO_2 during descent may cause a reverse in normal flow, with the CO_2 entering rather than leaving the capillary blood.[7]

While at dive depth, body consumption of oxygen continues, and lung pO_2 falls steadily. Carbon dioxide tends to stay constant.[8] This results from a lower production of carbon dioxide during apnea and from the high alveolar pCO_2 reducing the flow gradient from the tissues. During surface breath holding, carbon dioxide rises.

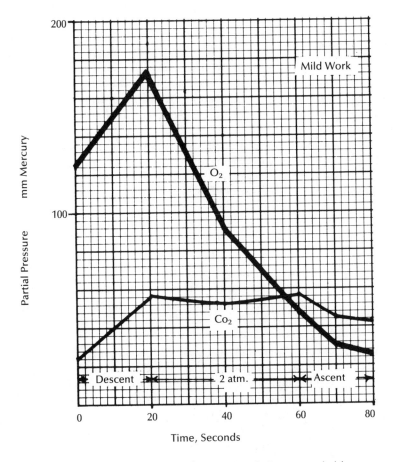

pO_2 and pCO_2 during 80 second simulated dives preceded by hyperventilation. Note the very low O_2 at the end of the dive. Compare this to breath holding without hyperventilation. From E. H. Lanphier and H. Rahn, "Alveolar Gas Exchange During Breath-Hold Diving." *Journal of Applied Physiology*, 18:471–477 May 1963. Used with permission.

Upon ascent, the partial pressures all fall as the lungs expand. At high ascent rates, alveolar pCO_2 falls more rapidly since there is less time for alveolar uptake from the blood. Oxygen pressure also drops much more quickly as speed increases. Symptomatic hypoxia (dizziness) may result. Nitrogen percentage at the end of the dive is higher than at the start of the descent, since it leaves the blood quickly and comprises a greater percentage of the lung volume.[9] Oxygen levels after a breath-hold dive are considerably lower than those for breath holding for the same period at the surface.[10] Carbon dioxide was slightly higher after exercise during surface breath holding than after a dive.[11] When a dive was made after hyperventilation, the above findings were exaggerated. Oxygen rose quickly and fell sharply. At the termination of the dive, pO_2 was less than pCO_2.[12] (This is not seen in normal breath-hold diving.) In a series of chamber dives, the terminal alveolar pO_2 was lower than venous in one case, and this suggests a loss of O_2 from the blood in the lungs—the reverse of normal.[13] This reversed O_2 flow was not demonstrated in open-water experiments with less hyperventilation.[14]

Underwater swimmers are not endangered by holding their breath unless they hyperventilate, because rising CO_2 will cause them to end their swim before oxygen is dangerously low. Skin divers have a greater risk, since their oxygen falls during ascent. Staying down until the very last moment may result in hypoxic unconsciousness near the surface. Hyperventilation makes breath holding very dangerous for both swimmers and divers.

Typically, hypoxia is not noted until it is too late. There are several reports of swimmers who continued to swim after they were unconscious—they had no memory of covering those last yards. Similarly, competitive spear fisherman often say they cannot recall the final feet of their ascent. These people are fortunate to have reached—or been brought to—the surface.

Unconsciousness from hypoxia is an especially dangerous way to drown. (See Chapter 18, Drowning.) The likelihood of permanent damage in drowning depends on the duration of impaired oxygenation. Craig has simulated breath-holding hypoxia and estimates that only about 2.5 minutes can be tolerated between hypoxic loss of unconsciousness and death.[15]

But it is difficult to predict how much hyperventilation will cause a problem. Slight reduction of predive carbon dioxide is not dangerous and does improve bottom dive. Posthyperventilation CO_2's were shown to vary from person to person and from day to day in the same person.[16] Caution is advisable.

There are several causes of unconsciousness in underwater swimming and diving. These include medical conditions such as heart disease, epilepsy, hypoglycemia (dietary or related to diabetes mellitus), and cerebral vascular accidents. Diving maladies such as nitrogen narcosis, air embolism, decompression sickness, or oxygen poisoning may be implicated. And of course, trauma can cause unconsciousness.

Derangements in normal blood-gas tensions are common in skin and SCUBA diving. Elevated carbon dioxide (see Chapter 7, Respiration) can by itself cause unconsciousness, or, more often, act together with nitrogen narcosis; or it may cause heart-rhythm disturbances. Hypoxia is less often a problem in SCUBA diving, assuming the tanks are clean and filled with clean air. The use of semiclosed or closed circuit SCUBA may result in problems of high carbon dioxide or low oxygen (high oxygen is a risk below shallow depths). Unconsciousness associated with these rebreathing SCUBAs has been termed shallow-water blackout. Hypoxia following hyperventilation is a common cause of unconsciousness in breath-hold swimming and diving. It has been termed underwater blackout, but this is an unfortunate name since there are many causes of blacking out under water.

NOTES: RESPIRATION IN SKIN DIVING

1. J. Mithoefer, "Breath Holding," in *Handbook of Physiology*, vol. 2, W. Fenn and H. Rahn, eds. (Washington, D.C.: American Physiological Society, 1965), pp. 1011–27.
2. A. Craig, Jr., "Causes of Loss of Consciousness During Underwater Swimming," *Journal of Applied Physiology*, 16: 583–86, 1961.
3. A. Craig, Jr., "Underwater Swimming and Loss of Consciousness," *Journal of the American Medical Association*, 176: 255–58, 1961.
4. Mithoefer, *op. cit.*
5. A. Craig, Jr., "Underwater Swimming and Drowning," *Journal of Sport Medicine*, 2: 23–26, 1962.
6. J. Davis, "Fatal Underwater Breath-Holding in the Trained Swimmer," *Journal of Forensic Science*, 6: 301–66, 1962.
7. E. Lanphier, H. Rahn, "Alveolar Gas Exchange During Breath-Hold Diving," *Journal of Applied Physiology*, 18: 471–77, 1963.

8. A Craig, Jr., A. Harley, "Alveolar Gas Exchanges During Breath-Hold Dives," *Journal of Applied Physiology,* 24: 182–89, 1968.

9. K. Schaefer, "The Role of Carbon Dioxide in the Physiology of Human Diving" in *Proceedings of the Underwater Physiology Symposium* (Washington, D.C., National Academy of Science, 1955).

10. Lanphier and Rahn, *op. cit.*

11. A. Craig, Jr., W. Medd, "O_2 Consumption and CO_2 Production During Breath-Hold Diving," *Journal of Applied Physiology,* 24: 190–202, 1968.

12. Lanphier and Rahn, *op. cit.*

13. *Ibid.*

14. Craig and Harley, *op. cit.*

15. A Craig, Jr., "Summary of 58 Cases of Loss of Consciousness During Underwater Swimming and Diving," *Medical Science of Sports,* 8: 171–75, 1976.

16. P. Landsberg, "Carbon Dioxide Changes in Hyperventilation and Breath-Hold Diving," *South African Medical Journal,* 48: 18–22, 1974.

9 | Respiratory Adaptation

Experienced divers adapt physiologically to the demands of the hyperbaric environment.

Dr. Karl Schaefer has studied the instructors at the U.S. Navy's New London Submarine Escape Training Tank.[1] These men are involved in frequent breath-hold descents—they actually drop rather than swim down—to as deep as 90 feet. After a year of experience, almost all the instructors had increased their maximum depth limit by 20 to 30 feet (from 60–70 to 90 feet). Measurements of lung volumes showed actual physical change with training. All volumes, except for residual, had increased; residual had fallen slightly.[2] After the men were transferred from tank work, these increases were lost.

The increase in lung volume is one factor in increased tolerance for breath holding. Furthermore, repeated diving appears to extend tolerance to elevated carbon dioxide. The New London instructors had less respiratory stimulation than normal with elevated inspired carbon dioxide and were found to have larger than normal body CO_2 levels.[3]

Carbon dioxide responsiveness in SCUBA divers has been somewhat more controversial than in breath-hold divers. Schaefer confirmed that carbon dioxide sensitivity was diminished in demolition divers.[4] This was contraindicated by subsequent investigation in SCUBA divers.[5,6] Controversy is com-

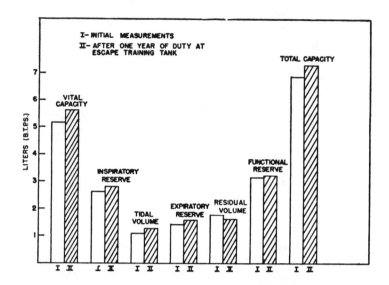

From K. E. Schaefer, "The Role of Carbon Dioxide in the Physiology of Human Diving" in *Proceedings of the Underwater Physiology Symposium*, (Washington, D.C.), National Academy of Sciences, 1955. Used with permission.

mon in respiratory physiology. English divers were compared to nondivers and were found to have reduced carbon dioxide responsiveness and, at rest, higher blood carbon dioxide tensions.[7] These divers did not have lung volumes different from the nondivers. With exercise there was a smaller increase in ventilation among divers than nondivers. This decreased responsiveness to carbon dioxide was not merely a reflection of physical training, because nondiving athletes were more reactive to CO_2 than divers.[8]

Trained underwater swimmers show breathing patterns compatible with increased CO_2 tolerance. Their breathing is deep and slow, with pauses after inspiration. This is desirable for alveolar ventilation with O_2 and for the reduction of airway resistance. However, it permits a CO_2 buildup, which in untrained swimmers causes rapid and shallow breathing. Similar responses to CO_2 have been found in pearl divers.[9]

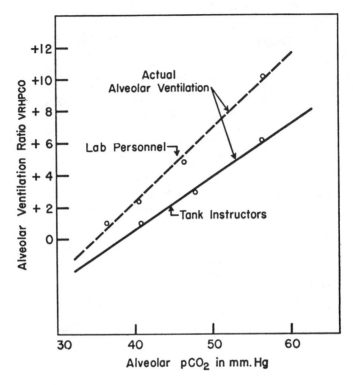

Ventilatory response as a function of alveolar pCO_2 in two groups of subjects, laboratory personnel and tank instructors.

From Schaefer, "The Role of Carbon Dioxide." Used with permission.

Schaefer suggests further an increased tolerance to low O_2 reflected in diminished respiratory response to low O_2, but this has not been firmly established.[10] It has been shown that trained underwater swimmers are more efficient in their consumption of O_2; they can remove greater quantities of O_2 from the same ventilatory quantity.[11] This ability is not unique to swimmers, for it is seen in all well-trained athletes.

Respiratory adaptation is not without hazards. Increased carbon dioxide can affect both state of consciousness and heart rhythm. A diver would be more subject to loss of consciousness if he were insensitive to carbon dioxide.

NOTES: RESPIRATORY ADAPTATION

1. K. Schaefer, "Effect of Prolonged Diving Training," in *Proceedings of Second Symposium on Underwater Physiology,* (Washington, D.C., National Acedemy of Sciences, 1963).

2. C. Carey, K. Schaefer, et al., "Effect of Skin Diving on Lung Volume," *Journal of Applied Physiology,* 8: 519–23, 1956.

3. K. Schaefer, "The Role of Carbon Dioxide in the Physiology of Human Diving," in *Proceedings of the Underwater Physiology Symposium* (Washington, D.C.: National Academy of Science, 1955).

4. Schaefer, "Effect."

5. H. Froeh, "Ventilatory Response of SCUBA Divers to CO_2 Inhalation," *Journal of Applied Physiology,* 16: 8–10, 1961.

6. L. Greenbaum et al., "Control of Ventilation in Underwater Swimmers: The Effect of Intermittent Exposure to Hyperbaric O_2," *Aerospace Medicine,* 49: 9–12, 1971.

7. J. Florio et al., "Breathing Pattern and Ventilatory Response to Carbon Dioxide in Divers," *Journal of Applied Physiology,* 46: 1076–80, 1979.

8. D. Lally et al., "Ventilatory Responses to Exercise in Divers and Non-Divers," *Respiratory Physiology,* 20: 117–29, 1974.

9. S. Song et al., "Lung Volumes and Ventilatory Responses to High CO_2 and Low O_2 in the Ama," *Journal of Applied Physiology,* 18: 466–71, 1963.

10. K. Schaefer, "Adaptation of Breath-Hold Diving," in *Physiology of Breath Diving and the Ama of Japan,* H. Rahn, ed. (Washington, D.C., National Academy of Science, 1965), pp. 237–52.

11. L. Greenbaum, "Respiratory Response of Underwater Swimmers to Oxygen," *Journal of Applied Physiology,* 15: 575–78, 1960.

10 | Circulation and the Skin Diver

Changes in heart and blood-vessel physiology are closely tied to respiratory function. The cardiovascular system carries the nutrients and waste products between the tissues and the lungs. Variation in one system directly affects the function of the other.

In SCUBA diving, cardiovascular changes are not usually marked. No consistent pattern has been demonstrated in either pulse or blood pressure. High O_2 tensions are commonly considered to result in cerebral vascular constriction, but Lambertsen showed that this does not occur unless CO_2 tension falls.[1] Conversely, high CO_2 causes cerebral vasodilatation. This increase in blood flow to the brain may be one reason that high CO_2 increases the risk of nitrogen narcosis and oxygen poisoning.

More consistently, cardiovascular changes accompany skin diving. Some of the most interesting work has been done with breath-holding animals: seals, ducks, whales, etc. Whales can hold their breath up to 2 hours and seals for over 20 minutes.[2] These animals have a higher blood capacity for O_2 than we humans. Diving animals are also more efficient in oxygen utilization.

The increased O_2 capacity of diving animals does not sufficiently explain their breath-holding capacity.[3] Blood flow to some organs is reduced during the animal's dive. Measurements of flow and pressure show a reduction in supply to the skin, kidneys, and intestines; this permits selective supply to the brain and heart muscle.[4] During dives, the pulse rate falls sharply in these animals.[5] (The pulse of seals goes from 80 to 7 or 8.) This reduction in supply can be endured since fewer organs must be supplied. Pulse slowing reduces cardiac work, so the heart needs less O_2.

Metabolic pathways also change, permitting work to be done without O_2. Metabolism without O_2 produces lactic acid; elevated excretion of it provides further evidence of reduced blood flow. During the dive, lactic acid accumulates in the muscles, but blood levels do not rise. Immediately after the dive, the blood level remains low; however, within a few minutes the lactic acid rises sharply.[6] This implies that the muscles are initially poorly perfused and that the blood is exposed to the high areas of lactic acid in the tissues only after the dive.

Humans experience similar changes during breath-hold dives. Most characteristic is the reduction in pulse rate; the slowing develops during the dive, but the low point may not be reached until after 50 seconds of submersion. The actual reduction in rate ranges from 17 percent to 50 percent.[7]

Studies in pearl divers show bradycardia to about 50 percent of surface rate.[8] (See graph on page 121.) The divers of the South Pacific, Korea, and Japan have provided a significant portion of the physiological data on breath-hold diving. These people (men in the South Pacific, chiefly women in Korea and Japan) dive as deeply as 120 feet in search of pearls and edible shellfish. Some make standard dives while others make weighted descents and are pulled back to the surface. The Oriental women divers (called Ama) make from thirty to sixty dives an hour, even in the winter with a water temperature of 50 degrees.

In animals, diving bradycardia (slow heartbeat) appears to result from reflexes initiated by facial wetting. The situation in man is more complex. Human diving bradycardia develops from at least two influences: breath holding and facial cooling. Breath holding alone causes the pulse to slow down, but facial immersion makes this more profound.

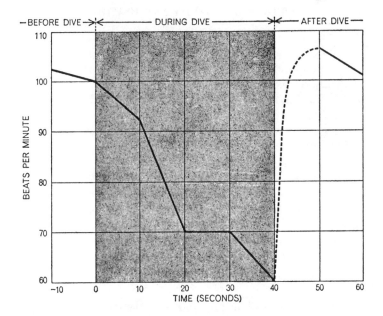

Facial immersion plus breath holding is as influential as total body immersion plus breath holding. Facial immersion while breathing through a snorkel will slow the heart, but much less than without breathing.[9]

Finally, cooling the face with air or an ice pack slows the heart without the influence of wetness.[10] Cold water augments the bradycardia,[11] but water may act more through its cooling properties than through its sheer wetness.

The pulse slowing of breath holding occurs through reflexes within the autonomic nervous system. It can be blocked by atropine, which implies that the final pathway is through the vagus nerve of the parasympathetic system.[12] Manipulation of the sympathetic system does not affect diving bradycardia.

In animals, bradycardia and vasoconstriction reduce oxygen consumption during the exercise of diving. Man, typically, has increased pulse rate during exercise on land or under water. Breath holding reduces this exercise tachycardia.[13] The comparative effect is the same under water as on land. Breath hold-ing does decrease blood flow in the arm, but this does not re-quire immersion. Cardiovascular changes in man do not evidently reduce oxygen consumption.[14]

Diving bradycardia cannot be well correlated with physical fitness.[15] Experienced divers may have more profound pulse slowing, but this may be related to mental adaptation. Mental activity attentuates bradycardia.[16]

Profound bradycardia causes reduced cardiac output. This is offset by vascular constriction, so blood pressure remains nor-mal or may be elevated. Measurements of heart action taken during breath-holding immersion show decreased performance of the heart's left ventricle.[17]

Measurements taken from pearl divers imply that humans can adapt usefully to frequent diving. In his work Scholander found an exponential decrease in metabolism as a dive pro-gressed.[18]

All of the preceding physiological adaptations may increase circulatory efficiency. Alteration in cardiac rhythm frequently accompanies breath holding. Several studies show an incidence of 50 percent to 70 percent.[19,20] These were not correlated with the length or depth of the dive. Profound bradycardia may con-tribute to these rhythm disturbances.[21] Several types of rhyth-mic changes occurred: early contraction of atria or ventricles, shift of center of rhythm control, uncontrolled rate, and many others detected only by analysis of electrocardiograms. A transient dysrhythmia is not necessarily dangerous; it can often be found in healthy persons. But one electrocardiographic change found by Olsen was similar to that seen in patients with impaired blood flow to the heart muscle.[22] For the average skin diver, little danger exists from these temporary changes. None of the people in the groups studied had any permanent changes; none had symptoms of cardiac malfunction. In a per-son with impaired cardiac health, the risk is greater, since dys-rhythmias may develop, and these may worsen heart function still further. Vigorous skin diving should be avoided by anyone with heart disease.

NOTES: CIRCULATION AND THE SKIN DIVER

1. C. J. Lambertsen, "Physiological Effects of Oxygen Inhalation at High Partial Pressures," *Fundamentals of Hyperbaric Medicine* (Washington, D.C.: National Academy of Science, 1966), pp. 12–20.

2. K. Schaefer, "Circulatory Adaptation to the Requirements of Life Under More Than One Atmosphere of Pressure," in *Handbook of Physiology*, vol. 8, P. Dow, ed. (Washington, D.C.: American Physiological Society, 1965), pp. 1843–73.

3. M. Strauss, "Physiological Aspects of Mammalian Breath-Hold Diving: A Review," *Aerospace Medicine* 41: 362–381, 1970.

4. P. Sholander, "The Master Switch of Life," *Scientific American*, 204: 42–106, 1963.

5. Strauss, *op. cit.*

6. *Ibid.*

7. P. Harding, D. Roman, et al., "Diving Bradycardia in Man," *Journal of Physiology* (London), 81: 401–09, 1965.

8. S. Hong, H. Rahn, "The Diving Women of Korea and Japan," *Scientific American*, 216: 34–43, 1967.

9. D. Speck, D. Bruce, "Effects of Varying Thermal and Apneic Conditions in the Human Diving Reflex," *Undersea Biomedical Research*, 5: 9–14, 1978.

10. *Ibid.*

11. B. H. Natelson, et al., "Roles of Stress and Adaptation in the Elicitation of Face-Immersion Bradycardia," *Journal of Applied Physiology*, 54: 661–65, 1983.

12. J. Finley et al., "Autonomic Pathways Responsible for Bradycardia on Facial Immersion," *Journal of Applied Physiology*, 247: 218–22, 1979.

13. A. Craig, Jr., W. Medd, "Man's Responses to Breath-Hold Exercise in Air and in Water," *Journal of Applied Physiology*, 24: 773–77, 1968.

14. *Ibid.*

15. S. Stromme, et al., "Diving Bradycardia During Rest and Exercise and Its Relation to Physical Fitness," *Journal of Applied Physiology*, 28: 614–21, 1970.

16. R. Ross, A. Septoe, "Attenuation of the Diving Reflex in Man by Mental Stimulation," *Journal of Physiology*, 302: 387–93, 1980.

17. M. Frey, R. Kenney, "Changes in Left Ventricular Activity During Apnea and Face Immersion," *Undersea Biomedical Research*, 4: 27–37, 1977.

18. P. Sholander et al., "Circulatory Adjustment in Pearl Divers," *Journal of Applied Physiology*, 17: 184–90, 1962.

19. C. Olsen at al., "Some Effects of Breath Holding and Apneic Underwater Diving on Cardiac Rhythms in Man," *Journal of Applied Physiology*, 17: 461–66, 1962.

20. T. Hughes, "Disorders of Cardiac Conduction Accompanying the Diver Reflex in Man," *Pavlovian Journal of Biological Science*, 16: 25–33, 1981.

21. S. Wolf, "Psychophysiological Influences on the Diver Reflex in Man," *Neural Mechanisms in Cardiac Arrhythmias*, P. Wchwartz et al. eds. (New York: Raven Press, 1978), pp. 237–50.

22. Olsen, *op. cit.*

11 | Air Embolism and Ascent

In general, pressure changes cause fewer problems in ascent than they do in descent. Ear squeeze is possible on ascent if the eustachian tube does not permit venting of the high middle-ear pressure. In such a case, middle-ear pressure would exceed ambient pressure, and the tympanic membrane would flex outward. The damage would be similar to the common ear squeeze of descent. Reverse ear squeeze is not common, since it is rare for the eustachian tube to be blocked in such a fashion that venting does not occur. Vertigo during ascent may result from unequal reduction in ear pressure. (See Chapter 6, Diving and the Ear.) If the sinuses do not allow free egress of high-pressure air, reverse sinus squeeze can develop—a condition which occurs far more frequently than reverse ear squeezes.

Gas in the intestine will occasionally increase during the dive, or it can be swallowed from a SCUBA rig. With rapid decompression, this gas may expand, causing discomfort before its expulsion. One case of stomach rupture has been reported in a scuba diving accident.[1]

In skin diving the air in the respiratory system expands during ascent. The maximum lung volume will be the volume at the time the dive started minus the volume of oxygen used in respiration. Overexpansion upon ascent cannot result, since final volume will always be less than the original volume.

CHEST WITH 6L OF AIR AT 100 FEET

If no exhalation, this volume
expands to 24L at the surface

Note the greater volume change
per foot in the shallow depths

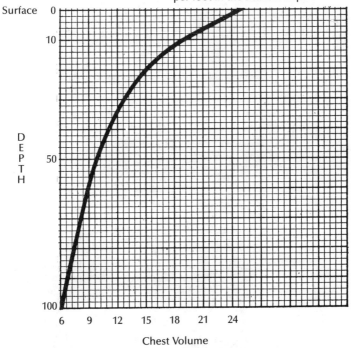

Chest Volume

In SCUBA diving, the situation differs. At depth the lungs
are filled with high pressure air; if during ascent there is no expiration, this quantity of gas will expand in accordance with
Boyle's law. The above graph shows the extent of expansion as
related to depth change. Note that the greatest change per foot
of ascent comes in the shallow depths. From 33 feet to the surface the volume doubles. If the elasticity of the lungs is exceeded, there can be actual rupture of the alveoli. The results
are as serious as could be imagined.

Alveolar air which has escaped into the lung tissue (interstitial emphysema) can follow several pathways. Air can move out of the lungs into the mediastinum (the space between the two lungs—see drawing below). From there, it may move into the subcutaneous spaces of the neck and upper chest. Also, it can enter into the pleurae themselves and cause pneumothorax (air in the chest cavity). When the air ruptures into small pulmonary veins, it will pass through the left heart and into the arterial circulation. These arterial air emboli may obstruct the blood supply of the brain or heart, and cause a stroke or infarction.

PATHWAYS OF AIR FROM RUPTURED ALVEOLUS

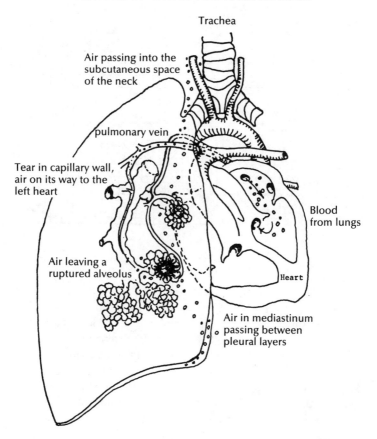

Trachea

Air passing into the subcutaneous space of the neck

pulmonary vein

Tear in capillary wall, air on its way to the left heart

Blood from lungs

Air leaving a ruptured alveolus

Heart

Air in mediastinum passing between pleural layers

Lung tearing comes from overexpansion secondary to a rapidly developing pressure gradient between the inner and outer lung surfaces. At diving depth, SCUBA air-supply pressure matches outside water pressure. During ascent, the water pressure, which tends to compress the chest, decreases. If normal free breathing continues, air pressure within the lungs falls also. If there is no free breathing, a pressure gradient develops; the air pressure remains high while the water pressure drops and the lungs expand. The restrictive forces of the lung tissue limit expansion until the intrathoracic pressure rises sufficiently to tear the walls of the alveoli and the capillaries.

The pressure gradient need not be large for alveolar and capillary rupture. Theoretical work showed that a difference of 50 to 70 mm mercury (Hg) between the inner and the outer lung surface is sufficient for rupture.[2] This equals only a 3-foot change in depth. Application of direct intratracheal pressures of 48 mm Hg in dogs caused lung rupturing.[3] More pressure can be tolerated if the chest or abdomen is splinted within a binder.

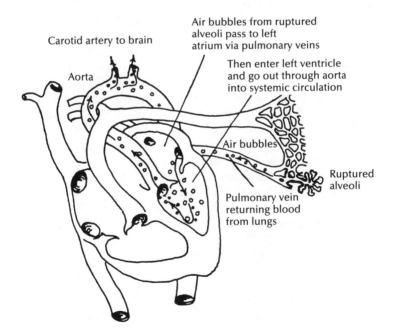

Carotid artery to brain

Air bubbles from ruptured alveoli pass to left atrium via pulmonary veins

Then enter left ventricle and go out through aorta into systemic circulation

Aorta

Air bubbles

Ruptured alveoli

Pulmonary vein returning blood from lungs

Apparently rupture results from lung distortion rather than just from expansion. Divers with a history of lung barotrauma had uneven elasticity of their lungs.[4]

Experiments with dogs have created alveolar tearing at gradients of 80 to 90 Hg (3.5 to 4 feet).[5] Guinea pigs have had lung ruptures in ascents from 10 feet.[6] Human cases have been documented within the same depth.[7] This means that alveolar rupture represents a potential danger even in shallow water or in pool training classes.

Gaseous emboli result from the introduction of gas bubbles into the veins, arteries, or capillaries; these are referred to as "gaseous" since any gas or combination thereof can be involved. The emboli travel in the bloodstream until they lodge at points of vessel narrowing, where they cause blockage of the local circulation system, partial or complete, depending on their size and number. Obstruction of blood flow to vital organs may be fatal. In decompression sickness, bubbles may form in arteries, veins, or capillaries. In pulmonary decompression sickness ("chokes"), interference with lung circulation results from bubbles that pass through the systemic veins to the right heart and thence to the lungs via the pulmonary artery; this disruption of capillary flow impairs gas exchange within the lung.

Air may also enter veins secondary to surgery or trauma. These emboli also lodge in the lung capillary bed unless the amount of gas suffices to impair the right heart's pumping action. Normally, no emboli travel from the right heart to the left heart, since the lung capillaries act as bubble traps. Rarely, a small perforation in the heart septum (chamber wall) permits direct passage, and the bubbles may enter the systemic arterial circulation from the left ventricle.

In traumatic embolization, resulting from alveolar injury, bubbles enter the small pulmonary veins, passing by these to the left atrium, then to the left ventricle, and finally out through the aorta into the systemic circulation. Since the bubbles are lighter than blood, they rise to the upper portions of the body, namely the brain. Results of obstructing blood flow to the brain range from localized weakness to unconsciousness and death, depending upon the amount of air involved. Cerebral air emboli may disrupt normal cardiac function.[8] Emboli may enter the coronary arteries and cause myocardial infarction (heart attack). The course is rapid; life may end within a few minutes after embolization.

Decompression sickness and traumatic cerebral embolization are both caused by gas bubbles; there are, however, significant differences: The gas in decompression sickness is nitrogen, while in cerebral embolization it is air. Decompression sickness most often results from bubbles in the systemic veins rather than from ones in the arteries. In embolization, the speed of onset and gravity of symptoms are greater. Air embolism results from normal lung air entering the blood vessels, while in decompression sickness the nitrogen bubbles can form in any part of the body. Moreover, decompression sickness requires deeper, longer diving than does embolization.

During ascent from a dive, overdistended lungs impede pulmonary circulation and thus keep emboli from moving to the heart.[9] But when the breathing is resumed at the surface, symptoms appear.

Air embolism most frequently results in unconsciousness. Because of its rapid onset, the diver rarely complains. Then, without warning, he may convulse or have localized impairment of motor and sensory functions. Occasionally, bloody froth will be found in the victim's mouth and throat.

There are other symptoms, depending upon the course of the air bubbles. Air from the ruptured alveoli can pass along the outside of the blood vessels and bronchi to reach the mediastinum. This space in the middle of the chest contains the trachea, main bronchi, major blood vessels, and the heart. Air in the mediastinum will cause severe pain under the sternum, radiating to the shoulders and down the arms. The expanding air can compress the respiratory passages, causing shortness of breath. The vena cava, which returns venous blood to the right heart, may be sufficiently compressed to compromise cardiac function.

Air from the mediastinum may escape up into the subcutaneous tissues of the neck. This results in a "puffy" appearance and voice change secondary to laryngeal compression. Pressure on the overlying skin results in a crackling sound, and airway compression may result.

From the mediastinum, air can break through the pleura, which lines the thoracic cavity and surrounds the lungs. The presence of air in the thoracic cavity (pneumothorax), pressing on the lungs from all sides, will result in lung collapse. (In theory, air could rupture directly from the alveoli into the pleural space, but this rarely happens.[10]) Pressure within the thoracic cavity defeats the pump action of the lungs in attempting to draw air in. Lung collapse allows the mediastinal structures (see above) to shift into the void, and this may cause airway and venous compression. Disaster piled on disaster. If, after ascending from a dive, a diver feels shortness of breath, chest pain, and unequal chest expansion, he may be experiencing pneumothorax. Any of these symptoms requires urgent medical consultation.

One case has been reported of air passing into the *abdominal* cavity during ascent.[11]

Ascent aggravates all the above-mentioned conditions. Ambient pressure reduction allows the extra-alveolar air volume to expand, causing more compression and obstruction. Most commonly, alveolar rupture occurs when a diver fails to exhale normally during ascent. Holding the breath while rising only a few feet can be dangerous.

Occasionally, air embolism develops in a diver who has apparently exhaled properly during his ascent. Autopsies in such cases have revealed partial obstruction of the respiratory passages.[12] During inspiration the air tubes expand in diameter, and air freely passes the partial block; during expiration, the tube size decreases, and air may be trapped behind the block. In this fashion, asthma patients as a rule have more trouble blowing air out than in inspiring. During an ascent, trapped air may expand sufficiently to tear lung tissue. Typically, "air trapping" can be caused by broncholiths ("stones," or concretions, impinging on the respiratory passageway), scars, or cysts resulting from past lung infections. Mucus plugs from asthma may sometimes be implicated. Weak areas in the lung (bullae) are not uncommon, and these increase the likelihood of lung rupture.

Alveolar rupture in diving can best be prevented by careful medical screening and adherence to safe ascent techniques. Prospective sport divers should have themselves checked out before they begin training as neophytes. Any past history of severe lung disease raises the suspicion that the diver may be susceptible to air trapping, as does a positive skin test for tuberculosis or any fungal pulmonary disease. Emphysema or asthma increases the risk of rupture. Anyone with a history of pneumothorax should avoid SCUBA diving. Even persons who have never experienced respiratory ailments should present themselves for a chest X ray before engaging in the sport.

Lung rupture can occur during an otherwise normal dive if the diver forgets to breathe normally while swimming up over a reef or after a fish. Most ruptures, however, occur during emergency ascents or during training for such ascents.

A SCUBA diver who finds himself out of air instinctively rushes toward the surface and has no inclination to exhale any of his precious air. One of the goals of training is to replace this dangerous instinct with calm, rational action. The safest solution to the out-of-air emergency is prevention. If a diver plans his dive properly and uses a submersible pressure gauge, running out of air should be rare. Well-maintained regulators are unlikely to fail. Even an apparently empty tank usually contains enough air for a normal ascent, since the remaining air expands as the diver ascends.

If a true emergency ascent should become necessary, there are several techniques for managing it safely. *Dependent* ascents require the air of a diving partner ("buddy") with an auxiliary second-stage regulator ("octopus") or a shared regulator for "buddy breathing"). *Independent* ascents are "swimming," "free,"* or buoyant. Diving organizations, through their National SCUBA Training Committee, have formulated policies for emergency-ascent training. Diving students will learn the advantages and disadvantages of various ascent techniques.

Any ascent risks lung rupture. About 20 percent of autopsied diving fatalities in the United States result from lung rupture.[13] Training is designed to reduce this incidence, and there are many sound arguments in support of emergency-ascent training. Unfortunately, such training is dangerous itself. From 1970 to 1976 there were eighty fatalities in organized diving classes, twenty from lung rupture.[14] (The statistical incidence is very low since over 2.5 million ascents were made in these classes. But we do not know the *total* number of lung ruptures; only the number of those that resulted in death and were autopsied.) Thus the risk of

---

*Free ascent is not recommended for sport diving. It involves floating to the surface without propulsion; it is difficult and is the most dangerous technique.

emergency-ascent training mandates that the risk-to-benefit ratio be carefully evaluated. The risk could be reduced by more careful selection of candidates and insistence on minimally dangerous techniques.

The most carefully supervised training ascents take place in the U.S. Navy's Submarine Escape Training Towers. Submarine trainees and crewmen simulate escapes by making ascents from air locks at varying depths. These ascents are different from the usual SCUBA ascents. Overall Navy experience between 1928 and 1957 was sixty-two casualties out of 250,000 ascents.[15] Of these, forty-four were air embolisms and the others involved noncerebral extra-alveolar air. Thus, the rate of air embolism was 0.018 percent. Eight of these forty-four died. In the New London Tank (1930–1965) 373,941 ascents gave thirty-nine embolisms with just four fatalities.[16]

James found a 1 percent incidence of extra-alveolar air when comparing pre- and posttraining chest X rays in a small group of trainees who had no symptoms.[17] In a Swedish study utilizing electroencephalograms a very high embolism incidence of 3.5 percent was found in a group of 112 submarine trainees.[18] The investigators suggested that their techniques permitted detection of mild cases.

TREATMENT OF LUNG RUPTURE

In any suspected case of lung rupture, a physician trained in diving medicine must be promptly consulted. Usually subcutaneous emphysema and mediastinal emphysema resolve spontaneously, but patients require careful observation. A pneumothorax, unless very small, is treated by suction reexpansion with a chest tube or valve. Recompression therapy is dangerous in pneumothorax unless chest drainage is provided, since the problem would recur during the decompression phase.

Air embolism must be treated with emergency recompression. The usual therapy is with Table 6A, which begins by compressing the patient to 6 atmospheres (165 feet seawater) for 30 minutes to shrink emboli. He is then decompressed to 60 feet, where oxygen breathing can be employed. Ancillary treatment with steroids and diuretics has been suggested because of the possibility of delayed cerebral edema.

NAVY TABLE 6A

MINIMAL RECOMPRESSION, OXYGEN BREATHING METHOD FOR TREATMENT OF DECOMPRESSION SICKNESS AND GAS EMBOLISM

Depth (feet)	Time (minutes)	Breathing Media	Elapsed Time (minutes)
165	30	Air	30
165 to 60	4	Air	34
60	20	Oxygen	54
60	5	Air	50
60	20	Oxygen	79
60	5	Air	84
60	20	Oxygen	104
60	5	Air	109
60 to 30	30	Oxygen	139
30	15	Air	154
30	60	Oxygen	214
30	15	Air	229
30	60	Oxygen	289
30 to 0	30	Oxygen	319

*US Navy Diving Manual

In mild cases, the victim may survive even if therapy is delayed. But if the diver is unconscious or has any other serious sign, delay in obtaining recompression therapy may be fatal. Any unconscious SCUBA diver should be *immediately* recompressed. Evaluation of the cause of his unconsciousness should be made only after recompression has started.

Severe decompression sickness may cause unconsciousness, but since the basic forms of therapy are identical, no time should be wasted trying to differentiate between the two diseases. Naturally, if the victim is not breathing or is in cardiac arrest, resuscitation must be carried out.

While the victim is being transported to the chamber he should breathe oxygen. His feet should be raised and his head lowered, so that new bubbles enter the legs rather than the brain. This will not displace any bubbles already in cerebral circulation. Usually the embolization process ceases soon after surfacing.

Lung rupture does not require *deep* water diving; it is an ever-present danger in all sport SCUBA diving. Prevention comprises the only effective means of control. Strict adherence to all safety precautions will reduce the danger to the diver.

NOTES: AIR EMBOLISM AND ASCENT

1. F. S. Cramer, R. D. Heimbach, "Stomach Rupture as a Result of Gastrointestinal Barotrauma in a SCUBA diver," *Journal of Trauma,* 22: 238–40, 1982.
2. K. Schaefer et al., "Mechanism in Development of Interstitial Emphysema and Air Embolism on Decompression from Depth," *Journal of Applied Physiology,* 13: 15–29, 1958.
3. R. Lenaghan et al., "Hemodynamic Alterations Associated with Expansion Rupture of the Lung," *Archives of Surgery,* 99: 339–43, 1964.
4. H. Colebatch et al., "Increased Elastic Recoil as a Determinant of Pulmonary Barotrauma in Divers," *Respiration Physiology,* 26: 55–64, 1976.
5. Schaefer, "Mechanism."
6. M. Denney, W. Glas, "Experimental Studies in Barotrauma," *Journal of Trauma,* 4: 791–96, 1964.
7. E. Lanphier, "Diving Medicine," *New England Journal of Medicine,* 256: 120–31, 1957.
8. D. E. Evans et al., "Cardiovascular Effects of Cerebral Air Embolism," *Stroke,* 12: 338–344, 1981.
9. Lenaghan, *op cit.*
10. M. Macklin, C. Macklin, "Malignant Interstitial Emphysema of the Lungs and Mediastinum as an Important Occult Complication in Many Respiratory Diseases and Other Conditions: An Interpretation of the Clinical Literature in the Light of Laboratory Experiment," *Medicine,* 23: 281–358, 1944.
11. D. Rose, P. Jarczyk, "Spontaneous Pneumoperitoneum After Scuba Diving," *Journal of the American Medical Association,* 239: 233, 1978.
12. A. Liebow et al., "Intrapulmonary Air Trapping in Submarine Escape Training Casualties," *U.S. Armed Forces Medical Journal,* 10: 265–90, 1959.
13. J. McAniff, U.S. Underwater Diving Fatality Statistics, 1970–78, Report URI-SSR-80-13, National Underwater Accident Data Center, University of Rhode Island, 1980.
14. J. McAniff, "Emergency Ascent Training and the Seven Year Record, 1970–76," in *Emergency Ascent Training,* M. Kent, ed. (Bethesda, Md.: Undersea Medical Society, 1979), pp. 31–33.
15. H. Moses, "Casualties in Individual Submarine Escape Training," U.S. Naval Submarine Medical Research Laboratory Report No. 438, 1964.
16. C. Waite et al., "Dysbaric Cerebral Air Embolism" in *Proceedings of the Third Symposium on Underwater Physiology,* (Baltimore: Williams and Wilkins, 1967), pp. 205–12.

17. E. James, "Extra-Alveolar Air Resulting from Submarine Escape Training: A Post Training Roentgenographic Survey of 170 Submariners," U.S. Naval Submarine Research Laboratory Report no. 550, 1968.

18. D. Ingvar, "Cerebral Air Embolism During Training of Submarine Personnel in Free Escape: An Electroencephalographic Study," *Aerospace Medicine,* 44: 628–35, 1973.

19. R. R. Pearson, R. F. Goad, "Delayed Cerebral Edema Complicating Cerebral Gas Embolism: Case Histories," *Undersea Biomedical Research,* 9: 283–96, 1982.

12

Introduction to Decompression Sickness

Decompression sickness—the bends—is probably the best-publicized of all diving maladies. Almost everyone has heard tales of deep sea divers bent over in pain and saved only by the presence of a recompression chamber. Bends can develop in a cautious SCUBA diver who never goes below 50 feet, with results as catastrophic as those from 300-foot dives by grizzled hard-hat divers. Although the fatality rate of decompression sickness falls below that of drowning or air embolism, it ranks first in incidence of serious ailments among sport SCUBA divers.[1]

Other expressions for decompression sickness include the bends, caisson disease, diver's itch, diver's paralysis, inkles, nigles, chokes, staggers, and aeroembolism (not to be confused with air embolism). Each of these terms refers to one of the malady's many manifestations, as will be elucidated. For convenience, "the bends" will be interchangeable with "decompression sickness."

Basically, bends results from rapid gas expansion, which forms bubbles in the blood vessels. During the dive, the tissues take up gas (chiefly nitrogen) under pressure and store larger-than-normal quantities of it. Upon ascent, gas stores decrease toward surface values, and the blood carries the excess gas to the lungs for elimination. But the blood can carry off only so much excess gas at a time. During a rapid pressure reduction—decompression—the amount of gas leaving the tissues may exceed the amount that can be dissolved in blood. Bubbles of gas form and may obstruct blood flow. (In a similar fashion, shaking a carbonated soft drink releases gas from solution.) Bubbling can be prevented by gradual ascent, which releases the excess tissue gas slowly and permits the blood to transport it in solution. Treatment of decompression sickness in a pressure chamber reduces bubble size and then permits slow decompression to the surface.

The time between the completion of the dive and the onset of decompression sickness depends largely on the type of involvement. Neurological disease generally develops faster than joint pain. Fifty to 85 percent of the cases present themselves within the first hour after surfacing; by 12 hours, 90 to 97 percent have been seen, but cases have delayed for 24 hours.[2] In the Dartford Tunnel, the "minor" cases had an average onset time of 3 hours, while the "serious" ones came on in 50 minutes or less.[3]

Aviators may get decompression sickness (called aeroembolism) if cabin pressure fails at high altitudes (above 17,000–25,000 feet), thus reducing ambient pressure to under surface values. The nitrogen (N_2) normally carried in the body leaves the tissues in response to the new low N_2 partial pressure, and bubbles can form. When a man goes SCUBA diving and then flying afterward, the risk of aeroembolism is increased, because excess nitrogen is added to the body by the dive. The problem of flying after diving is discussed in Chapter 14, Decompression Sickness in Sport Diving.

Caisson workers—sand hogs—work under water in dry chambers (pneumatic caissons) in which air pressure keeps water from entering. These chambers are used for tunneling and bridge building, are entered and left through an air lock, and permit dry work under water. The nature of caisson disease differs slightly from diver's decompression sickness.

CLINICAL FINDINGS IN DECOMPRESSION SICKNESS

Decompression sickness most often causes arm or leg pain, chiefly in the joints. The term "bends" applies to this manifestation and describes the severe pain, which may literally bend the diver in agony. Decompression sickness rarely develops without limb pain (only 5 to 8 percent of cases), and in 66 to 95 percent of cases, limb pain is the only symptom.[4] In civilian diving "pain only" cases are less common than serious cases of decompression sickness.[5] The pain, generally characterized as "deep and boring," is rarely accompanied by tenderness, swelling, or discoloration. Application of heat provides little, if any, relief.

Among divers, the pain of decompression sickness occurs almost twice as often in arms as in legs. Caisson workers have the opposite distribution. In his series on British tunnel workers, Golding found an incidence of 85 percent lower limb pain.[6] A number of dry chamber dives also caused more lower limb pain than upper. The reason for this difference remains unknown. Perhaps it relates to impaired circulation caused by the cramped positions of the men in tunnels, to the relative differences in exercise of arms and legs, or to the hydrostatic support of the legs in divers.

A prickly, itching sensation (diver's itch) often presents itself, especially after chamber dives. Probably the temperature rise during compression, followed by temperature fall in decompression, explains the higher incidence of itch in dry dives. This itch generally disappears in 15 to 20 minutes with no aftereffects. Less frequently, an irregular, mottled skin rash develops, accompanied by tenderness and a rise in the skin's temperature; chest, back of shoulders, upper abdomen, forearms, and thighs are most frequently involved. Tenderness may persist after the rash has resolved. No definite mechanism has been elucidated. Although not dangerous by themselves, skin symptoms serve as a warning that decompression may have been too rapid, that serious symptoms may soon develop.

Fatigue, beyond that expected from the amount of work done, may accompany deep dives. Following deep chamber runs, dry and wet, diving classes often have a 100 percent incidence of fatigue, far out of proportion to the minimal activity carried on or to natural inertia. Onset of this fatigue, typically, comes a few hours after the dive.

The most serious cases of decompression sickness are those affecting the nervous system. Both the central nervous system (brain and spinal cord) and the peripheral (cranial nerves and nerves coming off the spinal cord) are concerned. Nervous involvement develops more frequently among divers than among caisson workers.[7] This may be related to the depth of maximal exposure, but unfortunately, major neurological involvement can also result from a shallow dive. In general, the serious symptoms have a faster onset than the typical pain of the bends. The result of nervous involvement can be weakness of muscles, or actual paralysis, altered reflexes, and sensory abnormalities such as numbness or "pins and needles" sensations. Loss of bowel and bladder control is one of the most serious results. Brain involvement, though less common, can cause loss of consciousness, convulsions, nausea and vomiting, speech defects, personality changes, as well as paralysis.

Peripheral nerve damage gives signs similar to spinal lesions, though more localized. Cranial nerve involvement may cause deafness or visual impairment. Nervous system damage leading to vertigo is known as the staggers since the patient has difficulty with walking. Decompression sickness may involve the inner ear.[8]

Respiratory symptoms, "chokes," though less common* than other forms of decompression sickness, can be exceedingly serious. These symptoms are caused by nitrogen bubbles in the right ventricle, which block pulmonary circulation. The onset of chokes comes later than with neurological sickness, because of the time it takes for a bubble mass to become large enough to block circulation; about 60 percent of the pulmonary arterial system must be blocked before its function is impaired.

Initially, difficulty with deep breathing causes the diver to feel a "burning" sensation under his breastbone. The burning sensation may spread in the upper respiratory tract and cause reddening of the mucosal surfaces. (Chest soreness may persist even after recompression has relieved the pulmonary impairment.) Deep breathing or smoking brings on coughing, and this gradually worsens. Since shallow breathing does not hurt, the victim develops a pattern of shallow, rapid breathing, inadequate for good ventilation. Oxygenation of the blood fails, and cardiovascular collapse (shock) may be seen. Unless prompt recompression is instituted, the outcome may be fatal.

---

*Chokes appears in anywhere from 2 to 20 percent of cases of decompression sickness.[9] People susceptible to diver's mottled skin rash seem to have an increased incidence of chokes.[10]

Circulatory collapse (shock) occasionally develops from decompression sickness. It can result from chokes, bubble blockage of vital blood vessels, or damage to the central nervous system. Transient drops in blood pressure not infrequently accompany serious cases of decompression sickness. Careful measurements suggest that cardiac impairment may not be rare.[11]

The clinical appearance of decompression sickness varies widely between naval and civilian cases. In three large series of civilian cases, serious decompression sickness (as contrasted to pain only or skin rash) was present in 53 to 67 percent of the patients.[12,13,14] This results from two considerations. First, minor symptoms are more likely to be reported by naval divers, who have easy access to therapy and who will not be financially inconvenienced by missing a diving turn. Secondly, there are significant differences between the persons who dive and the types of diving done. Civilian divers (especially sport divers and diving fishermen) are less rigorously examined for diving fitness, and they tend to be much more casual about following standard decompression procedures. In an English group, fifteen of seventeen civilian victims of decompression sickness took less decompression time than required by Royal Navy Tables;[15] 4 percent of Hawaiian cases omitted more than 5 hours of required decompression.[16]

The majority of the signs of decompression sickness resolve with recompression therapy or with physical therapy following recompression. Chronic effects are limited to the nervous system and bones. But permanent neurologic damage from decompression sickness is more common than often realized.[17,18]

Chronic bone changes (called aseptic bone necrosis or dysbaric osteonecrosis) occur in divers and caisson workers. Areas of infarcted bone develop in the bone shaft or near the joints (juxtaarticular). The lesions have long been recognized in caisson workers and commercial divers, but in 1968 the first U.S. Navy case was reported.[19] Bone necrosis appears to be related to decompression, but a firm cause-and-effect principle is lacking. Cases typically appear only after years of diving. Divers with a history of decompression sickness have a higher incidence of bone lesions, than that of divers without such a history, but bone necrosis does occur among the latter nonetheless.[20]

It is difficult to establish the incidence of dysbaric osteonecrosis. One problem is that there are no statistics on the incidence of aseptic necrosis in the general population. A few facts are known: Those divers or caisson workers who have been careless in decompression are much more frequently involved than naval divers. In Hawaii and in Japan over 50 percent of diving fishermen may have osteonecrosis; naval divers have less than 2 percent.[21] Osteonecrosis is less common in air diving than in mixed gas, experimental, and saturation diving. One survey found osteonecrosis among sport divers.[22]

Generally, the necrosis is found only upon X ray. Only juxta-articular lesions cause disability. The possible relationship between chronic bone disease and marginal decompression is yet another reason for careful diving.

PHYSIOLOGICAL MECHANISM

Breathing air under high pressure raises the blood tensions of both O_2 and N_2; correspondingly, tissue levels rise in response to the higher blood levels. The oxygen is metabolized, but N_2 remains in the tissues under high pressure; when the tissue is completely saturated, there is no longer a N_2 capillary-to-tissue gradient.

Nitrogen solubility determines how much gas can be dissolved in a given tissue. Fat will absorb 5.3 times as much N_2 as will water; thus, saturation takes longer in fatty tissues. During a short dive, only the watery tissues will become saturated. Highest fat concentrations are found in the adipose tissue, bone marrow, and spinal cord.

Blood supply also influences the rate of uptake of gas. Areas with high blood flow receive more gas per minute and thus reach saturation sooner.

During decompression, the lung and blood N_2 pressures fall in coordination with diminishing water pressure. The excess N_2 leaves the tissues and enters the capillaries; it then passes into the veins and is eliminated in the lungs.

Because fat stores more N_2, it takes longer to lose its excess N_2 during decompression. Similarly, areas with poor circulation have prolonged desaturation times.

If decompression is rapid, the blood may not be able to carry the nitrogen in solution. Then gas forms bubbles. Sometimes

X rays, taken immediately after a dive, will show these bubbles. Areas with the most N_2 (fat and regions with poor circulation) have the most bubbles. Because of its watery composition, a given volume of blood can carry only one fifth as much N_2 as that released from the same volume of fat.

Bubbles in blood vessels were first noted by Robert Boyle in 1670, and he even postulated that these bubbles could obstruct blood flow.[23] At this time, decompression sickness did not exist because there was no compressed-air diving. (It began in 1819.) The first cases of decompression sickness were reported by Triger in 1841.[24] However, the possibility of gas bubbles causing the symptoms was not well accepted until the late nineteenth and early twentieth centuries.

Circulatory obstruction by nitrogen bubbles can cause tissue death. The capillaries may be distended behind the block and impinge on nerves, thus causing pain. Edema results from transudation through capillary walls. Bubbles sometimes form outside the blood vessels in fat and neural tissues.

Obese divers have a greater tendency than thin ones to develop bends, because of their large fat stores. In the spinal cord, those parts with the highest fat (lower thoracic, upper lumbar, lower cervical) are most frequently involved in decompression sickness. During ascents from *short* dives, the fat can take up N_2 released from lean tissues; it thus acts as a buffer in preventing bubble formation. During *long* dives, this property is eliminated by fat saturation.

Any condition that impairs circulation can be expected to increase the likelihood of bends by slowing gas elimination. Cold will cause peripheral vasoconstriction, and this may explain the frequent occurrence of "skin bends" in chamber dives, where the temperature falls markedly during decompression. The spinal cord has poorer circulation than the brain, and this may contribute to its more frequent involvement.

The mechanism of decompression injury is not always known. Venous or arterial occlusion is an obvious possibility. However, this may not explain limb and joint pain. Perhaps gas actually distorts tissue structure. Recent experiments suggest that spinal-cord injuries result from secondary venous obstruction.[25] Transport of venous bubbles to the right heart causes central venous pressure to rise. This impairs spinal cord venous drainage by slowing flow in the epidural venous plexus. Bubbles also may form in the sluggish spinal cord venous system.

Bubbles react with the blood to cause several derangements. In 1938, Edgar End reported that rapid decompression resulted in the clumping of red blood cells, which then impeded circulation in small blood vessels.[26] Current investigation has identified several other responses to gas/fluid interaction. Proteins are denatured,[27] platelets clump, and the blood coagulation system is affected.[28] Substances affecting the smooth muscle in blood vessels may be released.[29] Plasma loss in decompression enhances the impairment of blood flow.[30] Blood lipids (fat) may also be involved. Actual lipid emboli have been identified in decompression injury.[31] A complex interrelationship among intravascular mechanical effects, direct tissue distortion, and gas/blood interactions leads to the protean findings of decompression sickness.

BUBBLE FORMATION

The starting point for decompression sickness is the formation of bubbles. There are many theories about this complex subject. The site for bubble formation has not been resolved; there are proponents for bubble initiation within the tissues,[32] veins,[33] or arteries.[34] Bubbles formed in one region could migrate to another before causing injury.

Standard decompression theory, from the work of J. S. Haldane, assumes that tissues can hold excess gas pressures in solution.[35] Haldane theorized that a twofold reduction in ambient pressure would be tolerated without bubbling. This is the supersaturation theory, and it is incorporated in the commonly used decompression tables.

Ultrasonic bubble detectors, which utilize the Doppler principle, detect asymptomatic intravascular bubbles, which occur after decompression that should not result in bubbling, according to Haldanian theory.[36] In 1945 A. R. Behnke had postulated the presence of such bubbles and had called them "silent bubbles".[37] The significance of such bubbles is controversial, but they certainly do cast doubt on former concepts of bubble formation.

An unusual theory of decompression sickness is the thermodynamic approach of B. A. Hills, who believes that initial gas phase

BUBBLE FORMATION

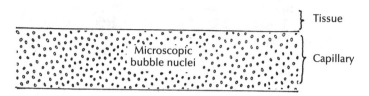

High N_2 in both tissue and capillaries;
Water pressure keeps bubble nuclei small

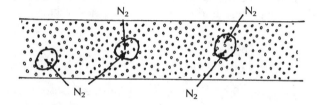

When water pressure is reduced, the N_2 leaves
the tissues and enter capillaries
Bubbles expand and gas flows into them

separation occurs within the tissues after most decompressions.[38] Gas phases coalesce to cause decompression sickness.

Bubble formation depends on total dissolved-gas tension. This includes not only N_2 but also carbon dioxide (CO_2) and O_2. Because O_2 is rapidly metabolized, it does not participate in bubble formation. In the beginning, CO_2 enters small bubbles because of its great solubility. High CO_2 thus may increase the tendency for bubble formation. With time, the CO_2 is less important, since N_2 stores are much larger. In Japanese caisson work, high environmental CO_2's were associated with high incidences of decompression sickness.[39]

Bubbles probably form from microscopic gas nuclei. With ambient pressure reduction, these nuclei expand, and gas diffuses into them to form bubbles. Brief high-pressure compression before a "dive" reduces bubble formation in gelatin and in animals.[40]

Investigators theorize this high pressure crushes gas micronuclei and prevents bubble formation. Below a critical size, the forces of surface tension collapse potential bubbles. During decompression, increasing bubble volume lowers gas pressure within the bubble (Boyle's law). Gas, under high pressure in solution, flows into this low pressure area, thus further increasing bubble size. The constrictive force of surface tension decreases as the bubble expands; therefore, bubbles grow because of reduction in water pressure and from inward flow of gas.

Venous blood and tissues have a lower total gas pressure than arterial blood, which is ambient. This occurs because (1) the body uses more O_2 than it produces CO_2, and (2) CO_2 is more soluble, so it raises venous and tissue pressure less when excreted in exchange for O_2 uptake from arterial blood. This desaturation of venous blood and tissues provides a carrying capacity for excess nitrogen during decompression. Bubbles are at ambient pressure, which is always higher than tissue or venous pressure. Thus, bubbles have a tendency to expel gas into venous blood. This partially affects the bubble expansion, which occurs during decompression.

Recompression compresses the bubbles and raises their internal gas pressure (Boyle's law). Gas pressure in the bubble then exceeds that in the surrounding fluid, and gas flows outward. Surface tension becomes important again as the bubble size decreases.

High temperatures decrease gas solubility (try heating a carbonated beverage) and have been indicated as a factor in decompression sickness.

Formerly, it was believed that exercise during decompression reduced the frequency of bends by increasing the circulation, thus hastening the rate of N_2 elimination. This was shown to occur only during the first thirty minutes of exercise. Furthermore, increased circulation secondary to exercise also increases gas supply to the tissues, thus speeding their saturation with N_2. Local pCO_2 built up in exercise may also aggravate bubble formation. Finally, the contraction of muscles causes low pressure areas, which hasten gas flow into bubble nuclei. One study indicated by controlled tests that exercised divers developed decompression sickness more frequently than rested divers.[41] In current practice, divers remain at rest during decompression. However, Vunn suggests that the timing of exercise determines its effect on gas elimination.[42] He found improved gas elimination in divers who exercised during decompression.

INDIVIDUAL SUSCEPTIBILITY

Individuals differ in their susceptibilities to the bends. Given the same exposure, one man may be "bent" while another feels no pain. Naturally, all diving organizations would like to determine what type of person is most likely to develop decompression sickness. Certain factors seem to modify sensitivity. Conditions that increase the amount of gas dissolved or that impair the elimination of this gas during decompression will raise the probability of bends. Obese divers carry more dissolved gas, since fat forms an excellent reservoir. Any condition that hinders circulation will reduce the efficiency of gas transport to the lungs during decompression. Older divers tend to have less adequate circulation and are more prone to the bends. A diver with an injury (e.g. sprained ankle) has an increased tendency for involvement of that area, because of circulatory impairment and prior tissue damage. One episode of decompression sickness may predispose the diver to another. Hence, repeat diving should be delayed. Postalcoholic state is also associated with a higher incidence of the bends through an unknown mechanism. Tolerance may evidently develop to bends; seasoned divers have a lower incidence. This could be due to natural selection: Bends-prone divers leave the field; furthermore, experienced divers have more awareness of the dangers and practice better techniques. Navy divers are fond of the familiar slogan: "There are old divers and there are bold divers, but there are no old, bold divers." Possibly, there is an actual physical adaptation, but this has not been established. Golding studied twenty-two new divers at the Dartford Tunnel project and found that, with increased experience, their incidence of bends fell. Interestingly, this "adaptation" was lost in those men who were away from compressed air work for one to two weeks. Adaptation to one depth did not confer bends resistance at deeper depths.[43]

INCIDENCE

The overall frequency of bends cannot be determined; many studies have tabulated total cases, but the number who dived and were not stricken during this period remains unknown. Also, the incidence depends upon the type of diving done.

Doll analyzed all U.S. Navy dives requiring decompression, in 1958, 1960, and 1961, and found sixty-two cases of decompression sickness out of 7,625 total dives (.81 percent). A revision was made of the Navy decompression tables in 1958, and for 1960 and 1961, thirty-eight cases were reported out of 5,453 (0.69 percent) dives.[44] Note that this series included only those dives needing decompression stops. Rivera reported 6.4 percent of his cases occurred in dives which supposedly required no decompression stops.[45] When Navy diving requirements were properly followed, the Navy incidence of decompression sickness, using air, was 0.047 percent.[46] This includes decompression dives, no-decompression dives, and repetitive dives. Unfortunately, no comparable studies have been done on the incidence among recreational divers. Navy experience is not necessarily transferable to sport diving, since the divers and diving vary so much.

NOTES: INTRODUCTION TO DECOMPRESSION SICKNESS

1. A. Dewey, "Decompression Sickness: An Emerging Recreational Hazard," *New England Journal of Medicine*, 267: 754–65, 812–20, 1962.
2. J. Rivera, "Decompression Sickness Among Divers: An Analysis of 935 Cases," *Military Medicine*, 129: 314–34, 1964.
3. F. Golding et al., "Decompression Sickness During Construction of the Dartford Tunnel," *British Journal of Industrial Medicine*, 17: 167–86, 1960.
4. Rivera, *op. cit.*
5. K. Kizer, "Dysbarism in Paradise," *Hawaii Medical Journal*, 39: 106–16, 1980.
6. Golding, *op. cit.*
7. Rivera, *op. cit.*
8. J. Farmer et al., "Inner Ear Decompression Sickness," *Laryngoscope*, 86: 1315–27, 1976.
9. A. Erde, C. Edmonds, "Decompression Sickness: A Clinical Series," *Journal of Occupational Medicine*, 17: 324–28, 1975.
10. Dewey, *op. cit.*
11. T. Neuman et al., "Cardiopulmonary Consequences of Decompression Stress," *Respiration Physiology*, 41: 143–53, 1980.
12. Kizer, *op. cit.*
13. Erde, *op. cit.*
14. J. How et al., "Decompression Sickness in Diving," *Singapore Medical Journal*, 17: 92–97, 1976.

15. R. Hanson, "Decompression Sickness in Civilian Divers," *Journal of the Royal Naval Medical Service*, 59: 77–80, 1973.
16. Kizer, *op. cit.*
17. A. Palmer et al., "Spinal Cord Degeneration in a case of 'Recovered' Spinal Decompression Sickness," *British Medical Journal*, 283: 288, 1981.
18. R. Vaernes, S. Eidsvik, "Central Nervous Dysfunction After Near-Miss Accidents in Diving," *Aviation Space Environmental Medicine*, 53: 803–07, 1982.
19. R. Uhl, "Aseptic Bone Necrosis in Divers," *Aerospace Medicine*, 39: 1345–47, 1968.
20. C. Wade et al., "Incidence of Dysbaric Osteonecrosis in Hawaii's Diving Fishermen," *Undersea Biomedical Research*, 5: 137–47, 1978.
21. W. Hunter et al., "Aseptic Bone Necrosis Among U.S. Navy Divers: Survey of 934 Non-randomly Selected Personnel," *Undersea Biomedical Research*, 5: 25–36, 1978.
22. B. Williams, I. Unsworth, "Skeletal Changes in Divers," *Australian Radiology*, 20: 83–94, 1976.
23. M. Goodman, "The Syndrome of Decompression Sickness in Historical Perspective," U.S. Naval Medical Research Laboratory Report No. 368, 1961.
24. *Ibid.*
25. J. Hallenbeck et al., "Mechanisms Underlying Spinal Cord Damage in Decompression Sickness," *Neurology*, 25: 308–16, 1975.
26. E. End, "The Use of New Equipment and Helium Gas in a World Record Dive," *Journal of Industrial Hygiene and Toxicology*, 20: 511–20, 1938.
27. D. H. Elliot, et al., "Acute Decompression Sickness," *Lancet*, 21: 1193–99, 1974.
28. R. Philip, "A Review of Blood Changes Associated with Compression Decompression: Relationship to Decompression Sickness," *Undersea Biomedical Research*, 1: 117–50, 1974.
29. Elliot, *op cit.*
30. A. Cockett et al., "Pathophysiology of Bends and Decompression Sickness," *Archives of Surgery*, 114: 296–301, 1979.
31. S. Pauley, A. Cockett, "Role of Lipids in Decompression Sickness," *Aerospace Medicine*, 41: 56–60, 1970.
32. B. Hills, "Biophysical Aspects of Decompression," in *Physiology and Medicine of Diving and Compressed Air Work*, P. Bennett and D. Elliot, eds. (Baltimore: Williams and Wilkins, 1975), pp. 366–91.
33. D. Elliot, J. Hallenbeck, "The Pathophysiology of Decompression Sickness," in *Physiology and Medicine of Diving and Compressed Air Work*, P. Bennett and D. Elliot, eds. (Baltimore: Williams and Wilkins, 1975), pp. 435–55.
34. H. Hempleman, "British Decompression Theory and Practice" in *Physiology and Medicine of Diving and Compressed Air Work*. P. Bennett and D. Elliot, eds. (Baltimore: Williams and Wilkins, 1969) pp. 291–318.
35. A. Boycott, C. Damant, J. Haldane, "The Prevention of Compressed-Air Illness," *Journal of Hygiene*, 8: 342–443, 1908.

36. Spencer, "Decompression Limits for Compressed Air Determined by Ultrasonically Detected Blood Bubbles," *Journal of Applied Physiology*, 40: 229–35, 1976.

37. A. Behnke, "Decompression Sickness Incident to Deep-Sea Diving and High Altitude Ascent," *Medicine*, 24: 381–402, 1945.

38. Hills, *op cit.*

39. Y. Mano, J. D'Arrigo, "Relationship Between CO_2 Levels and Decompression Sickness: Implications for Disease Prevention," *Aviation Space Environmental Medicine*, 49: 340–55, 1978.

40. R. Vann et al., "Evidence for Gas Nuclei in Decompressed Rats," *Undersea Biomedical Research*, 7: 107–12, 1980.

41. O. Van Der Aue, R. Kellar, "The Effects of Exercise During Decompression from Increased Barometric Pressures on the Incidence of Decompression Sickness in Man," U.S. Navy Experimental Diving Unit Report, 1949, pp. 8–49.

42. R. Vann, "Another View of the Fundamental Issues for Table Development," abstract presented at the Decompression Group Symposium, Undersea Medical Society, San Antonio, 1984.

43. Golding, *op. cit.*

44. R. Doll, "Decompression Sickness Among U.S. Navy Operational Divers: An Estimate of Incidence Using Air Decompression Tables," U.S. Navy Experimental Diving Unit Report 4–64n, 1965.

45. Rivera, *op. cit.*

46. R. Biersner, "Factors in 171 Navy Diving Decompression Accidents Occurring Between 1960–1969," *Aviation Space Environmental Medicine*, 46: 1069–73, 1975.

13 ‖ Prevention and Treatment of Decompression Sickness

Gradual decompression forms the basis for prevention of the bends. Haldane in 1908 determined that a sudden fall in ambient pressure from 2 to 1 atmospheres could be tolerated.[1] That is, the amount of excess nitrogen (N_2) dissolved at 2 atmospheres (33 feet) can be tolerated if the ambient pressure is suddenly reduced to 1 atmosphere (the surface). This ratio, though not exact, demonstrates the theoretical basis of the decompression tables. It is the pressure ratio that is important, not the number of atmospheres changed. For example, rapid decompression can safely occur from 6 to 3 atmospheres (a ratio of 2:1) but not from 3 to 1. Reductions in excess of 2 to 1 will result in the N_2 leaving solution to form bubbles. As will be discussed, Haldane's decompression concepts have been extensively reevaluated.

During a dive, alveolar N_2 rises, leading to heightened arterial nitrogen tension. This larger quantity of gas enters the tissues; tissue level rises toward blood level. When tissue level, blood tension, and alveolar partial pressure of nitrogen are all equal, the tissue can be called saturated. At that partial pressure, no more N_2 can be stored. Increasing the lungs' N_2 partial pressure by diving deeper will raise the tissue's capacity. The time it takes for saturation to be reached depends on the fat content of the tissues and circulation; fatty tissues with a high capacity for N_2 naturally require longer for saturation, and a good blood supply permits faster gas uptake and quicker saturation.

Initially, the blood level is much higher than the tissue level, and gas flows rapidly. The rate of gas uptake decreases with time, since the pressure of the blood and that of the tissue become closer. Once the blood/tissue differential is reduced, the rate of gas transfer slows proportionately. (See graph below.) The time between 0 and 50 percent of saturation is termed halftime; after six periods, each equal to one halftime, the tissues will be 98.5 percent saturated. For example, if a tissue requires 10 minutes for 50 percent equilibration, it will be virtually completely saturated in 60 minutes.

The U.S. Navy Standard Decompression Tables were formulated using several arbitrary "tissue units." These representative units range in halftime from 5 minutes to 2 hours. They reflect different combinations of N_2 capacity and circulations;

CHANGES IN RATE OF GAS UPTAKE WITH TIME

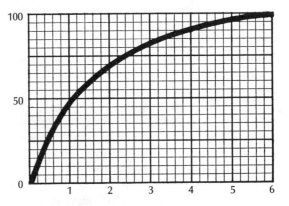

Here the halftime is 1 hour.
By 6 hours saturation is
virtually complete.

they do not represent any actual organ. The fastest tissue saturates almost completely in 30 minutes, while the longest requires 12 hours.[2] In theory, after 12 hours, at any depth, the tissues would not be able to take up more gas. In fact, gas uptake after 12 hours does exist, and current thinking advances the time for complete saturation to more than 24 hours. The U.S. Navy tables utilize Haldane's principles but do not use his constant tissue ambient pressure ratio. Instead, representative tissue gas concentrations (M values) control ascent.[3]

The extent of time, not the depth, determines the degree of saturation. At 33 feet, blood/tissue equilibration requires approximately the same amount of time as at 330 feet; however, the total quantity of gas increases with depth; equilibration occurs to a higher pressure. For example, at 33 feet the alveolar N_2 of air approximates 1,200 mm Hg, and tissue N_2 will rise toward this level. At 330 feet, the tissue N_2 tension approaches 6,600 mm.

During ascent, gas elimination follows the same pattern: Those tissues which took up gas most rapidly also lose it most quickly. Initial rate of elimination exceeds the subsequent rate. Theoretically, gas elimination rate should mirror uptake. This is not true. Elimination of nitrogen during decompression depends on the depth at which it takes place; this may be related to bubble formation.[4]

The decompression tables were designed so that tissue to blood gradient, during ascent, never exceeded a safe limit. Some fast tissues can tolerate a ratio slightly above the basic 2 to 1. Short dives permit rapid ascent, since the percentage of saturation remains low; less gas must be eliminated. Long dives—even to relatively shallow depths—permit tissue saturation, so that the tissue gas pressures are more than twice those at the surface.

When a dive raises tissue gas level above the tolerable surfacing value, ascent must be gradual. This allows time for gas elimination. In staged decompression, stops are made to permit this elimination. At the last stop before surfacing, the tissue N_2 tension falls sufficiently to permit surfacing. As dive depth or duration lengthens, the first stop must be made longer, and the stop periods must be lengthened. The longer the dive to a given depth, the greater the gas uptake, so that the initial ascent becomes more limited. Similarly, deeper dives of a given duration raise tissue gas and require deeper stops. The first stop involves an approximately

50 percent reduction in the gradient of ambient pressure to tissue pressure. Subsequent stops are made at 10 foot intervals to the surface. The time at each stop permits sufficient gas elimination to ascend.

Because gas elimination slows with time, the later stops require a longer time to give up the same amount of gas.

In the early part of ascent, the slowly saturating tissues may still take up gas, while the fast tissues are eliminating it. Later, in ascent, the fast tissues will be almost completely desaturated while the slow tissues contain large amounts of gas.

A different form of gradual ascent is continuous decompression. Once ascent starts, it continues to the surface, without stops. This slow rate substitutes for the staged stops. The rate of ascent decreases as the surface is neared because of the slowing of gas elimination. Continuous ascent requires less time since it more closely matches desaturation rate; however, the difficulty in maintaining accurate ascent speed makes it a difficult system to practice. For routine use, the U.S. Navy uses staged decompression. In saturation diving continuous ascent is employed.

USING THE TABLES

In theory, dives less than 33 feet require no gradual decompression, since maximum gas pressure cannot exceed twice surface pressure, regardless of dive length; however, cases of bends in dives less than 33 feet have been reported. Rivera noted that three out of 835 bends cases developed above this depth.[5] During the BART project, Behnke reported cases of decompression sickness after long exposures to pressures equivalent to 30 feet of seawater.[6] A sport diving case of bends developed during diving to 25 feet.[7]

At depths below 33 feet, direct ascent can be made from dives of limited duration. If time down is limited, the overall gas tension will not exceed surfacing N_2 pressures. The column "No Decompression Limits" on the Repetitive Group Designation Table shows the maximum time allowable at different depths without the need for gradual decompression. As the graph indicates, deep dives permit proportionately shorter dive times. For example, a dive can be made to 50 feet for 100 minutes but to 100

NO-DECOMPRESSION LIMITS AND REPETITIVE GROUP DESIGNATION TABLE FOR NO-DECOMPRESSION AIR DIVES

Depth (feet)	No-decompression limits (min)	Group Designation														
		A	B	C	D	E	F	G	H	I	J	K	L	M	N	O
10		60	120	210	300											
15		35	70	110	160	225	350									
20		25	50	75	100	135	180	240	325							
25		20	35	55	75	100	125	160	195	245	315					
30		15	30	45	60	75	95	120	145	170	205	250	310			
35	310	5	15	25	40	50	60	80	100	120	140	160	190	220	270	310
40	200	5	15	25	30	40	50	70	80	100	110	130	150	170	200	
50	100					10	15	25	30	40	50	60	70	80	90	100
60	60		10	15	20	25	30	40	50	55	60					
70	50		5	10	15	20	30	35	40	45	50					
80	40		5	10	15	20	25	30	35	40						
90	30		5	10	12	15	20	25	30							
100	25		5	7	10	15	20	22	25							
110	20			5	10	13	15	20								
120	15			5	10	12	15									
130	10			5	8	10										
140	10			5	7	10										
150	5			5												
160	5				5											
170	5				5											
180	5				5											
190	5				5											

US Navy Diving Manual

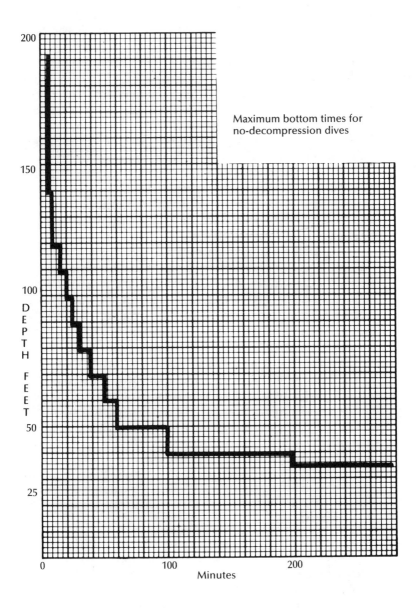

Maximum bottom times for no-decompression dives

feet for only 25 minutes. A smaller percentage of saturation is allowable at deep depths, since each increment adds a greater total amount of gas. SCUBA divers should stay within the no-decompression limits for maximum safety.

If the limits of the no-decompression table are exceeded, gradual ascent must be made. The Navy standard decompression table and air compression table for exceptional exposure are the references. As depth or duration increases, the time required for decompression lengthens. Total decompression time does not rise linearly with depth or time. Again, the total amount of gas for elimination increases faster with additional depth or lengthening of time spent below. Initial ascent is limited, and the time required at each step lengthens disproportionately.

A twofold increase in time at 100 feet increases decompression time more than seven times, while a 1.5 increase in depth for 60 minutes augments it by almost three times.

In using the tables, remember that the bottom time consists of the total time from leaving the surface to the beginning of the ascent. Obviously, not all of the bottom time is spent on the bottom; the amount spent in descent increases with the depth of the dive. *"Depth"* refers to the deepest point reached, regardless of the time spent there. A SCUBA diver, spending 30 minutes at 50 feet and 4 minutes at 75 feet, must regard his dive depth as 75 feet for the whole dive. Time and depth cannot be interpolated. That is, a dive of 52 minutes at 85 feet must be decompressed on the schedule for 60 minutes at 90 feet. These rules aid safety by their allowances. They help to equalize the effects of possible miscalculations of depth and time, high individual susceptibility, or heavy exertion.

DEPTH AND TIME INFLUENCES ON DECOMPRESSION REQUIREMENTS

Depth of dive	100 feet	100 feet	150 feet
Duration	30 minutes	60 minutes	60 minutes
Total decompression	4.5 minutes	38.3 minutes	111.8 minutes
Depth of first stop	10 feet	20 feet	40 feet
Length of first stop	3 minutes	9 minutes	3 minutes

Ascent to the first stop—or to the surface in no-decompression dives—is made at the rate of 60 feet per minute. Some divers feel that they add to their safety by slowing their rate and increasing decompression time; however, at depth, a slow ascent provides more time for saturation of the slow tissues and thus actually raises the possibility of bends. If ascent is made faster than 60 feet per minute, the time should be made up at 10 feet in no-decompression dives or at 10 feet below the first stop in dives requiring decompression stops. The rate of ascent between stops is not critical. Well-meaning instructors sometimes advise slight increases in decompression stops for added "safety," but this too may permit added gas uptake.

For the sport diver the most important tables deal with repetitive dives. Since complete desaturation does not occur for over 24 hours, multiple dives within one day continue to add to the total gas tension. Repeated no-decompression dives can result in bends from this accumulation. Thus, the repetitive dive tables are used when more than one dive is made. The U.S. Navy repetitive dive tables consider dives made within 12 hours of each other to be repetitive dives. No repeat dive within 12 hours is permitted after a dive covered by the extreme exposure table. The amount of gas remaining after decompression from a dive is represented by repetitive groups. These groups are simply a means of expressing the amount of excess N_2 remaining in the body. The amount of excess gas progresses through the alphabet, A being the smallest remaining and Z the greatest.

While on the surface, the diver slowly eliminates this gas so that the amount present at the time of the next dive is lower than when the first dive ended. Navy Table 1-7 takes this interval desaturation into account. An interval under 10 minutes is treated as though there were no break between dives; after 12 hours, desaturation may be considered essentially complete. Reference to this table shows how staying longer at the surface lowers the repetitive group's letter in effect at the time of the next dive. For surface intervals between categories on the table *the next greater* interval is used. For example, a group N dive after 41 minutes on the surface becomes group L, not group M. Up to this point, only the initial dive has been considered.

Next, in Navy Table 1-8, the depth of the repetitive dive is balanced against the repetitive group (from Table 1-7) to obtain a

REPETITIVE GROUP AT THE END OF THE SURFACE INTERVAL

	Z	O	N	M	L	K	J	I	H	G	F	E	D	C	B	A
Z	0:10-0:22	0:34	0:48	1:02	1:18	1:36	1:55	2:17	2:42	3:10	3:45	4:29	5:27	6:56	10:05	12:00*
O		0:10-0:23	0:36	0:51	1:07	1:24	1:43	2:04	2:29	2:59	3:33	4:17	5:16	6:44	9:54	12:00*
N			0:10-0:24	0:39	0:54	1:11	1:30	1:53	2:18	2:47	3:22	4:04	5:03	6:32	9:43	12:00*
M				0:10-0:25	0:42	0:59	1:18	1:39	2:05	2:34	3:08	3:52	4:49	6:18	9:28	12:00*
L					0:10-0:26	0:45	1:04	1:25	1:49	2:19	2:53	3:36	4:35	6:02	9:12	12:00*
K						0:10-0:28	0:49	1:11	1:35	2:03	2:38	3:21	4:19	5:48	8:58	12:00*
J							0:10-0:31	0:54	1:19	1:47	2:20	3:04	4:02	5:40	8:40	12:00*
I								0:10-0:33	0:59	1:29	2:02	2:44	3:43	5:12	8:21	12:00*
H									0:10-0:36	1:06	1:41	2:23	3:20	4:49	7:59	12:00*
G										0:10-0:40	1:15	1:59	2:58	4:25	7:35	12:00*
F											0:10-0:45	1:29	2:28	3:57	7:05	12:00*
E												0:10-0:54	1:57	3:22	6:32	12:00*
D													0:10-1:09	2:38	5:48	12:00*
C														0:10-1:39	2:49	12:00*
B															0:10-2:10	12:00*
A																0:10-12:00*

REPETITIVE GROUP AT THE BEGINNING OF SURFACE INTERVAL (FROM PREVIOUS DIVE)

(Rev. 1958)

INSTRUCTIONS FOR USE

Surface interval time in the table is in hours and minutes ("7:59" means 7 hours and 59 minutes). The surface interval must be at least 10 minutes.

Find the repetitive group designation letter (from the previous dive schedule) on the diagonal slope. Enter the table horizontally to select the listed surface interval time that is exactly or next greater than the actual surface interval time. The repetitive group designation for the end of the surface interval is at the head of the vertical column where the selected surface interval time is listed. For example — a previous dive was to 110 ft. for 30 minutes. The diver remains on the surface 1 hour and 30 minutes and wishes to find the new repetitive group designation: The repetitive group from the last column of the 110/30 schedule in the Standard Air Decompression Tables is "J". Enter the surface interval credit table along the horizontal line labeled "J". The 1 hour and 47 min. listed surface interval time is next greater than the actual 1 hour and 30 minutes surface interval time. Therefore, the diver has lost sufficient inert gas to place him in group "G" (at the head of the vertical column selected).

*NOTE: Dives following surface intervals of more than 12 hours are not considered repetitive dives. Actual bottom times in the Standard Air Decompression Tables may be used in computing decompression for such dives.

Navy Table 1–7

Surface interval credit table.

Used with permission. U.S. Navy Diving Manual, Part I.

REPET. GROUPS	REPETITIVE DIVE DEPTH (Ft.)															
	40	50	60	70	80	90	100	110	120	130	140	150	160	170	180	190
A	7	6	5	4	4	3	3	3	3	3	2	2	2	2	2	2
B	17	13	11	9	8	7	7	6	6	6	5	5	4	4	4	4
C	25	21	17	15	13	11	10	10	9	8	7	7	6	6	6	6
D	37	29	24	20	18	16	14	13	12	11	10	9	9	8	8	8
E	49	38	30	26	23	20	18	16	15	13	12	12	11	10	10	10
F	61	47	36	31	28	24	22	20	18	16	15	14	13	13	12	11
G	73	56	44	37	32	29	26	24	21	19	18	17	16	15	14	13
H	87	66	52	43	38	33	30	27	25	22	20	19	18	17	16	15
I	101	76	61	50	43	38	34	31	28	25	23	22	20	19	18	17
J	116	87	70	57	48	43	38	34	32	28	26	24	23	22	20	19
K	138	99	79	64	54	47	43	38	35	31	29	27	26	24	22	21
L	161	111	88	72	61	53	48	42	39	35	32	30	28	26	25	24
M	187	124	97	80	68	58	52	47	43	38	35	32	31	29	27	26
N	213	142	107	87	73	64	57	51	46	40	38	35	33	31	29	28
O	241	160	117	96	80	70	62	55	50	44	40	38	36	34	31	30
Z	257	169	122	100	84	73	64	57	52	46	42	40	37	35	32	31

(Rev. 1958)

INSTRUCTIONS FOR USE

The bottom times listed in this table are called "residual nitrogen times" and are the times a diver is to consider he has <u>already</u> spent on bottom when he <u>starts</u> a repetitive dive to a specific depth. They are in minutes.

Enter the table horizontally with the repetitive group designation from the Surface Interval Credit Table. The time in each vertical column is the number of minutes that would be required (at the depth listed at the head of the column) to saturate to the particular group.

For example – the final group designation from the Surface Interval Credit Table, on the basis of a previous dive and surface interval, is "H". To plan a dive to 110 feet, determine the "residual nitrogen time" for this depth required by the repetitive group designation: Enter this table along the horizontal line labeled "H". The table shows that one must <u>start</u> a dive to 110 feet as though he had already been on the bottom for 27 minutes. This information can then be applied to the Standard Air Decompression table or "No Decompression" Table in a number of ways:

(1) Assuming a diver is going to finish a job and take whatever decompression is required, he must add 27 minutes to his actual bottom time and be prepared to take decompression according to the 110 foot schedules for the sum or equivalent single dive time.

(2) Assuming one wishes to make a quick inspection dive for the minimum decompression, he will decompress according to the 110/30 schedule for a dive of 3 minutes or less (27 + 3 = 30). For a dive of over 3 minutes but less than 13, he will decompress according to the 110/40 schedule (27 + 13 = 40).

(3) Assuming that one does not want to exceed the 110/50 schedule and the amount of decompression it requires, he will have to start ascent before 23 minutes of actual bottom time (50 - 27 = 23).

(4) Assuming that a diver has air for approximately 45 minutes bottom time and decompression stops, the possible dives can be computed: A dive of 13 minutes will require 23 minutes of decompression (110/40 schedule), for a total submerged time of 36 minutes. A dive of 13 to 23 minutes will require 34 minutes of decompression (110/50 schedule), for a total submerged time of 47 to 57 minutes. Therefore, to be safe, the diver will have to start ascent before 13 minutes or a standby air source will have to be provided.

Navy Table 1–8   *Repetitive dive timetable.*

Used with permission. U.S. Navy Diving Manual, Part I.

time figure. This time, added to the actual bottom time of the repetitive dive, determines the total time to be used for calculating decompression for the second dive. This added time is equivalent to the time at that depth which would give that amount of N_2 and is represented by the group letter. As the repetitive group increases, the amount of time at a given depth increases; however, as depth increases within a given group, added time decreases. For example, a dive to 60 feet by a group B diver adds 11 minutes

---

REPETITIVE DIVE WORK SHEET

    I. PREVIOUS DIVE:

       20 minutes   see Table 1-5 or 1-6 for

       60 feet   repetitive group designation   Group D

    II. SURFACE INTERVAL:

       1 hour 20 minutes on surface   see Table 1-7

       Group D (from I.)   for new group   Group C

    III. RESIDUAL NITROGEN TIME:

       100 feet (depth of repetitive dive)   see Table

       Group C (from II.)   1-8   10 minutes

    IV. EQUIVALENT SINGLE DIVE TIME:

           10 minutes (residual nitrogen time from III.)

      (add) 15 minutes (actual bottom time of repetitive dive)

      (sum) 25 minutes   Thus the second dive is considered a

                    100 ft. dive for 25 mins.

    V. DECOMPRESSION FOR REPETITIVE DIVE:

       25 minutes (equivalent single dive   see Table

             time from IV.)   1-5 or 1-6

       100 feet (depth of repetitive dive

           ☒No decompression required

           or

           Decompression stops:____feet____minutes

                       ____feet____minutes

                       ____feet____minutes

                       ____feet____minutes

Work sheet from U.S. Navy Diving Manual. Original problem. Used with permission. U.S. Navy Diving Manual, Part I.

to his bottom time; a 100 foot dive in group B would add only 7 minutes. At first glance this seems unsafe since deeper dives add less time; nevertheless, this table only determines the amount of time required to accumulate a given amount of gas, and increasing the depth speeds the uptake. Thus, the repetitive group represents the amount of gas already present when the second dive begins. Obviously, less time would be required for its accumulation at deeper depths.

A sequence of dives can be worked out in the same fashion. The second dive determines the new repetitive group, etc. The technique is shown on the accompanying work sheets.

This system can be used from different approaches in planning repeat dives. Its biggest value is in establishing limits for no-decompression dives. If a first dive to 100 feet for 15 minutes requires no decompression and equals group E, a second dive to 100 feet after two hours on the surface puts the diver in group C, adding 10 minutes to his bottom time. In order to stay within no-decompression limits for 100 feet, the actual dive can then last only 15 minutes and the diver will enter group H. After another 2 hour surface period, he moves to group E and has 18 minutes added, thus reducing bottom time to 7 minutes. It can be seen that no-decompression limits are quickly reached. A short, 15 minute dive to 100 feet, followed by a 30 minute rest and another 100 feet, 15 minute dive, would mean that the diver would have to make a decompression stop at 10 feet. Ignorance of the residual action of N_2 makes bends possible in divers who are careful to make only short, shallow dives.

One interesting case, treated at Pearl Harbor, involved a coral diver who required treatment after making 6 dives from 60 to 165 feet, with a maximum surface interval of 55 minutes. The timing of the dives is shown below. Computation shows that he would have spent 390 minutes in decompression stops had he followed the repetitive dive system. Instead, he spent no time in decompression stops. His last dive was an attempt at a homemade "treatment" dive because of nausea in prior dives, but he sighted sharks and this shortened the duration of the dive.

Although the repetitive dive system seems complicated, it can be easily mastered with a little practice. It affords a great deal of savings in decompression time over simply adding the bottom time from the first dive to the second in order to determine de-

TIMING OF CORAL DIVER

Dive Depth	Bottom time	Surface interval	Time for Decompression of each dive
60 feet	30 minutes	55 minutes	0
110	5	15	3
165	20	15	79
165	20	10	150
165	15	10	107
70	15	—	51

compression requirements. In planning dives of varying depths, time will be saved by making the deepest one first.

Because of the many variable factors in diving, some cases of decompression sickness will result when using decompression tables. Individual susceptibility, prolonged work, rough seas, inaccurate depth and time measurements—all make protection incomplete. To rule out all risk would make the schedule overly restrictive; an expected failure rate of 2 to 3 percent was accounted for in the tables' design.[9] Actually, failure rate has been below 1 percent when the tables are properly used.

EVALUATION OF DECOMPRESSION TABLES

The work of Haldane revolutionized diving. Modification of his concepts led the U.S. Navy to devise its decompression tables, which have been the most commonly used ones in the world. Decompression sickness has been shown to be a complex disease, but the role of bubbles remains central. Thus, the goal of preventing bubble formation and growth is still sought.

A major problem is that U.S. Navy tables do not prevent nitrogen bubbling. Ultrasonic investigations have repeatedly demonstrated intravascular bubbles under supposedly safe diving conditions. Quite often bubbles occur without any findings of decompression sickness. The significance of these "silent bubbles" is still not known. Spencer has not found decompression sickness in the absence of ultrasonically detectable bubbling.[10]

Ultrasonic bubble detection offers an exciting way to monitor decompression. An ideal decompression schedule would permit surfacing without bubbling. In fact, this would be unnecessarily restrictive. It is hoped that further investigation will define the degree of tolerable bubbling and the means to achieve this consistently.

As noted, the Navy tables were not intended to eliminate decompression sickness completely. Proper Navy use of the tables results in a decompression sickness incidence of about 0.047 percent.[11] The incidence varies with dive profile. Long shallow dives have a higher than expected occurrence of bends. In fact, Spencer had bubbling in 75 percent and bends pain in 25 percent of long exposures to 30 feet.[12] It appeared that the Navy tables were less conservative than desirable for long, shallow dives and more conservative than necessary for short, deep dives.

Considerations in decompression theory have suggested decompression table modification. These have been based on models, in vitro experimentation, animal experiments, and ultrasonic bubble monitoring. There is evidence that initial decompression stops should be deeper than in the U.S. Navy schedules.[13, 14]

Despite imperfections the Navy tables remain the standard guide. They are definitely the tables of choice for sport divers today. Many techniques can be used to design decompression regimens, but only through regular use can table safety be established. The intrinsic failure rate for Navy decompression tables is much less than failures from table misuse. The highest incidence of failure develops at the extreme depth and time portions of the tables.

DIAGNOSIS AND TREATMENT

The possibility of bends must be considered in the case of any person becoming ill after a dive. Claims that the dive was neither long enough nor deep enough to cause decompression sickness should be taken with a grain of sand. Poor record keeping or failure to follow repetitive dive techniques are frequent. Unfortunately, bends symptoms can easily be confused with other maladies. Joint pain may come from sprains, falls, or tight equipment; a tight wrist strap or wet suit cuff may result in numbness and tingling in the arms. Joint and muscle pain from the mere exertion of diving may resemble the pain of bends. Onset, after 12 hours following a dive, makes bends a less likely possibility, but cases have occurred after 36 hours.[15] When symptoms are indefinite and the history makes decompression sickness possible, trained medical counsel should be sought. Careful examination is necessary to detect unsuspected lesions.

Since the late 1800s, recompression has been the preferred treatment in decompression sickness. Through recompression the bubbles are compressed and the gas in them reenters the body fluids. Reduction of bubble size relieves circulatory blockage and decreases tissue compression by extravascular bubbles. Following relief of symptoms, the patient is slowly decompressed to the stage at which the gas can be eliminated without bubbling. Bubble reduction follows the reverse pathway of bubble formation. With rapid recompression, the high pressure decreases bubble size. This raises bubble pressure over surrounding fluid gas tension, and results in diffusion of gas from the bubble, further reducing bubble size. Outward diffusion continues as long as internal bubble pressure remains above tissue gas tension.

The reduction of bubble size by compression gives the first symptomatic relief. Lasting relief depends upon diffusion from the bubble so that the excess gas can be eliminated from the body. This process takes longer. Diffusion depends on the surface area of the bubble. Compression reduces bubble radius by a greater proportion than surface area; small bubbles still have adequate area for diffusion.

In accordance with Boyle's law, volume decreases directly with pressure, while the bubble's diameter is inversely proportional to the cube root of pressure. The chart that follows shows the much greater reduction in volume than diameter at increasing pressures. At 165 feet, volume is one sixth of surface while diameter has been cut less than 50 percent. Bubble radius rather than volume determines the extent of vessel occlusion. Increases in pressure above 165 feet bring little symptom relief since they cause little decrease in radius.

Diffusion can be speeded by reducing the amount of N_2 in the blood, thus increasing the gradient from bubble to blood. Substituting O_2 for air as the breathing medium provides the most effective method. Breathing O_2 for about 7 minutes virtually eliminates N_2 from the lungs, and the blood level will fall accordingly. High inspired O_2's give high arterial O_2 tensions. Metabolism sharply reduces venous oxygen tension. This difference in blood gas tensions provides carrying capacity for N_2 and hastens its elimination (Behnke's oxygen window).[16] Unfortunately, the toxicity of pure O_2 under pressure limits the depth of its use; generally it is begun only after decompression reaches 60 feet. Helium oxygen mixes have been used since they, too, will increase N_2 gradient and have no depth limit. However, the tissues take up helium as they give up N_2, thus maintaining excessive tissue gas tensions. Bubbling can result from this combination of N_2 and helium. This is not a problem when breathing pure oxygen because the body burns O_2 before it can form bubbles.

After recompression relieves the symptoms, gradual decompression is made to the surface pressure. Rapid decompression would allow for reexpansion of any bubble that had not been completely eliminated. The recompression treatment actually acts as a repetitive dive and results in further uptake of N_2 by the tissues. The longer the treatment, the greater the new saturation.

The biggest advantage of maximal recompression is the rapid reduction in bubble size; however, decompression must then be slower, and high pressure increases the possibility of new decompression sickness. Lower pressure therapy may take longer to give complete relief, but it has a lower incidence of new sickness resulting from the therapy.

Dissatisfaction with results of using the old treatment Tables 1–4 led to development of "minimal-recompression, oxygen-

CHANGES IN BUBBLE VOLUME AND DIAMETER RELATED TO DEPTH

Depth	Volume	Diameter
surface	100	100
33 feet	50	79.3
66 feet	33.3	69.3
99 feet	25	63.0
132 feet	20	58.5
165 feet	16.7	55.0
297 feet	10	46.2

breathing" treatment schedules.[17] These tables maximize oxygen use and are shorter than former schedules. With the exception of Table 4, the older tables are used only when oxygen is unavailable. Table 4 is used under certain conditions when the new schedules are not satisfactory.

For decompression sickness the patient is taken to 60 feet for 20 minutes of oxygen breathing. If the findings are "pain only" and resolve in 10 minutes, therapy is continued on Table 5. Serious disease or pain only failing to respond in 10 minutes is treated with Table 6. Table 6A (see page 133) is used for air embolism and includes an initial air exposure at 165 feet. Therapy on the new schedules alternates oxygen breathing with air breathing to reduce the risk of oxygen poisoning. (See Chapter 16, Oxygen Poisoning.)

Besides speeding bubble resolution, breathing oxygen under pressure improves tissue oxygenation. Limiting depth of treatment reduces new inert gas uptake and reduces the risk of decompression sickness caused by therapy.

The hazards of this new technique are failure to achieve sufficiently prompt reduction in bubble diameters and the possibility of oxygen toxicity. Massive decompression sickness, as seen in explosive decompression (diver rises, out of control) may re-

NAVY TABLE 5

MINIMAL RECOMPRESSION, OXYGEN BREATHING METHOD FOR TREATMENT OF DECOMPRESSION SICKNESS AND GAS EMBOLISM

Depth (feet)	Time (minutes)	Breathing Media	Total Elapsed Time (minutes)
60	20	Oxygen	20
60	5	Air	25
60	20	Oxygen	45
60 to 30	30	Oxygen	75
30	5	Air	80
30	20	Oxygen	100
30	5	Air	105
30 to 0	30	Oxygen	135

U.S. Navy Diving Manual

quire immediate recompression to 165 feet for adequate reduction of bubble size. Oxygen toxicity may be seen especially when the tables are extended. In clinical trials, the failure rate—even in serious cases—was about 9 percent.[18] Use of the minimal recompression tables, more than ever, requires specialized medical personnel and equipment.

Effectiveness of recompression therapy is limited by the conflicting considerations of bubble-size reduction, oxygen toxicity, oxygen diffusion, and inert gas uptake. The physics of bubble dissolution makes sufficiently prompt bubble resolution difficult.[19]

One other use of the treatment tables is for "trial by pressure." In doubtful cases of bends, pressurization is performed. If no relief occurs, the cause probably is not decompression sickness. This trial by chamber represents a repetitive dive and must follow decompression standards. Preventive recompression may be used when a diver knows he has skipped decompression times during a dive or series of dives.

NAVY TABLE 6

MINIMAL RECOMPRESSION, OXYGEN BREATHING METHOD FOR TREATMENT OF DECOMPRESSION SICKNESS AND GAS EMBOLISM

Depth (feet)	Time (minutes)	Breathing Media	Total Elapsed Time (minutes)
60	20	Oxygen	20
60	5	Air	25
60	20	Oxygen	45
60	5	Air	50
60	20	Oxygen	70
60	5	Air	75
60 to 30	30	Oxygen	105
30	15	Air	120
30	60	Oxygen	180
30	15	Air	195
30	60	Oxygen	255
30 to 0	30	Oxygen	285

U.S. Navy Diving Manual

Not surprisingly, the success of therapy depends largely on the severity of the case. Residual impairment from edema and compression may persist after severe neurological involvement. Follow-up hyperbaric oxygen therapy is often used when residual signs are present following recompression therapy. Physical therapy generally results in later improvement, but the injury may be permanent. *Fatalities are rare if recompression is prompt.* Rivera recorded three deaths, but none of these had received standard therapy.[20]

Because recompression therapy is not always successful, there has been an intensive effort to improve on standard treatment techniques. The oxygen treatment tables have options for extension in the event of treatment failure. Often, therapy facilities devise their own treatment table modifications. Since oxygen toxicity limits these tables, a system utilizing O_2 enriched nitrogen was devised which permits long saturation therapy in difficult cases.[21]

A variety of ancillary treatment techniques are used with recompression and during transport to recompression chambers. These are based on the demonstrated disruptions in circulation that occur with significant decompression sickness. During transport oxygen should be breathed to speed nitrogen elimination. Conscious victims are given large quantities of oral fluids. Seriously ill divers receive intravenous fluids. Dextrans have been popular because of purported ability to (1) reexpand circulatory volume, (2) improve blood flow in small vessels, and (3) clear lipids from the blood. Actually no proof exists that Dextrans are superior to other intravenous fluids. Steroids are often used in central nervous system decompression sickness to reduce damage from edema. Their value is somewhat controversial.[22] Heparin has been proposed for its lipid clearing properties. Its value is debatable, and it is dangerous when inner ear damage may be present.[23],[24] Other emergency medical therapy is used as necessary.

The major development in therapy of decompression sickness is the realization that serious cases require critical care therapy at its best, not just pressure.

The treatment of sport diving decompression sickness is often less satisfactory than treatment in professional diving. Divers need to know that use of approved decompression regimens may not prevent decompression sickness. Part of dive planning is ascertaining the location and availability of the nearest recompression facility. Thought should be given to methods of emergency transport before the diving begins. If symptoms develop, the recompression facility should be promptly contacted. Serious injuries may be masked by the presence of joint pain. It is useful to carry oxygen on diving trips since its use during transport of an injured diver may relieve symptoms and prevent progression of the disease.[25] Ancillary treatment may be very successful,[26] but any victim of decompression sickness should be examined by a physician experienced in diving medicine.

Some persons suggest that during transport the victim should be positioned on the left side with the body tilted head down. This helps keep any mobile bubbles out of the pulmonary circulation. In an unconscious person the risk of pulmonary aspiration of vomitus is reduced with this posture. Enhanced venous return from the legs supports blood pressure. The head-down tilt makes breathing more difficult (abdominal contents push against the diaphragm) and venous pressure in the head is increased. This is undesirable in the presence of brain injury. The importance of body position has not been determined.

Attempts to treat decompression sickness by putting the diver back in the water for recompression generally meet with failure. Managing a sick SCUBA diver in these circumstances is virtually impossible. Depth control and air supply present two of the major difficulties. Limited communication impairs the rescuer's ability to monitor the victim's condition. This attempt at treatment allows further N_2 intake, thus worsening the bubble danger. Water treatment may, then, harm the diver, in addition to delaying definitive chamber therapy. Water therapy using oxygen has been described for use in remote areas.[27] It is quite complex and not suitable for sport diving.

It is difficult to evaluate treatment success. The response is generally excellent in cases that are promptly and correctly treated. Unfortunately treatment, especially in recreational diving, is frequently delayed. In too many cases, the diver does not report his symptoms, waiting to see if they will not disappear spontaneously. Attempts at therapy with whiskey or with water recompression often add to the delay in instituting therapy. Air Force treatment of diving accidents with an average treatment delay of about 16 hours had a 90 percent success rate.[28] However, central nervous system decompression sickness had almost 20 percent incidence of permanent damage. This is comparable to results in Hawaii.[29] Very careful testing suggests residue from nervous system decompression sickness is more common than generally realized.[30] The potential seriousness of decompression sickness makes prevention far preferable to therapy.

See page 219 about Divers Alert Network, which can provide emergency information.

NOTES: PREVENTION AND TREATMENT OF DECOMPRESSION SICKNESS

1. A. Boycott, C. Damant, J. Haldane, "The Prevention of Compressed Air Illness," *Journal of Hygiene,* 8: 342–443, 1908.
2. R. Workman, "Calculation of Decompression Schedules for Nitrogen-Oxygen and Helium-Oxygen Dives," U.S. Navy Experimental Diving Unit Research Report 6-65, 1965.
3. *Ibid.*
4. E. Kindwall et al., "Nitrogen Elimination in Man During Decompression," *Undersea Biomedical Research,* 2: 285–97, 1975.
5. J. Rivera, "Decompression Sickness Among Divers: An Analysis of 935 Cases," *Military Medicine,* 129: 314–34, 1964.
6. A. Behnke, "Medical Aspects of Pressurized Tunnel Operations," *Journal of Occupational Medicine,* 12: 101–12, 1970.
7. E. Beckman, "Decompression Sickness," *Aviation Space Environmental Medicine,* 48: 996–97, 1977.
8. Kindwall, *op. cit.*
9. E. Lanphier, J. Dwyer, "Diving with Self Contained Underwater Breathing Apparatus," U.S. Navy Experimental Diving Unit Special Report Series, 1954.
10. M. Spencer, "Decompression Limits for Compressed Air Determined by Ultrasonically Detected Blood Bubbles," *Journal of Applied Physiology,* 40: 229–35, 1976.
11. R. Biersner, "Factors in 171 Navy Diving Decompression Accidents Occurring Between 1960–1969," *Aviation Space Environmental Medicine,* 46: 1069–73, 1975.
12. Spencer, *op. cit.*
13. R. Strauss, "Bubble Formation in Gelatin: Implications for Prevention of Decompression Sickness," *Undersea Biomedical Research,* 3: 121–30, 1974.
14. T. Neuman et al., "Gas Phase Separation During Decompression in Man: Ultrasound Monitoring," *Undersea Biomedical Research,* 3: 121–30, 1976.
15. Rivera, *op. cit.*

16. A. Behnke, "Early Quantitative Studies of Gas Dynamics in Decompression," *Physiology and Medicine of Diving and Compressed Air Work*, P. Bennett and D. Elliot, eds. (Baltimore: Williams and Wilkins, 1967), pp. 398–416.

17. M. Goodman, "Minimal-Recompression, Oxygen-Breathing Method for the Therapy of Decompression Sickness," in *Proceedings of the Third Symposium on Underwater Physiology* (Baltimore: Williams and Wilkins, 1975) pp. 165–82.

18. *Ibid.*

19. T. Kunkle, E. Beckman, "Bubble Dissolution Physics and the Treatment of Decompression Sickness," *Medical Physiology,* 10: 184–90, 1983.

20. Rivera, *op. cit.*

21. J. Miller et al., "Nitrogen-Oxygen Saturation Therapy in Serious Cases of Compressed-Air Decompression Sickness," *Lancet,* 2: 169–71, 1978.

22. "Emergency Use of Drugs," discussion in *Interaction of Drugs in the Hyperbaric Environment,* J. M. Walsh, ed., (Bethesda, Md.: Undersea Medical Society, 1980), pp. 80–81.

23. E. Kindwall, "Role of Adjunctive Drug and Fluid Therapy," in *Treatment of Serious Decompression Sickness and Arterial Gas Embolism,* J. Davies, ed. (Bethesda, Md.: Undersea Medical Society, 1979), pp. 45–49.

24. A. Bove, "The Basis for Drug Therapy in Decompression Sickness," *Undersea Biomedical Research,* 9: 91–111, 1982.

25. A. Dick et al., "Early Oxygen Breathing for SCUBA Injuries: A Highly Effective Therapy," *Undersea Biomedical Research,* 11 (Supplement): 20–21, 1984.

26. R. Saumerez, "Neurological Decompression Sickness Treated Without Recompression," *British Medical Journal,* 1: 151–52, 1973.

27. C. Edmonds et al., *Diving and Subaquatic Medicine,* 2nd ed. (Sydney, Aust.: Diving Medical Centre, 1981), pp. 171–80.

28. J. Davis, "Treatment of Decompression Accidents Among Sport SCUBA Divers with Delay Between Onset and Compression," in *Treatment of Serious Decompression Sickness and Arterial Gas Embolism,* J. Davis, ed., (Bethesda, Md.: Undersea Medical Society, 1980), pp. 3–9.

29. K. Kizer, "Dysbarism in Paradise," *Hawaii Medical Journal,* 39: 106–16, 1980.

30. B. Peters et al., "Neurologic and Psychologic Manifestations of Decompression Illness in Divers," *Neurology,* 27: 125–27, 1977.

14 Decompression Sickness in Sport Diving

Because of the possible severity of decompression sickness and the difficulties of treatment, the sport diver's first interest should be to prevent the bends. It was once believed that decompression sickness could not be caused by breath-hold diving since there was no exposure to high pressure air. However, Paulev reported a case of decompression sickness in himself resulting from multiple "bottom drops" in a submarine escape training tank and noted that three Norwegians had had similar experiences.[1] Paulev's case involved about sixty "dives" of two minute durations to 50 to 66 feet, separated by surface intervals of a few seconds to 2 minutes. Within 30 minutes after the last dive, he had hip pain, which progressed to near shock within 6 hours. Recompression therapy gave good relief.

A group of male skin divers in the South Pacific makes closely spaced dives to 100 to 130 feet in search of pearls. These men sometimes are afflicted by a disease called taravana, which bears a certain resemblance to classic decompression sickness.[2] Pearl divers in other regions do not have a similar problem; this has been attributed to their more widely spaced dives.

During skin diving, lung compression does raise the partial pressure of N_2. In theory, if the dives are closely spaced, this N_2 will accumulate and could result in bubbling. For the average skin diver, however, the fatigue of the repeated dives will halt the diving before dangerous amounts of N_2 can accumulate.

Limiting exposure obviously provides the best method of prevention. In SCUBA diving, no dives should be made that exceed the no-decompression limits. Most importantly, these dives have a lower incidence of bends; furthermore, in SCUBA diving, adequate air supply for decompression presents a real problem. In all but the shortest dives, the original tank will be inadequate for the dive plus the decompression stops. Leaving the water to obtain a new bottle lengthens decompression along with raising the chance of bends. If dives are kept within the no-decompression limits, emergency surfacing can be made under unforeseen circumstances such as shark attack, rough waters, illness, or exhausted air supply. Abruptly terminating a dive which calls for decompression stops necessitates later chamber recompression.

Unfortunately, some diving books assert that decompression sickness cannot result if the diver uses only one single tank. The graph on page 174 shows that below 110 feet, air supply duration exceeds the time limit for no-decompression dives. Since bends has been seen even during no-decompression dives, the risk certainly does exist with a single tank.

THE SPORT DIVER AND DECOMPRESSION TABLES

There are two somewhat contradictory classes of problems with standard decompression tables. They are not completely safe, and they are quite restrictive. It is essential that SCUBA divers realize that *the tables were not intended to be an absolute prevention for decompression sickness.*

Cases occur even when the tables are used properly by the men for whom they were intended. It is small wonder that improper use by civilian divers results in decompression sickness.

Individual susceptibility to bubbling (as detected ultrasonically) and to decompression sickness must be acknowledged. Several possible contributing factors such as age and obesity have been identified. Statistically, it is difficult to make satisfactory correlations.[3] Older naval divers have more bends, but they also

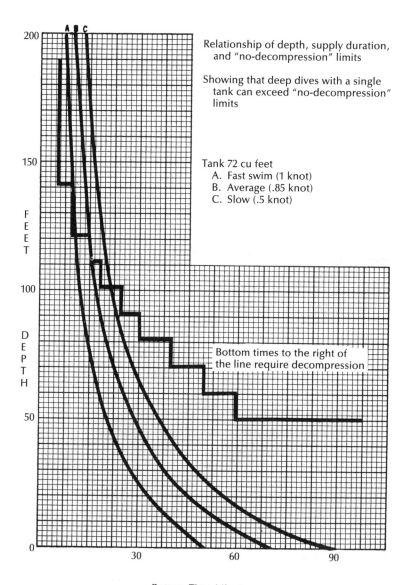

Relationship of depth, supply duration, and "no-decompression" limits

Showing that deep dives with a single tank can exceed "no-decompression" limits

Tank 72 cu feet
A. Fast swim (1 knot)
B. Average (.85 knot)
C. Slow (.5 knot)

Bottom times to the right of the line require decompression

Bottom Time Minutes

tend to dive deeper and use experimental equipment. Body build has not been shown as a factor in naval decompression sickness. Would this be true if the more diverse sport diving population could be investigated? Sexual susceptibility to decompression sickness has been postulated. A small sample of Air Force altitude physiology candidates revealed a 10 times higher incidence of decompression sickness in women than in men.[4] This is not entirely comparable to diving, and other Air Force data contradict the observed difference.[5] A retrospective survey of sport diving instructors also suggested a greater occurrence of bends in women.[6] Again, the small sample size and the investigative technique employed means that the conclusion cannot be considered firmly established.

Diving during pregnancy is discussed in Chapter 20, Health Requirements.

A major problem in evaluating decompression sickness is the small number of cases that occur. Also, individuals are not consistent from day to day in their susceptibility to bubbling. In the previous chapter some considerations in decompression table improvement were discussed. Sport divers and diving instructors sometimes try to make their own improvements on the Navy tables. One way to modify use of the tables is to employ the next greater bottom time for a given depth dive. A similar change would be to use the next deeper depth. Either change would shorten dive time and raise the repetitive group letter. It is not necessarily safe to add decompression stops or to slow ascent, since gas elimination and uptake may occur simultaneously. It has been fairly popular to make a short stop at 10 feet before surfacing. This is not inherently dangerous, but it will not necessarily be useful. There is experimental evidence that deep, rather than shallow, stops are best to prevent bubbling.[7]

Decompression tables were designed for one-depth diving as is common in hard-hat work. SCUBA divers are really underwater swimmers and typically visit several depths during one dive. For safety, the entire dive must be considered to have taken place at the deepest depth. This clearly makes the Navy tables restrictive for sport SCUBA use. Divers sometimes try to escape this restrictiveness by ignoring very brief depth excursions—as in 2 minutes at 150 feet during a 100 foot dive—or by mathematically calculating equivalent depth and time combinations for multilevel dives.

Either approach is dangerous. The tables were not constructed in a way that permits rearrangement of time and depth constraints. Furthermore, gas elimination varies from uptake and is depth dependent.[8] This makes extrapolation unsafe. During multidepth diving, the deepest excursion should be made first. This enhances decompression safety since the remainder of the dive serves as a decompression period for the deep excursion.

DECOMPRESSION METERS

It would be useful to have a device that could measure N_2 uptake and elimination and calculate safe decompression patterns. This would eliminate the restrictiveness of treating multilevel dives as single level dives and could reduce the dangers incurred through manual timing and depth recording of single repetitive dives. Until recently there was only one commercially available type of decompression meter.[9] Unfortunately, this meter is so flawed that it is not a valuable piece of diving equipment. It is more conservative than Navy schedules for shallow diving, but is less conservative for deep diving. It is thoroughly useless in repetitive diving, and it is in repetitive diving that a meter could be most valuable.

A new generation of decompression meters using computer technology has been introduced. These meters continuously compute gas uptake and elimination. They facilitate repetitive diving and make multilevel diving more efficient. One of the meters utilizes a new decompression schedule designed to minimize bubble formation. Time will be required to validate the safety of the meters, but the concepts are sound.

DIVING AND FLYING

In the modern world many diving trips involve airplane rides. Flying after a dive reduces ambient pressure and adds to decompression stress. If the nitrogen tension on the surface is sufficiently great and if the altitude of the flight is sufficiently high, bubbling may occur, and decompression sickness may develop.

The actual incident of decompression sickness from altitude exposure after diving is low. Divers rarely fly immediately after diving. Commercial airplanes are pressurized so that physiological altitude is much less than flying altitude. Of course, accidental cabin decompression, though rare, does occur.

It is difficult to define the risk of flying after diving. Considerations include the dive depth, dive duration, number of dives, diving surface intervals, surface interval from last dive to flight, rate of ascent to altitude, altitude reached, and the diver's physical status.

The earliest standards for flying after diving ignored the protective effects of cabin pressurization. In modern airliners, flying at 40,000 feet, cabin pressure is usually maintained at 0.74 ATA (8.000 feet equivalent). Efforts to facilitate flying after diving led to testing of a variety of schedules. The conclusion was that flying was safe to commercial altitudes after 2 hours on the surface.[10] This, however, is a minimal requirement and does not apply to repetitive or decompression dives. Mild symptoms of decompression sickness were ignored in these experiments. Recent ultrasonic bubble detection investigation has shown marked bubbling with 3-hour surface intervals before commercial flights.[11]

Another approach has been extrapolation of diving surfacing ratios for nitrogen. Using this technique a diver is presumed safe to fly in a commercial plane once he has reached repetitive group D. Testing of this system showed it to be unreliable.[12]

Currently the trend is toward more conservative practice. Minimum surface intervals of 8 hours are recommended for no-decompression dives; 24 hour intervals are suggested after decompression diving.[13] For greater safety the 8 hour interval should be lengthened.

Flying after diving is especially a problem when victims of decompression sickness or air embolism must be transported by plane. The advantage of speed often overrules the risk of further decompression. Either pressurized aircraft are used or flight altitude is kept to a minimum. Interestingly, in helicopter evacuation it was possible to determine empirically a safe altitude ceiling.[14] Mountain driving after diving can also cause decompression sickness.[15]

HIGH ALTITUDE DIVING

Some divers utilize mountain lakes for fun or work. Decompression requirements are modified since surface pressure is reduced. Surfacing from a given dive depth will create more stress in the mountains, since the ratio of accumulated N_2 to surface N_2 pressure is greater. There are basically two approaches to altitude diving. New tables can be formulated.[16] [17] or standard tables can be used if an equivalent sea level dive depth is used instead of the actual altitude depth.[18] For example, a lake dive made to 100 feet at 6,000 feet equals diving to 122 feet in the ocean.

The problem with new tables is validation. No altitude tables have the proved reliability of standard Navy tables.

Transforming sea-level tables for altitude diving is theoretically safe.[19] The commonly used transformed tables unfortunately did not correct for the lower density of fresh water (which reduces the equivalent depth) or correct the ascent rate. In altitude diving the same amount of time is used to ascend a shorter distance. Hence, actual ascent rate is slower. Transformed tables fail when decompression stops must be made.[20] The criteria used for Navy decompression stop duration are not met by simply establishing depth ratios. In altitude diving, using the same decompression stop time as called for in the equivalent sea level table would give a longer than necessary stop. Of course, this is a failure in the direction of safety. Since SCUBA divers should not make dives requiring decompression stops, this problem is not important for sport diving.

A simple way to do altitude diving is to use a capillary depth gauge.[21] These gauges indicate deeper depth than actual water depth when used at higher altitudes since they function by compression of a small volume of trapped air. Thus, the capillary gauge will give an equivalent sea level dive depth reading, which can be used directly in dive planning. Similarly, the capillary gauge will indicate more ascent distance than is actually traversed. This permits easy ascent timing (at 6,000 feet actual 50 feet/minute ascent will appear to be 60 feet/minute). The capillary gauge technique will give longer than necessary decompression stops as seen with table transformation.

Upon arrival at altitude from sea level the diver's tissues contain higher nitrogen tensions than are present in the atmosphere.

This is equivalent to flying or to surfacing from a dive. A period of at least 12 hours is required to eliminate this excess nitrogen. Only then can diving calculations be safely made.

Divers are advised to obtain special training before attempting altitude diving. Dive techniques vary from ocean diving.

SUMMARY

If bends does result, the prognosis for sport divers is less favorable than in Navy diving, where treatment facilities are convenient. The sport diver's case may be diagnosed only after a long delay; then, transportation causes further procrastination in treatment.

Good planning and careful record keeping play an essential part in bends prevention. Time and depth limits must be understood *before* the dive—not after it! Careful attention must be paid in calculating residual nitrogen after repetitive dives. Decompression sickness is a fascinating but dangerous affliction which should, and could, be a rarity among sport divers.

NOTES: DECOMPRESSION SICKNESS IN SPORT DIVING

1. P. Paulev, "Decompression Sickness Following Repeated Breath Hold Dives," *Journal of Applied Physiology,* 20: 1028–31, 1965.
2. E. Cross, "Taravana-Diving Syndrome in the Tuamotu Divers," in *Physiology of Breath Hold Diving and the Ama of Japan* (Washington, D.C.: National Academy of Science, 1965).
3. R. Biersner, "Factors in 171 Navy Diving Decompression Accidents Occurring Between 1960–1969," *Aviation Space Environmental Medicine,* 46: 1069–73, 1975.
4. B. Bassett, "Decompression Sickness in Female Students Exposed to Altitude During Physiological Training," in Proceedings, *PADI Women in Diving Seminar* (Santa Ana, Calif.: PADI, 1978) pp. 52–53.
5. *Effects of Diving on Pregnancy,* M. B. Kent, ed. (Bethesda, Md.: Undersea Medical Society, 1980), pg. 8.
6. *Ibid.*
7. R. Strauss, "Bubble Formation in Gelatin: Implications for Prevention of Decompression Sickness," *Undersea Biomedical Research,* 1: 169–74, 1974.
8. E. Kindwall et al., "Nitrogen Elimination in Man During Decompression," *Undersea Biomedical Research,* 2: 285–97, 1975.

9. R. Howard et al., "Theory of Evaluation of the Single Pneumatic Resistor Decompression Computer," *Medical Biological Engineering* 14: 570–79, 1976.

10. P. Edel et al., "Interval at Sea-Level Pressure Required to Prevent Decompression Sickness in Humans Who Fly in Commercial Aircraft After Diving," *Aerospace Medicine,* 40:1105–10, 1969.

11. J. Balldin, "Venous Gas Bubbles While Flying with Cabin Altitudes of Airliners or General Aviation Aircraft 3 Hours After Diving," *Aviation Space Environmental Medicine,* 51: 649–52, 1980.

12. B. Bassett, "Results of Validation Testing of Flying After Diving Schedules," *Abstracts of the Seventh Symposium on Underwater Physiology,* Athens, 1980.

13. R. Goad, "Letters re: Flying After Diving," *Pressure,* 5: 6–7, 1976.

14. E. Reddick, "Movement by Helicopter of Patients with Decompression Sickness," *Aviation Space Environmental Medicine,* 49: 1229–30, 1978.

15. R. DiLibero, A. Pilmanis, "Spinal Cord Injury Resulting from Scuba Diving," *American Journal of Sports Medicine,* 11: 24–33, 1983.

16. M. Boni et al., "Diving at Diminished Atmospheric Pressure: Air Decompression Tables for Different Altitudes," *Undersea Biomedical Research,* 3: 189–204, 1976.

17. R. Bell et al., "The Development and Testing of High Altitude Diving Tables Using Extrapolated U.S. Navy Critical Tissue Pressure Criteria," *Abstracts of the Seventh Symposium on Underwater Physiology,* Athens, 1980.

18. E. Cross, "High Altitude Decompression," *Skin Diver,* November 1970, pg. 17.

19. *Ibid.*

20. R. Bell, R. D. Borgwarrdt, "The Theory of High-Altitude Corrections to the U.S. Navy Standard Decompression Tables, The Cross Corrections," *Undersea Biomedical Research,* 3: 1–23, 1976.

21. P. Mackay, "Automatic Compensation by Capillary Gauge for Altitude Decompression," *Undersea Biomedical Research,* 3: 399–402, 1976.

15 | Nitrogen Narcosis

Nitrogen narcosis—so-called rapture of the deep—is a significant danger in SCUBA diving since it may lead to drowning. Breathing compressed air below 100 feet causes impairment of judgment and coordination. A diver may remove his mouthpiece, take off his equipment, or dive aimlessly to the point of unconsciousness or exhaustion of his air supply. To the narcotized diver, the sea world is pleasant indeed; he is all powerful, there are no dangers, everything seems amusing. The fish around him do not have air bottles, so why should he? One such man "became so disturbed at a depth of 270 feet that he attempted to unscrew the faceplate from his helmet in order to escape from the diving suit."[1]

Nitrogen intoxication has reportedly occurred at 30 feet, but this is not well-documented or common. Usually, nitrogen narcosis manifests itself around 100 feet. The intoxication may be so subtle that the diver feels unimpaired; however, Kiessling found changes at 100 feet in conceptual reasoning (most affected) reaction time, and mechanical dexterity (least affected).[2] In the 150 to 250 foot range, poor judgment and diminished reflexes are readily apparent. Mental and motor function deteriorate markedly below 300 feet. Convulsions and loss of consciousness may occur. High nitrogen pressure modifies normal EEG (brain wave) patterns.

Alcoholic intoxication follows a similar clinical course. In the use of general anesthetics, a stage of delirium may precede unconsciousness. The central nervous system is probably affected in basically the same fashion by all these forms of narcosis. Several theories have been proposed to explain the mechanism of narcosis. None completely satisfies.

Nitrogen (N_2), known as an inert gas since the body does not metabolize it, enters the bloodstream and the tissues, but leaves the tissues, breathed out again without being used by the cells. In this aspect, it resembles the gases used for anesthesia. Other inert gases are found in trace amounts in air. These are hydrogen, helium, krypton, argon, neon, and xenon. If the partial pressure of any of these gases reaches sufficient levels, narcosis results. Anesthetics are effective at atmospheric pressure, but N_2 pressure must be raised before it is narcotic. At 100 feet inspired N_2 pressure is 4 times surface value (2,400 mm). When the neural tissues become equilibrated with this new level, their function is impaired. Increasing depth raises N_2 pressure, thus intensifying the narcotic effect.

The Myer-Overton theory of anesthesia relates anesthetic action to gas solubility in fat. It states that when any inert substance reaches a sufficient concentration in the fatty part of the nervous system, depression will result.[3] This theory has its faults, but it is useful as a model in understanding inert gas narcosis. Gases with high fat (or oil) solubility can be expected to be the most intoxicating.

The chart that follows shows the solubility of the inert gases along with values for two anesthetic agents as a comparison. The most soluble inert gas, xenon, can actually cause surgical anesthesia at atmospheric pressure.[4]

There is a complex relationship between pressure and narcosis that has been used to study the mechanism of anesthesia. High

DEPTH AND NITROGEN PRESSURE

Depth	Total Pressure	Nitrogen Pressure (air with 79 percent N_2)
surface	760 mm Hg.	600 mm Hg.
33 feet	1,520	1,200
100 feet	3,060	2,420
200 feet	5,360	4,230
500 feet	12,300	9,700
1000 feet	23,760	18,800

GAS SOLUBILITY AT 37°C

Gas	Molecular Wt.	Water Solubility	Fat Sol.	oil to H_2O ratio
Cyclopropone	42	0.204	7.14	35
Nitrous oxide	44	0.47	1.4	3.2
Nitrogen	28	0.013	0.067	5.2
Xenon	131.3	0.085	1.7	20
Krypton	84	0.045	0.43	9.6
Argon	40	0.026	0.14	5.3
Radon	222	0.15	0.19	1.25
Neon	20	0.0097	0.019	2.07
Hydrogen	2	0.016	0.048	3.1
Helium	4	0.0085	0.015	1.7
Oxygen	32	0.024	0.12	5.0
Carbon Dioxide	44	0.56	0.876	1.6

This table is a composite of information taken from:

P. Bennett, "Performance Impairment in Deep Diving Due to Nitrogen, Helium, Neon and Oxygen," *Proceedings of the Third Symposium on Underwater Physiology.* C. Lambertsen, ed. (Baltimore: Williams & Wilkins), 1967, Pp. 327-8.

Lawrence et al., "Preliminary Observations on the Narcotic Effect of Xenon with a Review of Values for Solubilities of Gases in Water and Oils," *Journal of Physiology,* 105:197-209, 1946

S. Miles, *Underwater Medicine* (Philadelphia: Lippincott), 1969.

pressures reverse the action of gaseous anesthetics.[5] The "critical volume hypothesis" asserts that anesthesia results from expansion due to absorption of the anesthetic.[6] Pressure reverses this expansion. Presumably this occurs in nervous system membranes. The validity of this theory is not completely established.

Pressure itself affects the nervous system. Divers breathing helium at very great depths have tremors that can progress to convulsions. This is called the high pressure nervous syndrome (HPNS).[7] The extension of deep diving has been complicated by the existence of HPNS. Helium has not been shown to have narcotic properties.[8] Interestingly, HPNS can be offset by the inhalation of very small concentrations of narcotic gases such as nitrogen or nitrous oxide. Hydrogen has less HPNS potency than helium, and this is probably related to H_2's slight narcotic potency.[9] Proponents of the "critical volume hypothesis" suggest that high pressure compression of membranes causes HPNS and that narcotic gas reverses this by causing reexpansion.[10] The sites of action may be different for HPNS and narcosis. Sport divers will not be affected by HPNS.

Nitrogen narcosis limits the effective depth of air-supplied diving to shallower than 200 feet. Substitute breathing mixes using O_2 and a less narcotic inert gas must be used for deeper diving. Helium O_2 is the most commonly used mix. Small quantities of nitrogen may be added to the helium oxygen. Hydrogen, too, has a low potential for intoxication, but the problem of explosiveness makes its use complicated. Hydrogen can be used safely in deep dives where O_2 percentage is reduced since it is nonexplosive used with less than 4 percent O_2.[11] Neon's expense and its greater effect on respiratory efficiency have restricted its use despite its low tendency for narcosis.

People vary greatly in their sensitivity to nitrogen narcosis. The question of acclimatization to depth lies unanswered. Experienced divers claim that they are more resistant, but testing often reveals unsuspected impairment. Certainly, trained divers do have greater ability to work at depths. The neophyte's greater anxiety can increase his tendency toward poor performance.[12] Furthermore, the old hand is familiar with the "narcs" and knows that he must concentrate harder on his work.

One question, not often discussed, is the relationship of alcoholic tolerance to resistance toward inert gas intoxication: ". . . there is some evidence that a man who can take alcohol and remain clear headed has, therefore, some similar resistance to the narcosis."[13]

The elevated carbon dioxide sometimes found in deep dives has been considered as a cause of narcosis. Carbon dioxide does have potent narcotic properties. However, CO_2 alone does not suffice to narcotize in the concentrations usually present. Blood gas measurements revealed low pCO_2's coexisting with nitrogen narcosis.[14] Shallow working dives may cause a greater rise in CO_2 than deep, resting dives, but narcosis will not be seen in the former.[15] At a given depth intoxication is more common in water dives than in chamber exposures. This discovery, made during the salvage of the U.S.S. *Squalus* in 1939, led to the first use of HeO_2

equipment.[16] Diving suits retain carbon dioxide and may explain the difference between sea and chamber dives. Oxygen has been investigated as a contributer to narcosis;[17] it may act through its influence on CO_2 elimination.

Symptoms of narcosis disappear with lowered gas pressure, as for example during an ascent. Time is required for gas elimination so narcosis at 250 feet may not be fully resolved until decompression reaches 50 feet.

Narcosis dulls the perception of danger; a SCUBA diver may be lost before he even considers the need to ascend. Anxiety and cold stress compound the risk of nitrogen narcosis.[18] Poor surface-to-diver communications makes deep diving hazardous for the sport diver. Avoiding deep dives will prevent narcosis. The buddy system is of little value since both divers may be totally affected. Sport divers should not go beneath 125 feet, the U.S. Navy standard SCUBA limit. Attempts at depth records must be firmly discouraged.

NOTES: NITROGEN NARCOSIS

1. E. End, "The Use of New Equipment and Helium Gas in a World Record Dive," *Journal of Industrial Hygiene and Toxicology,* 20: 511–20, 1938.
2. R. Kiesling, C. Maag, "Performance Impairment as a Function of Nitrogen Narcosis," U.S. Navy Experimental Diving Unit Research Report 3-60.
3. F. Carpenter, "Inert Gas Narcosis," in *Proceedings of the Underwater Physiological Symposium,* (National Academy of Sciences, Washington, D.C., 1955), pp. 124–128.
4. S. Cullen, E. Gross, "The Anesthetic Properties of Xenon in Animals and Human Beings, with Additional Observations on Krypton," *Science,* 113: 580–82, 1951.
5. M. Lever et al., "Pressure Reversal of Anaesthesia," *Nature,* 231: 368–71, 1971.
6. K. Smith, "Inert Gas Narcosis, the High Pressure Neurological Syndrome, and the Critical Volume Hypothesis," *Science,* 185: 867–69, 1974.
7. W. Hunter, Jr., P. Bennett, "The Causes, Mechanisms, and Prevention of the High Pressure Nervous Syndrome," *Undersea Biomedical Research,* 1: 1–28, 1974.
8. R. Brauer, R. Way, "Relative Narcotic Potencies of Hydrogen, Nitrogen, and Their Mixtures," *Journal of Applied Physiology,* 29: 23–31, 1970.
9. R. Brauer, "N_2, H_2, and N_2O Antagonism of High Pressure Neurological Syndrome in Mice," *Undersea Biomedical Research,* 1: 59–72, 1974.
10. Smith, *op. cit.*
11. A. Zetterstrom, "Deep-Sea Diving with Synthetic Gas Mixtures," *Military Surgery,* 103: 104–06, 1948.

12. F. Davis, "Diver Performance: Nitrogen Narcosis and Anxiety," *Aerospace Medicine,* 43: 1079–82, 1972.

13. S. Miles, *Underwater Medicine* 3rd ed. (Philadelphia: Lippincott, 1969), pg. 112.

14. P. Bennett, G. Blenkarn, "Arterial Blood Gases in Man During Inert Gas Narcosis," *Journal of Applied Physiology,* 36: 45–48, 1974.

15. E. Lanphier, "Influence of Increased Ambient Pressure upon Alveolar Ventilation" in *Proceedings of the Second Symposium on Underwater Physiology* (Washington, D.C.: National Academy of Science, 1963), pp. 124–33.

16. A Behnke, T. Willman, "Medical Aspects of the Rescue and Salvage Operations and the Use of Oxygen in Deep Sea Diving," U.S. Navy Medical Bulletin 37: 629–40, 1939.

17. C. Hesser et al., "Roles of Nitrogen, Oxygen, and Carbon Dioxide in Compressed Air Narcosis," *Undersea Biomedical Research,* 5: 391–400, 1978.

18. Davis, *op. cit.*

16 Oxygen Poisoning

It may be difficult to believe that too much oxygen can be harmful, but exposures to abnormally high amounts of oxygen (O_2) have proved poisonous to plants and animals as well as to isolated cellular preparations. As a minor example, elevated oxygen concentration will block the light production by fireflies. In 1878 Paul Bert showed the convulsive effects of elevated O_2 in man. Twenty-one years later, Lorrain Smith demonstrated that pulmonary damage resulted after long exposure to moderate O_2 elevations. More recently, oxygen has been indicted as the cause of blindness in some premature babies.

The O_2 partial pressure (percentage of O_2 in the breathing mix multiplied by the ambient pressure) determines oxygen toxicity. In a space capsule, where total pressure is low, pure oxygen can be breathed, and the O_2 partial pressure will not be above normal. Conversely, with increased total gas pressure in diving a smaller percentage of O_2 is required to maintain a given O_2 pressure. At surface pressure, air contains 21 percent O_2, which thus constitutes 159 mm of the total atmospheric pressure of 760 mm. Doubling the ambient pressure by descending to 33 feet raises the O_2 pressure to 318 mm, although O_2 concentration remains constant at 21 percent. Oxygen, like all other gases, enters the blood and tissues in proportion to pressure, not percentage. The elevated pressure drives more O_2 into the body.

Prolonged inhalation of pure O_2 at atmospheric pressure can damage the respiratory system. Pure O_2 breathed at 760 mm will cause pulmonary and nasopharyngeal irritation after twenty-four hours.[1] Lower percentages can be tolerated longer: 60 percent O_2 (456 mm) is much less irritating, but will still cause pulmonary problems if administered over a period of weeks. Volunteers breathing O_2 at 2 atmospheres developed symptoms of pulmonary oxygen toxicity after 3 to 8 hours.[2] Vital capacity progressively decreased after 4 hours. If air is supplied under pressure, the O_2 percent must be lowered in order to keep the O_2 pressure at a safe level. Prolonged O_2 poisoning will permanently damage the lungs.

High O_2 levels in incubators have been indicted as the cause of blindness from retrolental fibroplasia in premature infants. Reduction of O_2 concentration eliminates the disorder. Adults are not susceptible to retrolental fibroplasia, but high O_2 tensions cause transient constriction of retinal blood vessels and limitation of peripheral vision.[3]

Long-term exposure to moderately elevated O_2 does not crop up as a problem in standard diving, but it is a major consideration in long-term, underwater residences. At 450 feet, 2 percent O_2 provides an O_2 partial pressure of 220 mm, well above that produced by the 21 percent O_2 on the surface. Pressures even in this range have been well tolerated in protracted dives. During ascent and descent the gas mix must be altered so that hypoxia will not develop at shallow depths.

Oxygen toxicity in standard diving involves shorter exposures to O_2 tensions well above 760 mm. The pressure at which oxygen is acutely toxic cannot be dogmatically stated. Prior to World War II, it was considered safe to use pure O_2 to 99 feet for 30 minutes, or to 66 feet for 3 hours. During the war, swimmers from the OSS were allowed to stay 2 hours at 33 feet and 30 minutes at 60 feet.[4] Today, U.S. Navy standards for normal operations limit divers to 75 minutes at 25 feet when breathing pure oxygen. Exceptional operations may permit 10 minute dives to 40 feet. Convulsions have occurred at only 33 feet.[5] In general, with increasing depth on O_2, the incidence of seizures increases while the latent period (time between start of dive and convulsion) decreases. Lengthening the exposure time at a given depth increases the risk of poisoning.

As a way of studying toxicity, men have been exposed to varying O_2 pressures. Some studies set definite exposure times and then record the number and type of symptoms produced. On

OXYGEN PARTIAL PRESSURE RELATED TO DEPTH

Depth	Total Pressure	Partial Pressure O_2
40,000 feet	152mm Hg.	32mm Hg.
18,000 feet	380	80
Surface	760	160
33 feet	1520	319
66 feet	2280	480
99 feet	3040	638
132 feet	3800	798
165 feet	4560	958

Note: Air contains 21 percent oxygen.

the other hand, the exposure can be continued until the induction of poisoning in all subjects.

In one British experiment, 100 men were exposed underwater to 50 feet on pure O_2 for 30 minutes.[6] Twenty-six convulsed, and the remaining 24 had other symptoms. This is a much higher incidence of convulsion than is usually experienced. Two other large studies gave convulsion percentages of 4 and 9 percent, respectively.[7]

Generalized convulsions are the most dramatic result of oxygen poisoning; they may come on without warning, but more commonly minor symptoms precede them. Some of these are nausea, muscle twitching (particularly lips), vertigo, visual abnormalities (especially reduction of peripheral vision), irritability, and numbness. The first two exceed the others in frequency.[8]

Oxygen convulsions are of the same nature as grand mal epilepsy. They last about 2 minutes and are followed by amnesia for the seizure; commonly, a period of sleep and general mental depression follows. In the initial phase, the body is tonic (rigid), and consciousness is lost. Breathing stops. After about 30 seconds the clonic phase begins with spasmodic movement of the head, neck, trunk, and limbs. Breathing resumes. During the seizure, the electroencephalograph (brain wave) shows a pattern typical of grand mal epilepsy. Residual changes have not been demonstrated from O_2 convulsions if the oxygen exposure is promptly terminated. Of course, a seizure under water may cause other problems such as drowning, due to a lost mouthpiece, or head injuries, from the inside of a hard hat.

The mechanism of oxygen poisoning remains theoretical.[9, 10] Possible processes include enzyme inhibition or hormonal changes. Metabolism of O_2 forms free radicals, which may disrupt cellular function and structure. Elevated carbon dioxide increases the sensitivity to oxygen poisoning. Oxygen poisoning does not require high CO_2, however.[11] It may well be that there is not one single mechanism of action, but a combination.

Interspersing periods of air breathing with oxygen breathing delays the onset of pulmonary toxicity. At 2 atmospheres the tolerable oxygen breathing time can be doubled by breathing air for 5 minutes after each 20 minute O_2 exposure.[12] Apparently, the air periods permit some recovery from O_2 poisoning. This has not been studied experimentally at higher pressures to prevent central nervous system toxicity. There is evidence that visual effects are attenuated by intermittent exposure.[13] This principle of intermittent O_2 exposure is employed in the oxygen recompression tables.

Susceptibility to O_2 poisoning varies widely among different persons; in fact, it is not even constant for the same person on separate days.[14] All the influencing factors are not known, but several have been confirmed. As mentioned previously, elevated CO_2 increases the risk, as does elevated temperature. Exercise greatly reduces tolerance to high O_2; divers have been poisoned mainly when doing heavy work.[15] Submersion in water seems to hasten the onset of seizures. Oxygen, it has been shown, can be tolerated in a dry chamber for a longer period than under similar conditions beneath the water.

"In corroboration of previous work, it was found that in 20 exposures in the dry chamber at rest at a simulated depth of 60 ft. symptoms did not occur during a period of two hours. However, at the same depth underwater at rest, 32 of the 107 exposures were terminated prior to 60 mins."[16]

Treatment of O_2 poisoning is simple: Reduce the O_2 tension. Unfortunately, a convulsion may be unheralded by warning signs. In a chamber or a hard-hat rig the breathing mixture must be immediately shifted to air. Since with convulsions breathing stops, and there is frequently airway obstruction, the patient should not be decompressed during a convulsion. The result might be intrathoracic—air expansion sufficient to cause air embolism. Rarely the shift from O_2 to air will briefly intensify the symptoms.

Because there may be no warning and because the air mixture in closed-circuit SCUBA cannot be changed by a convulsing diver, prevention is more relevant than treatment. All U.S. Navy diving candidates must breathe O_2 at 60 feet in a chamber for 30 minutes as a test for O_2 tolerance. Regrettably, a man may pass the test one day and convulse another as tolerance for O_2 is not constant. Anticonvulsant drugs may prevent the actual seizure, but they do not prevent the toxic action of O_2.[17] If convulsions are masked so that exposure continues, there may be permanent central nervous system damage. The best way to prevent O_2 poisoning is to follow conservative exposure standards.

For the recreational diver O_2 poisoning ought not to be a problem as when using air in open-circuit SCUBA, the O_2 pressure will not reach the equivalent of 2 atmospheres, the accepted maximum pressure for O_2 use, until a depth of nearly 300 feet. However, the use of pure O_2 systems is extremely dangerous. If open circuit tanks are filled with pure O_2, rather than air, dives below 33 feet are unsafe, even for brief periods. Closed circuit SCUBA equipment allows O_2 rebreathing after CO_2 removal. Any malfunction in the absorbent system permits a rise in CO_2, which intensifies the risk of O_2 toxicity. Synthetic gas mixes for semiclosed SCUBA permit deeper dives, but miscalculations in O_2 percentages may result in too little O_2 at shallow depths, or too much on the bottom. Closed and semiclosed SCUBA were not designed for recreational diving and should not be used for it because of the possible danger of oxygen poisoning.

The oxygen recompression tables introduce the possibility of O_2 toxicity to recreational divers. These tables maximize O_2 exposure for its therapeutic value. In so doing, they approach toxic oxygen doses. This is especially true when the tables must be extended. Generally, the oxygen is well tolerated, but cases of pulmonary and central nervous system poisoning have occurred.

NOTES: OXYGEN POISONING

1. C. J. Lambertsen, "Oxygen Toxicity," *Fundamentals of Hyperbaric Medicine* (Washington, D.C.: National Academy of Science, 1966), pp. 21–32.
2. J. Clark, C. Lambertsen, "Rate of Development of Pulmonary O_2 Toxicity in Man During O_2 Breathing at 2.0 Ata," *Journal of Applied Physiology,* 30: 739–752, 1971.
3. C. Nichols, C. Lambertsen, "Effects of High Oxygen Pressures on the Eye," *New England Journal of Medicine,* 281: 25–30, 1969.
4. C. Lambertsen, "Problems of Shallow Water Diving: Report Based on Experiences of Operational Swimmers of the Office of Strategic Services," *Occupational Medicine,* 3: 230–45, 1947.
5. K. Donald, "Oxygen Poisoning in Man," *British Medical Journal,* 1: 667–72, 712–17, 1947.
6. *Ibid.*
7. O. Yarborough et al., "Symptoms of Oxygen Poisoning and Limits of Tolerance at Rest and at Work," U.S. Navy Experimental Diving Unit, Project x–337 (sb. No. 62), Report No. 1, 1947.
8. *Ibid.*
9. J. Clark, C. Lambertsen, "Pulmonary Oxygen Toxicity: A Review," *Pharmacological Review,* 23: 37–133, 1971.
10. L. Frank, D. Massaro, "Oxygen Toxicity," *American Journal of Medicine,* 69: 117–26, 1980.
11. Donald, *op cit.*
12. P. L. Hendricks et al., "Extension of Pulmonary O_2 Tolerance in Man at 2 AtA by Intermittent O_2 Exposure," *Journal of Applied Physiology:* 42: 593–99, 1977.
13. Nichols, *op. cit.*
14. Donald, *op. cit.*
15. Yarborough, *op. cit.*
16. *Ibid.*
17. Lambertsen, "Oxygen Toxicity,"

17 | Carbon Monoxide

Carbon monoxide (CO) poisoning can result from the use of impure air in SCUBA tanks. It represents a serious form of poisoning, which may cause unconsciousness and death or lead to death from drowning.

Carbon monoxide (CO) competes with oxygen in the body and results in impairment of tissue oxygenation. The site of this competition is debatable.

Carbon monoxide competes with oxygen (O_2) for combination with hemoglobin in the blood. The combination of carbon monoxide with hemoglobin forms carboxyhemoglobin. Tissue metabolism depends on oxygen transport in the form of oxyhemoglobin. As carboxyhemoglobin increases, oxyhemoglobin decreases. Carbon monoxide has a 200 to 300 times greater affinity for hemoglobin than does O_2. Thus, even CO in small amounts preferentially binds with hemoglobin. For example, assuming 220 times greater affinity, .01 percent CO in air will result in 50 percent carboxyhemoglobin. Tissue anoxia results from this reduction in hemoglobin's oxygen-carrying capacity.

Furthermore, CO interferes with the release of O_2 from hemoglobin to the tissues. The oxyhemoglobin that does remain has an impaired function. Carbon monoxide, thus, reduces the amount of O_2 which can be transported, and it hinders the availability of O_2 to the cells.

Recent investigation suggests there is important competition within the cells between CO and O_2. Within the mitochondria (sites of metabolism) CO binds to one of the enzymes (cytochrome A_3) and disrupts oxygen metabolism. After dog experiments, Goldbaum et al. concluded that this cellular toxicity was more important than carboxyhemoglobin formation.[1] This conclusion is, however, not universally accepted.[2,3]

Arterial O_2 tension (pressure) remains near normal despite the reduction of O_2 carrying capacity. Because of normal O_2 tension, there will be no respiratory stimulation.[4]

The impaired release of O_2 from oxyhemoglobin masks the blueness usually seen in the skin of hypoxia victims. However, the "cherry red" appearance of carbon monoxide victims is not as common as formerly described.[5]

Carboxyhemoglobin levels of 3 to 40 percent are associated with unconsciousness and levels of 70 percent are often fatal. These figures are not extremely reliable. Lower concentrations may also be fatal.

The toxic dose of CO is not easily defined. Its effects are cumulative with prolonged inhalation. Because of its high toxicity CO is measured in parts per million (ppm) rather than by percentage. One ppm equals .0001 percent. A concentration of 400 ppm (.04 percent) will give symptoms in one hour. At 1200 ppm (.12 percent) only 20 minutes can be tolerated.[6] Equilibration at 700 ppm (.07 percent) would give approximately 30 percent carboxyhemoglobin.

The relationship between tolerable CO concentration and increasing diving depth is still disputed. Depth, with its higher pressure, will increase the partial pressure of a given CO percent but it also proportionately raises the O_2 partial pressure. The ratio of CO to O_2 thus remains constant with increased pressure. Since CO acts through competition with O_2, it would seem logical that an unchanging ratio would cause no increase in toxicity.[7] Also at high pressures, blood plasma can carry significant amounts of O_2 in simple solution. However, some workers maintain that CO of a given concentration is more toxic at depth.[8]

Early symptoms of CO poisoning include headache (described as feeling like a tight band around the head), weakness, and dizziness. Unconsciousness may develop, at times without these warnings.

Exposure to the fresh air is the first step in treating CO poisoning. In diving, other causes of unconsciousness such as decompression sickness or air embolism must be considered.[9]

Artificial respiration may be required. As soon as possible, pure O_2 should be administered. High O_2 speeds the displacement of carbon monoxide from hemoglobin. Hospitalization is essential in all but the mildest cases. Hyperbaric oxygenation has proved of value for two reasons: It increases the rate of carboxyhemoglobin dissociation and adds to the amount of O_2 which can be carried in physical solution to the plasma. At oxygen pressures between 2 and 3 atmospheres absolute, plasma O_2 alone can supply basic metabolic requirements.

Carbon monoxide poisoning will not be a problem if a reliable air source is used for charging SCUBA bottles. The usual purity standard for CO under 20 ppm (.002 percent) can be tolerated indefinitely as shown by submarine crew exposures. Unfortunately, in some regions there are no effective air purity standards or inspections of air stations. A random investigation of twenty-five SCUBA tanks by Breysse showed five with levels over 25 ppm and eighteen between 10 and 25 ppm.[10] Carbon monoxide enters SCUBA air from three main sources. If a gasoline compressor is used, the exhaust fumes may be drawn in the intake chamber. Charging air in an area of high fume level (a garage or near the street) may result in impure air. At high temperatures, lubricating oil in a compressor may be partially burned ("flashed"), thus giving off CO. Water lubricated compressors are safest, but if oil must be used, the pump should not be overheated and high stability oil should be used.

In diving, elevated carbon monoxide may intermix with carbon dioxide and/or nitrogen. Thus the effect of a given CO may be greater than predicted. Small decrements in performance can be very significant under water.

Fortunately, carbon monoxide poisoning does not often occur in SCUBA diving. Its serious effects, however, make careful control of air purity mandatory.

NOTES: CARBON MONOXIDE

1. L. M. Goldbaum et al., "What Is the Mechanism of Carbon Monoxide Toxicity?" *Aviation Space Environmental Medicine*, 46: 1289–91, 1975.
2. R. Coburn, "Mechanisms of Carbon Monoxide Toxicity," *Preventive Medicine*, 8: 310–22, 1979.

3. J. S. Urbanetti, "Carbon Monoxide Poisoning," *Progress in Clinical and Biological Research,* 51: 355–85, 1981.

4. C. Klassen, "Nonmetallic Environmental Toxicants: Air Pollutants, Solvents and Vapors, and Pesticides," *Goodman's and Gilman's The Pharmacological Basis of Therapeutics,* 6th ed. (New York: The Macmillan Company, 1980), pp. 1641–43.

5. E. Kindwall, "Carbon Monoxide Poisoning and Cyanide Poisoning," *HBO Review,* 1: 115–22, 1980.

6. W. Glass, W. Meldrum, "Carbon Monoxide Poisoning in Skin Divers—A Short Report of Two Cases," *New Zealand Medical Journal,* 62: 41–42, 1963.

7. J. Bloom, "Some Considerations in Establishing Divers' Breathing Gas Purity Standards for Carbon Monoxide," *Aerospace Medicine,* 43: 633–36, 1972.

8. R. Workman, "Other Medical Problems Associated with Exposure to Pressure," *Fundamentals of Hyperbaric Medicine* (Washington, D.C., National Academy of Science, 1966), pp. 110–14.

9. F. Furgang, "Carbon Monoxide Intoxication Presenting as Air Embolism in a Diver: A Case Report," *Aerospace Medicine,* 43: 785–86, 1972.

10. P. Breysse, "Safe Practices for Industrial Scuba Diving," Industrial *Medicine and Surgery,* 34: 870–73, 1965.

18 Drowning

Drowning ranks third among the causes of accidental death in the United States. In the age range of one to forty-four, only motor vehicles cause more accidental deaths than drowning.[1] Worldwide, drowning kills 150,000 people yearly.[2] In the United States 8,000 people die each year from drowning.[3] Drowning is by far the most common cause of death in skin and SCUBA diving.

About 70 percent of autopsied diving fatalities result from drowning.[4] In New Zealand about 90 percent of SCUBA deaths were from drowning.[5] Diving accounted for 4 percent of California water sport drownings,[6] 77 percent of diving deaths were drownings.

Virtually any diving accident can end in drowning. Causes include

1. exhaustion
2. pain from animal injury
3. incapacitation from injury
4. panic
5. intoxication or drug actions
6. nitrogen narcosis
7. air embolism
8. medical disorders such as heart attack, stroke, or epilepsy
9. equipment malfunction
10. running out of air

11. entanglement in weeds, a cave, wrecks, or being trapped under ice
12. unconsciousness

THE PHYSIOLOGY OF DROWNING

Drowning is death resulting from immersion in a liquid. Near-drowning refers to immersion accidents that are reversed before death supervenes.

The physiology of drowning in humans has been radically reevaluated by scientists. Former theories were based on experimental drownings of dogs. In dogs, the findings depended mainly on whether the water was fresh or salty. Careful analysis of human immersion accidents failed to demonstrate changes found in dogs.[7]

Upon submersion the alert person voluntarily and reflexly stops breathing. Typically, there will be struggling to get to the surface for a breath of air. Water in the throat causes a reflex closure of the vocal cords (laryngospasm). With time, voluntary breath holding becomes impossible, and there will be gasping breathing efforts. As body oxygen content falls (hypoxia) the vocal cords relax, and water enters the trachea and passes to the lungs.

Severe hypoxia may develop without aspiration of water into the lungs. Animal experiments and observations in humans, however, suggest that it is unlikely that death will occur before the vocal cords open and permit water entry.[8][9]

Displacing lung air with water makes gas exchange impossible. Thus, the basic problem in drowning is the rapid development of hypoxia. Without sufficient oxygen no part of the body can function normally. The heart soon stops functioning (cardiac arrest). Within 5 minutes of cardiac arrest, permanent damage occurs within the brain.

Large quantities of water are not required to disrupt lung function. In dog experiments high mortality rates were seen with instillation of 22 ml of seawater per kilogram body weight.[10] Fresh water was only half as deadly on a volume per weight basis. Measurements in human drowning and near-drownings suggest that most persons aspirate less than 22 ml/Kg.[11] Even volumes less than this impair blood oxygenation.

Salt water in the alveoli of the lungs tends to draw fluid from the blood into the lungs because of the higher osmotic pressure of salt water. In some animal salt-water drownings, it has been possible to recover more fluid from the lungs than was initially instilled. Fresh water tends to enter the blood since blood's osmotic pressure is greater. Also fresh water disrupts the function of the surfactant that lines the alveoli. Hypoxic damage itself causes fluid accumulation in the lungs (pulmonary edema). Direct and indirect water effects may cause lung damage that persists after initial recovery from near-drowning.

Animals given large volumes of water may have changes in concentration of the electrolytes (especially sodium and potassium) in their blood.[12] Salt water tends to concentrate sodium because fluid volume decreases. Fresh water may expand fluid volume, thus decreasing sodium concentration. The absorption of fresh water can cause the destruction of red blood cells. This releases cellular potassium, which raises the plasma concentration of potassium. Electrolyte changes are brief in duration and require large volume aspiration. Most human victims do not have these changes.

The havoc wrought by immersion accidents results from the primary and secondary effects of hypoxia.

TREATMENT

The transition from health to death caused by drowning is not sudden. With immersion, hypoxia begins. If the drowning sequence is not interrupted, the heart will arrest and the pace of hypoxia accelerates. The brain begins to suffer with the onset of hypoxia and quickly fails when blood flow totally stops. Within seconds of cardiac arrest, consciousness is lost.[13] It is impossible to put firm time values on each step of a drowning. If a normal person suddenly has a cardiac arrest, permanent brain damage ensues within 4 to 5 minutes. However, the drowning victim usually does not suffer a sudden cardiac arrest. Because of struggling, blood oxygen may already be low before the victim begins to aspirate water. This decreases tolerance for cardiac arrest. A diver who drowns because of an exhausted air supply also starts with suboptimal oxygenation. Air embolism can cause brain injury, which adds to that associated with hypoxia of drowning. There are considerations in diving that may occasionally favor survival, and these are discussed in "prolonged immersion."

The main goal in treating the nearly drowned is to restore the inhalation of air promptly. Early interruption of the drowning sequence greatly increases the likelihood of survival. Time wasted during the initial resuscitation of a victim cannot be offset by the most sophisticated medical care.

Contact with the drowning victim is the key to resuscitation. Unfortunately, this is often poorly managed. In fatal SCUBA accidents more than 10 minutes passed from the time of the accident to the recovery of the body in over two thirds of the cases.[14] Victim recovery took over an hour in half the fatal accidents. On land, successful resuscitation of ventricular fibrillation was 8 times more successful when begun within 5 minutes of occurrence.[15]

The method of initial contact depends on the victim's state of consciousness. An impaired diver who is still conscious has a better prognosis than an unconscious diver. But the conscious diver may represent a threat to the rescuer. People who find themselves in danger often act instinctively. A struggling swimmer typically grabs at any floating object and may cause the drowning of a would-be rescuer. Of note, most divers in trouble fail to drop their weights or to inflate their buoyancy equipment. Thus, the first step in rescue is to encourage the victim loudly to drop weights and inflate his vest. After this, the buoyancy problem will be solved. Never swim into the arms of a confused diver. Instead push your diving float to him and approach only when the victim has been calmed.

Unconscious victims may be found either on the surface or under water. In approaching an unconscious diver under water, beware of any entanglements such as weeds, fishing line, etc. An unconscious person should be brought immediately to the surface. Position of ascent is not as important as efficiency. Once on the surface a prompt check must be made to determine if the victim is breathing. If not, resuscitation begins immediately. The chart on page 201 sets out the proper steps in the rescue of an unconscious swimmer.

It is essential to begin artificial ventilation in the water. With the exception of experimental techniques, mouth to mouth venti-

---

RESCUING AN UNCONSCIOUS SWIMMER

If the victim is underwater, bring him to the surface.

If victim is breathing	If victim is not breathing
1. Adjust buoyancy;	1. Begin artificial ventilation;
2. Check for injuries;	2. Adjust buoyancy;
3. Transport to shore;	3. Check for injuries;
4. Provide follow-up care.	4. Transport to shore while ventilating;
	5. On shore, begin cardiac compression if necessary; continue to ventilate;
	6. Provide follow-up care.

---

lation is the only feasible method for in-water use. Four quick breaths can significantly reoxygenate the victim's blood. After a brief period of cardiac arrest, ventilation alone may restart the heart.[16] Delays in artificial ventilation increase the likelihood of permanent damage. It has been estimated that delaying resuscitation until reaching shore eliminates three eighths of possible survivors.[17]

Artificial ventilation in the water is not easy. Major problems are maintaining contact, verifying adequacy, and controlling buoyancy.

After establishing ventilation, a quick check should be made for associated injuries. The only one that would affect transport of a nonbreathing diver would be the possibility of a spine injury. Persons thrown against rocks or into the sand may have broken necks or backs. Care must be taken to minimize movement that could cause spinal cord injuries. It would, however, not be wise to avoid artificial ventilation if the victim is not breathing.

During transport to shore, or rescue boat, constant assessment must be made of the victim's condition. Obviously, no injured diver should be sent off to shore by himself even if he appears to be recovered. An initially conscious victim may have suffered injuries that will cause unconsciousness within a few minutes. Likewise, a breathing, nearly drowned diver may stop breathing. Artificial ventilation during transport is a challenge, but it is essential! Any lapse in artificial ventilation allows the deadly hypoxia sequence to begin again. The only permissible time to interrupt artificial ventilation, briefly, is in the crossing of a rough surf line. If there is only one rescuer, it would be better to miss a few breaths than to lose contact with the victim. In a multirescuer situation, one person can maintain ventilation while others provide propulsion and support.

Once ashore (or on a boat) the victim should be placed on his back. On a beach the head is ideally placed down the slope to increase blood return to the heart and to facilitate drainage of water or vomitus. At least 50 percent of victims will vomit.[18] A pulse is quickly sought to determine the need for cardiac resuscitation. Because of blood vessel constriction in cold water and tight wet suit cuffs, it is easiest to seek the carotid pulse in the neck. This naturally requires the removal of any wet suit that covers the neck. If there is no palpable pulse, cardiac compression begins.

TECHNIQUES OF CARDIOPULMONARY RESUSCITATION

Mouth to mouth ventilation has been the accepted method of artificial ventilation since 1958. Closed-chest cardiac compression (or "massage") was clinically introduced in 1960 but was first used only by physicians and then slowly approved for use by paramedical personnel. Now complete cardiopulmonary resuscitation (CPR) is taught to nonmedical people.[19]

Every sensible diver should be taught CPR on a formal basis. Divers are subject to water accidents, and they often enjoy their sport in areas remote from formal rescue facilities. Courses in CPR are available through schools, the Red Cross, and the American Heart Association. Some progressive diving instructors have become certified CPR instructors in order to augment the value of their diving courses. No one can learn CPR properly by just reading about it. The techniques require actual practice. Furthermore, it has been found that CPR skills are quickly lost without the provision for regular practice.

The use of CPR in a diving rescue

The following list deals with some salient points in connection with CPR and diving. It is not intended to replace formal instruction and practice.

Artificial Ventilation

1. If the victim is not breathing, begin ventilation in the water.
2. Open the airway by tilting the head back. Forward displacement of the lower jaw is difficult in the water. If the likelihood of cervical spine injury is high, it is safer to push the jaw forward without tilting the head.
3. You may *quickly* clear the victim's mouth of debris, if necessary.
4. Seal the nose with fingers or cheek.
5. Give 4 full quick breaths into the victim. Do not allow time for full exhalation by the victim of these initial breaths. There is nothing magic about the number 4. A few quick breaths do give a quick rise in blood oxygenation.

6. Be sure that the victim's chest rises with each breath. Breaths that don't expand the chest are wasted.
7. Ventilate about 12 times per minute during transport. Children require 20 breaths each minute. Each breath should be a full one. Faster ventilation will quickly tire the rescuer.
8. Any interruption must be very brief.

Cardiac Compression

1. Standard chest decompression is not feasible in the water. Therefore it is foolish to waste time looking for a pulse. This time would be better spent moving toward shore. There are experimental techniques for aquatic chest compression[20] but they have not been proved effective.[21]
2. Improperly performed chest compression can cause sternal fractures, rib fractures, pneumothorax, lung and liver lacerations, etc. These are minimized by attention to proper detail.
3. The hands of the rescuer are locked together and only the heel of the hand is placed over the lower half of the sternum. Pressure on only the very bottom of the sternum (the xiphoid process) can easily tear the liver.
4. By placing his shoulders over the victim's sternum and locking his elbows, the rescuer can use his weight to depress the sternum 1½ to 2 inches. This straight vertical compression minimizes complications and preserves the rescuer's strength for prolonged resuscitation.
5. Blood flow occurs during compression so the compression phase should be 50 percent of the cycle.
6. During the relaxation phase, all pressure should be removed from the sternum.
7. Rate for one rescuer CPR is 2 breaths and then 15 compressions with a compression rate of 80/minute. Two-person CPR gives one breath after 5 compressions with compression rate of 60/minutes. Breaths are interspersed between chest compressions.

Cardiopulmonary resuscitation has certainly been proved valuable. In a long study of ventricular fibrillation, usually from heart attacks, prompt out-of-hospital care by firemen paramedics allowed 21 percent of victims to leave the hospital. All of these would have died or have been severely impaired without this care. In a follow-up study, the survival rate was 43 percent, if resuscitation was immediately begun by outstanders.[22]

The techniques of CPR have become quite standardized, and this aids in mass education. It is wrong, however, to think that specific methods are necessarily perfect. Current investigations reevaluating the actual physiology of chest compression have, for example, suggested that the compression phase should ideally be 60 percent of a cycle.[23] There are also theories about better ventilatory patterns.[24] Basic CPR does have some significant weakness. The hypoxic victim requires maximal inspired oxygen but mouth-to-mouth ventilation can provide only about 16 percent inspired oxygen. Cardiac output with CPR is only 25 percent of normal. Fortunately, the blood flow to the brain may be 90 percent of normal and the heart receives 35 percent of normal flow.[25]

It can be fairly said that the institution of prompt, proper CPR is essential to the intact survival of the nearly drowned. Many studies have been made of groups of near-drowning victims. Survival ranges from under 50 percent to over 90 percent. Refinement of these gross survival percentages show that the number who survive without any neurological deficit is small in those victims who reach the hospital still comatose and still requiring CPR.[26 27 28] Prompt resuscitation greatly increases the likelihood that the victim will respond quickly. "The best indicator for a favorable neurologic prognosis has been the time to first spontaneous gasp after extraction from the water, . . ."[29]

FOLLOW-UP CARE

Once begun, CPR should continue until the victim responds or until medical personnel take over care. Because of the limitations of CPR, it is important that advanced therapy be instituted quickly. Bystanders should be utilized to obtain emergency transportation to the hospital. Resuscitation is, of course, continued during transport.

Any person who requires even brief CPR should be admitted to the hospital for careful observation. Even a person who has been well immersed without losing consciousness should be admitted. Only the victim of a very trivial dunking can be safely dismissed.

Hypoxia that does not cause unconsciousness, or only brief unconsciousness, may be severe enough to cause unsuspected lung impairment. In Fuller's series of resuscitated near-drownings, 25 percent succumbed after initially appearing well.[30] The conscious person may actually have severely impaired blood oxygenation with profound acidosis. Initial chest X rays may be normal and then become abnormal. All those admitted to hospitals should be given supplemental oxygen and have serial measurements of blood gases, electrolytes, and hematocrit.

If ventilation fails, as evidenced by falling oxygen and rising carbon dioxide with acidosis, intubation and mechanical ventilation may be necessary. It is better to treat too aggressively than too conservatively. The use of positive expiratory pressure is widely recommended when mechanical ventilation is necessary. Most authorities do not advise routine steroid use or antibiotics unless sputum cultures grow pathogens.[31]

Other medical care follows standard intensive-care practices. Current therapy techniques are very successful in those victims who are conscious on arrival at the hospital.[32]

A major controversy centers on the use and value of cerebral resuscitation. The grim outlook for severely injured near-drowned persons has led some to suggest that care be limited.[33] In Toronto, the other road is taken with aggressive therapy directed toward improving cerebral function by using fluid restriction, hypothermia, ventilation with high oxygen percentages, and profound sedation.[34]

PROLONGED IMMERSION

Generally the prognosis for complete recovery decreases as the time of immersion lengthens. There have been several cases reported, however, of survival from immersion from 10 to 40 minutes.[35] These cases not unexpectedly receive quite a lot of attention. Unfortunately, some persons have been misled into thinking that prolonged immersion is not as dangerous as previously believed. The old concept of prolonged immersions being worse than short ones is not invalid. The number of survivors is very small.

Most of the prolonged immersion survivors have been found in very cold water. Generally they are children. Profound cold (hypothermia) reduces the rate of brain metabolism and permits longer episodes of cardiac arrest. Upon sudden immersion in very cold water, both hypoxia and hypothermia begin. If hypoxia becomes quickly profound, the heart stops, and the brain begins to die. If temperature falls quickly, before hypoxia does its damage, the small amounts of oxygen may be sufficient to sustain life. Of course, on rewarming, increased amounts of oxygen will be required. Children cool faster than adults, and this probably partially explains their better survival.

This mechanism has its limitations. Hypothermia is not an instant occurrence. Chilling may cause fatal rhythm abnormalities in the heart, and the protection provided by cold is limited. First the water must be colder than usually used by divers. Moderate degrees of cold actually increase metabolic rate. Also there is a time after which hypoxia cannot be tolerated even in hypothermia. In Scandinavia those victims with the lowest rectal temperatures actually had the worst outcomes.[36]

Another occurrence in immersion has been theorized as part of the explanation for prolonged survivable immersions. When air breathing animals are immersed, they have a reflex inhibition of breathing, and their pulse rate slows. In diving animals this slow heart rate together with changes in regional blood flow reduces oxygen demand and prolongs breath holding. It is not established that immersion bradycardia prolongs survivable immersion in man. Immersion bradycardia does not necessarily conserve oxygen.[37]

Victims of cold water immersion should be managed somewhat differently from the normal near-drownings. Pulses may be slow, and because of vasoconstriction they may be virtually impossible to feel. Vigorous CPR in a hypothermic but regularly beating heart may cause ventricular fibrillation. Oxygenation is still important. These persons should be admitted to a hospital for rewarming with careful cardiac monitoring. It may take more than a day before their eventual prognosis can be determined.

PREVENTION OF DROWNING

The diver's attention should be directed to prevention of drowning. Rescue and resuscitation are both difficult and unpleasant. Even with excellent care, survival is far from universal.

Divers, of all people in the water, should be able to avoid trouble. Proper training will eliminate those who are weak swimmers and should teach good water skills. But it is practice rather than knowledge of theory that makes the difference. Those who push themselves and their equipment increase the likelihood of an accident.

Divers need training and practice in water rescue and resuscitation. The prolonged times for victim recovery show that divers are careless in their buddy-diving techniques.

NOTES: DROWNING

1. Metropolitan Life Insurance Co., "Accidental Drownings by Age and Activity," *Statistical Bulletin*, 58: 1–25, 1977.
2. V. D. Plueckhahn, "Alcohol and Drowning—The Geelong Experience, 1957–1980," *Medical Science and Law*, 21: 265–72, 1981.
3. Metropolitan Life, *op. cit.*
4. J. McAniff, *U.S. Underwater Diving Fatality Statistics, 1970–78*, Report URI-SSR-80-13, National Underwater Accident Data Center, University of Rhode Island, 1980.
5. P. Lewis, "Skin Diving Fatalities in New Zealand," *New Zealand Medical Journal*, 89: 472–75, 1970.
6. J. Lansche, "Deaths During Skin and Scuba Diving in California," *California Medicine*, 116: 18–22, (June) 1972.
7. R. Fuller, "The Clinical Pathology of Human Near-Drowning," *Proceedings of the Royal Society of Medicine*, 56: 33–38, 1963.
8. C. Dueker, "Pulmonary Aspiration in Drowning" in *Proceedings of the Sixth International Congress on Hyperbaric Medicine*, G. Smith, ed. (Aberdeen, Scotland: Aberdeen University Press, 1979), pp. 371–72.
9. F. Golden, J. Rivers, "The Immersion Incident," *Anaesthesia*, 30: 364–73, 1975.
10. J. Modell et al., "The Effects of Fluid Volume in Seawater Drowning," *Annals of International Medicine*, 67: 68–80, 1967.
11. J. Modell, J. Davis, "Electrolyte Changes in Human Drowning Victims," *Anesthesiology*, 30: 414–20, 1969.
12. Modell et al., "The Effects."
13. J. Criley, "Cough-Induced Cardiac Compression," *Journal of the American Medical Association*, 236: 1246–50, 1976.
14. H. Schenk, J. McAniff, *U.S. Underwater Fatality Statistics—1976*, National Underwater Accident Data Center, University of Rhode Island, 1978.
15. H. Alvarez, L. Cobb, "Experiences with CPR Training of the General

Public," in *Proceedings of the National Conference on Standards for CPR and Emergency Cardiac Care* (Washington, D.C.: National Academy of Science, 1973), pp. 33–37.

16. P. Safar et al., "Ventilation and Circulation with Closed Chest Cardiac Massage in Man," *Journal of the American Medical Association,* 176: 574–76, 1961.

17. L. Buchanan, "Rescue Breathing for the Partly Drowned," *Medical Journal of Australia,* 47: 405–12, 1960.

18. Anonymous, "Near Drowning," *Lancet,* 2: 194–95, 1978.

19. Anonymous, "Standards for Cardiopulmonary Resuscitation (CPR) and Emergency Cardiac Care (ECC)," *Journal of the American Medical Association,* 227 (Supplement): 833–68, 1974.

20. N. March, M. Matthews, "New Techniques in External Cardiac Compression," *Journal of the American Medical Association,* 244: 1229–32, 1980.

21. K. W. Kizer, "Aquatic Rescue and In-Water CPR," *Annals of Emergency Medicine,* 11: 166–67, 1982.

22. R. Thompson et al., "Bystander-Initiated Cardiopulmonary Resuscitation in the Management of Ventricular Fibrillation," *Annals of Internal Medicine,* 90: 737–40, 1979.

23. G. Taylor et al., "Importance of Prolonged Compression During Cardiopulmonary Resuscitation in Man," *New England Journal of Medicine,* 296: 1515–17, 1977.

24. N. Chandra et al., "Simultaneous Chest Compression and Ventilation at High Airway Pressure During Cardiopulmonary Resuscitation," *Lancet,* 1: 175–78, 1980.

25. W. Vorhess et al., "Regional Blood Flow During Cardiopulmonary Resuscitation in Dogs," *Critical Care Medicine,* 8: 134–36, 1980.

26. J. Modell et al., "Clinical Course of 91 Consecutive Near-Drowning Victims," *Chest,* 70: 231–38, 1976.

27. B. Peterson, "Morbidity of Childhood Near-Drowning," *Pediatrics,* 59: 364–70, 1977.

28. R. C. Frates, Jr., "Analysis of Predictive Factors in the Assessment of Warm-Water Near-Drowning in Children," *American Journal of Diseases of Children,* 135: 1006–08, 1979.

29. J. Pearn et al., "Neurologic Sequelae After Childhood Near-Drowning: A Total Population Study from Hawaii," *Pediatrics,* 64: 187–91, 1979.

30. Fuller, *op. cit.*

31. Modell et al., "Clinical Course."

32. *Ibid.*

33. Peterson, *op. cit.*

34. A. Conn et al., "Cerebral Salvage in Near-Drowning Following Neurological Classification by Triage," *Canadian Anesthesiology Society Journal,* 27: 201–10, 1981.

35. T. Sekar et al., "Survival After Prolonged Submersion in Cold Water Without Neurologic Sequelae," *Archives of Internal Medicine,* 140: 775–79, 1980.

36. S. Kruss et al., "The Prognosis of Near-Drowned Children," *Acta Paediatrica Scandinavica,* 68: 315–22, 1979.

37. A. Craig, W. Medd, "Man's Response to Breath-Hold Exercise in Air and in Water," *Journal of Applied Physiology,* 24: 773–77, 1968.

19 | First Aid

Since dives are frequently made in isolated areas far from medical facilities, it is incumbent on all divers to be well versed in the theory and practice of first aid. Proper techniques of first aid require practice which can only be obtained in a supervised class. First-aid methods have been discussed with the separate diving illnesses and accidents.

The first step is an evaluation of the patient's general condition. Check for consciousness, breathing, heartbeat, bleeding, head or spine injuries, and fractures. Unconscious divers require special attention. In general, the safest course is to assume that any unconscious person is suffering from a head or spine injury. In addition, SCUBA divers must be treated as though they have had an air embolism. Transportation to the nearest recompression facility must be instituted, but because of possible neck or back injury, the patient must be moved with extreme care. Firm support should be provided for the entire spine with a rigid stretcher so that there is no rotation or flexion. In emergencies, the patient can be carried on a wide board; the head should be placed between pillows or cloth rolls to prevent rotation.

Resuscitative measures have been discussed in the chapter on drowning. Remember that artificial resuscitation must begin *during—not after—*the rescue.

Bleeding can be controlled best by putting direct pressure on the wound with a sterile dressing. Tourniquets should be avoided, if at all possible, since these may cause permanent limb damage through their restriction of blood flow. *Minor* lacerations and scrapes are best treated by careful washing and the application of a sterile bandage. Antibiotic ointments are not required if the wound has been well cleansed. All other wounds should be seen by a physician, since suturing and tetanus prophylaxis may be required. Those wounds that require suturing should be treated within 6 to 8 hours in order to reduce the possibility of infection. Because of the risk of infection, dirty wounds, like those from stingrays, are often packed open rather than closed immediately.

In the case of fractures, the patient should be moved as little as possible. Open fractures may require pressure to control bleeding. The affected limb should be splinted to prevent motion during transportation.

Help the patient by keeping calm yourself, keeping crowds away, moving him only when required, and keeping him warm (assuming that the weather is not excessively hot already). *Don't give the injured person food or oral fluids* as this will complicate the situation if emergency surgery must be performed.

For basic needs, a first-aid kit should be taken on dives and should contain at least the following:

a blanket
splint
assorted sterile bandages
roller gauze bandages
elasticized wrap
adhesive tape
scissors
triangular sling
tourniquet
safety pins
soap
fresh water
tweezers
brush and gloves (for removing jellyfish tentacles)
vinegar (for jellyfish stings)

This kit has been designed for the layman and does not include equipment that physicians may find useful such as laryngoscope, endotracheal tube, oxygen resuscitation equipment, IV fluids, injectable steroids, antihistamines, calcium, vasopressors, morphine, local anesthetics, etc.

For boat dives or an expedition, an oxygen tank with an administration set is a worthwhile piece of gear. It can be used for resuscitation or for first aid therapy of decompression sickness or air embolism. Advanced first-aid training is advisable for oxygen use.

The most valuable piece of equipment—good training and calmness—cannot be packed into a kit!

In addition to the major diseases that have been discussed in previous chapters, divers are subject to a few other illnesses. Exposure to the sun can be expected to cause sunburn. Exposing oneself in gradual doses provides the best prevention, since protective lotions are usually washed off. Mild cases with skin reddening require no treatment except for soothing ointments and avoidance of the sun until healed. If blisters do develop, they should be left unopened; if they open by themselves, the skin must be kept clean. Cases of sunburn severe enough to cause nausea or fever should be treated by a physician.

Newer sunscreens, which contain para-aminobenzoic acid (PABA), provide significant protection. These are available in varying strengths and can be matched to climatic and individual needs. PABA sunscreens do cause contact dermatitis in some persons.[1]

Remember that bright sun can burn unprotected winter skin within 10 to 20 minutes. On a bright day the majority of the sun's burning ultraviolet rays pass through clouds and can penetrate 2 to 3 feet of water.

Seasickness has spoiled many a diving day. This occurs not only in getting to a diving site by boat but also while actually diving. Motion sickness is more than a nuisance. It distracts the diver and can impair performance. Vomiting underwater can be very dangerous. People vary both in their susceptibility to seasickness and in their ability to function when they are seasick. Adaptation to motion is an effective motion sickness preventive.[2] Unfortunately, this adaptation is soon lost when motion ceases. The diver must then begin all over again on the next diving trip.

Prevention of seasickness is variably successful.[3] Interestingly, the time between a meal and motion exposure doesn't affect susceptibility.[4] Nonetheless, most divers avoid large, complex meals before diving. Several medicines are available for seasickness prevention. The most commonly used ones are antihistamines. Some people are made drowsy by antihistamines, but pressure does not appear to intensify their action. More effective drugs include promethazine, scopolamine, amphetamines, and ephedrine (used in combination with promethazine or scopolamine). These drugs are dangerous for diving since they impair performance.

The notorious stomach cramps have disappeared from all but the oldest of old wives' tales, but leg and arm cramps do occur and can be extremely dangerous. Pain and restriction of movement may make swimming impossible. Cramps come on most often in cold water with sudden exertion, or after eating, when muscle blood flow is reduced. Avoidance of these circumstances will reduce the incidence. If a muscle does cramp, gentle massage may give relief. Flexing the foot upward often relieves a lower leg cramp.

Frequent diving may result in fungal or bacterial infection of the external ear canal (otitis externa). This is discussed in Chapter 6, Diving and the Ear.

Failure to keep SCUBA equipment clean can cause serious respiratory infections.

First aid preparation for the treatment of the injured diver includes familiarization with the peculiar problems of diving.

NOTES: FIRST AID

1. Anonymous, "Sunscreens," *The Medical Letter on Drugs and Therapeutics,* 16: 60, 1974.
2. K. Money, "Motion Sickness," *Physiology Review* 50: 1–39, 1970.
3. A. Graybiel, et al., "Human Assay of Antimotion Sickness Drugs," *Aviation Space Environmental Medicine,* 46: 1107–18, 1975.
4. Money, *op. cit.*

20 ‖ Health Requirements

Almost anyone with a pair of fins can paddle about in shallow water with impunity. Trouble arises when a poor swimmer literally gets in over his head and has inadequate skill to remove himself from danger. There is certainly nothing wrong with the nonathlete enjoying a paddle in clear, calm water, if he is well supervised and mature enough to know his limits. But a true diver cannot afford to be anything but physically and mentally fit.

Diving is a vigorous activity and ". . . the combination of exertion and breathholding can place more strain on the cardiovascular-respiratory system than almost any other type of activity."[1] Fins make swimming easy for the skin-diver, but repeated dives require much energy. The SCUBA diver can dive and stay down, but he is burdened with bulky equipment and may have trouble maintaining proper buoyancy. At increased depths, breathing with a regulator becomes harder work. After the dive, the swimmer often must forge his way back through the obstacle course of heavy surf, rocks, or coral. Unsuspected currents may take him out to sea or down the beach to an inhospitable landing site. In short, what starts out to be an easy dive can turn into a terrifying experience. The diver must have the physical and mental capabilities to deal with the unexpected.

In addition to general safety, fitness is important, since it reduces the incidence of diving maladies. Decompression sickness plagues fat, old divers with hearty appetites for alcohol, more frequently than it does young, fit divers. The risk of air embolism is markedly increased in people with past or present pulmonary disease.

For recreational diving, the strict U.S. Navy and commercial diving standards may be modified. Professional divers have to be ready at all times for deep dives; they must work in water that would never be entered for pleasure. At the same time, a sport diver should not risk health or life when medical considerations prevent safe diving.

Any person contemplating learning to dive should have a complete physical examination and an interview with a physician. The doctor must be made fully aware of the physical demands of diving. A current chest X ray is mandatory; any abnormality, whether active or residual, increases the risk of respiratory failure or air embolism.

Regretfully, the public cannot undergo the pressure test administered to all Navy diving candidates. An exposure to 110 feet in a pressure chamber eliminates those persons especially prone to sinus and ear squeeze. Being locked in the hot, noisy chamber also tests for claustrophobia.

A person does not have to be young to take up recreational diving; however, with advancing age the circulatory system becomes less efficient and exercise tolerance may fall. The propensity for decompression sickness increases with circulatory impairment. The older diver needs more frequent physical examinations, but while in sound health, diving can be enjoyed by him.

Most recognized diving schools have minimum age requirements for SCUBA instruction. As a general policy this is probably reasonable since mature judgment is essential for safe diving. Unfortunately, maturity does not always increase proportionately with age. Snorkel training can be a good introduction for the younger diver. Conscientious adult supervision will ensure that the child can become an old diver.

Personal habits of drinking and smoking can affect suitability for diving. Smoking may reduce exercise tolerance and impair respiratory function. Drinking during a diving day is obviously not wise.

Stable mental health has great importance for the diver. A tendency toward recklessness may be fatal. The mature diver gets into trouble less often and can remove himself more efficiently from unexpected dangers.

Any disease that interferes with normal activity can be expected to be more troublesome while diving. Because of the work of breathing under water, the respiratory system must be carefully evaluated. Asthma and emphysema are aggravated by the restrictive nature of SCUBA equipment and they increase the risk of lung rupture. Diseases such as tuberculosis and serious pneumonia may leave residual damage that predisposes the person to air embolism and associated maladies. Any occurrence of spontaneous pneumothorax (lung collapse in the absence of chest injury) would be disqualifying as it suggests the presence of air pockets (blebs) on the lung surface, which might well rupture again.

A person with symptomatic heart disease should definitely avoid diving. Swimming is not like climbing stairs. It is not always practical to stop in the event of fatigue or chest pain.

The advisability of diving for people who have had myocardial infarctions (heart attacks) is a frequent source of controversy. Clearly, symptomatic coronary artery disease makes diving dangerous. Some diving physicians permit symptomless postinfarction patients to dive, if they have normal stress electrocardiograms. Unfortunately, these tests are not completely accurate. The person who would dive must be aware of the physical exertion required in diving and of the increased risk of cardiac rhythm disturbances. A diver who is willing to dive only in warm, calm waters would be a more suitable candidate than a diver planning unrestricted excursions.

Hypertension (high blood pressure) is a common ailment. It has many causes and varies widely in severity. Often it is the therapy employed that makes diving inadvisable. (See Chapter 4, Diving and Drugs.) A hypertensive who uses no dangerous medicines and who has no functional impairments may be considered for recreational diving.

Gastrointestinal diseases are not significant in diving unless they involve a tendency toward vomiting, or if ulcer disease is active. The stresses of diving could lead to hemorrhage or perforation. Seasickness must be considered here since its significant features involve the gastrointestinal system. Those people who become seasick in small boats may expect to be affected by the gentle rolling of the sea while diving. Nausea under water is dangerous.

Diabetes mellitus is frequently noted as being incompatible with diving, but this is not always true if the patient is well controlled. Exercise may require changes in diet and drug dose, but the diabetic can learn this through gradual exposure. Athletics are no longer closed to the diabetic; this includes recreational diving. Complicated cases with circulatory or neurological changes make diving inadvisable. Diabetic divers must be aware of the risks and must dive accordingly. Medical consultation is essential.

Convulsive disorders (epilepsy) are disqualifying if there have been recent seizures, or if anticonvulsant medicines are used. It takes no imagination to picture the results of a convulsion 50 feet under water, or one in heavy surf. Cases that are seizure-free without medication are the subject for careful consideration by the physician.

The question of whether pregnant women should dive seems to be an increasingly popular one. In late pregnancy size considerations may limit agility and stability on land. Many pregnant women find swimming comfortable. In pregnancy the cardiovascular and respiratory systems are more active than normal. The further demands of vigorous exercise may be difficult to meet.

Is decompression sickness risk increased in pregnant women or their fetuses? There is no definite answer to this important question. Experiments in sheep have suggested an increased fetal risk.[2] However, further investigation suggested that experimental manipulations artificially caused the problem.[3] The type of dive made may affect fetal health.[4]

In the first third of pregnancy the baby's organs are formed. A variety of influences during this time can cause defects in organ formation. Animal experiments have not shown that air diving increases fetal abnormalities.[5,6] No firm data are available for humans despite attempts to study the problem through retrospective surveys.[7]

There is a potential risk of oxygen toxicity to the fetus if a pregnant woman requires recompression therapy. Again, this risk has not been defined. Hamster fetuses tolerated simulated hyperbaric therapy well.[8]

In summary, diving during pregnancy introduces potential dangers. But the likelihood of these remains undetermined. Because of the importance of fetal good health, a conservative program is worthwhile. An Undersea Medical Society workshop concluded: "Until further studies are made, we recommend that women who are or may be pregnant not dive."[9]

Two common ailments in diving are ear squeeze and sinus squeeze. Infections of the middle ear or of the sinuses may make diving temporarily impossible. The common cold frequently causes obstruction of the eustachian tube. With such plugging, equalization cannot occur. Fortunately, these ailments last only a short time. There should be no diving if an eardrum is perforated, since infection may develop, or water in the ear may cause vertigo. Middle-ear reconstructive surgery may make diving a risk since pressure changes can disrupt the prosthesis.

Medicines ought to be used with caution while diving. Any that cause drowsiness or inattentiveness must be avoided. A physician should be consulted before starting any new medicines. See Chapter 4, Diving and Drugs, for more information.

Passing a diving physical does not establish lifelong diving fitness. Acute illnesses may make diving unwise. This is especially true for the respiratory system. Pneumonia or bronchitis limit exercise capacity and increase the risk of lung rupture.

The diver should evaluate his physical and emotional readiness before every dive. Emotional distress, fatigue, illness, or recent drug use may make it advisable to postpone diving.

The Divers Alert Network (DAN) at Duke University offers a valuable service to sport divers, providing emergency information and facilitating diving-accident therapy through its regional consultants. The emergency number is (919) 684-8111. DAN depends on diver support. Information is available at Box 3823, Duke University Medical Center, Durham, North Carolina 27710.

NOTES: HEALTH REQUIREMENTS

1. E. Lanphier, J. Dwyer, "Diving with Self Contained Underwater Breathing Apparatus," U.S. Navy Experimental Diving Unit Special Report Series, 1954.
2. Fife et al., "Susceptibility of Fetal Sheep to Acute Decompression Sickness," Undersea Biomedical Research, 5: 287–92, 1978.

3. J. Rankin et al., "Scuba Diving in Pregnancy" in *Abstracts of the Seventh Symposium on Underwater Physiology,* Athens, 1980.
4. J. R. Wilson et al., "Hyperbaric Exposure During Pregnancy in Sheep: Staged and Rapid Decompression," *Undersea Biomedical Research,* 10: 11–15, 1983.
5. M. E. Bolton-Klug et al., "Lack of Harmful Effects from Simulated Dives in Pregnant Sheep," *American Journal of Obstetrics and Gynecology,* 146: 48–51, 1983.
6. M. E. Bolton, A. L. Alamo, "Lack of Teratogenic Effects of Air at High Ambient Pressure in Rats," *Teratology,* 24: 181, 1981.
7. M. Bolton, "Scuba Diving and Fetal Well-Being: A Survey of 208 Women," *Undersea Biomedical Research,* 7: 183–89, 1980.
8. S. C. Gilman et al., "Fetal Development: Effects of Simulated Diving and Hyperbaric Oxygen Treatment," *Undersea Biomedical Research,* 9: 297–304, 1982.
9. M. Kent, ed., *Effects of Diving on Pregnancy* (Bethesda, Md.: Undersea Medical Society, 1980), pg. 19.

Index